Dude, You're a Fag

Dude, You're a Fag

*Masculinity and Sexuality
in High School*

C. J. Pascoe

UNIVERSITY OF CALIFORNIA PRESS

Berkeley   Los Angeles   London

University of California Press, one of the most distinguished university presses in the United States, enriches lives around the world by advancing scholarship in the humanities, social sciences, and natural sciences. Its activities are supported by the UC Press Foundation and by philanthropic contributions from individuals and institutions. For more information, visit www.ucpress.edu.

University of California Press
Berkeley and Los Angeles, California

University of California Press, Ltd.
London, England

Library of Congress Cataloging-in-Publication Data

Pascoe, C. J., 1974–.
    Dude, you're a fag : masculinity and sexuality in high school / C.J. Pascoe.
        p.   cm.
    Includes bibliographical references and index.
    ISBN-13: 978-0-520-24862-5 (cloth : alk. paper), ISBN-10: 0-520-24862-7 (cloth : alk. paper)
    ISBN-13: 978-0-520-25230-1 (pbk. : alk. paper), ISBN-10: 0-520-25230-6 (pbk. : alk. paper)
    1. Teenage boys—California—Social conditions.   2. High school students—California—Social conditions.   3. Masculinity.   4. Heterosexuality.   5. Gender identity.   6. Identity (Psychology) in adolescence.   7. Socialization.   I. Title.

HQ797.P37   2007
306.76'40835109794—dc22   2006023537

Manufactured in the United States of America

15   14   13   12   11   10   09   08
10   9   8   7   6   5   4   3

*For Genevieve, Lacy, Riley, Ricky, Jessie,
Rebecu, Michelle, Valerie and other youth
at River High who are brave enough to
teach adults a thing or two about
challenging inequality*

CONTENTS

ACKNOWLEDGMENTS

Writing this book has been anything but an individual project. As I write these acknowledgments I realize the impossibility of including all those who have shepherded me along this journey. So to those I have recognized and those I haven't, thank you.

I am exceedingly grateful to the following organizations for providing generous financial support for this research. The Graduate Division, the Center for Working Families, the Center for the Study of Sexual Cultures, the Center for the Study of Peace and Well Being, the Abigail Reynolds Hodgen Fund, and the Department of Sociology at the University of California, Berkeley, have all funded the research and writing of this project. My affiliations with the Center for Working Families and the Center for the Study of Sexual Cultures provided me with varied intellectual communities with whom to share my work.

It is fitting, given that high school is the topic of this book, that I too return to high school in these acknowledgments. I doubt that this book would exist were it not for the support and mentoring of my two high school English teachers, Mrs. Sheila Kasprzyk, who, quite simply, taught me how to write, and Mrs. Sharon Spiers, who introduced me to the social topics that still drive my research—power, inequality, gender, psychological processes, and feminism. Not surprisingly, during my time at

River High I often thought back to the analysis of *Lord of the Flies* that I had written while in her class.

While I was an undergraduate at Brandeis University, talented, caring, and insightful mentors introduced me to sociology and feminist theory. Eli Sagan, Gordon Fellman, Michael Macy, Bernadette Brooten, Pamela Allara, Karen Hansen, and Irving Zola all taught me important lessons about being a scholar, thinking about the social world, and addressing inequality.

I was similarly blessed to work with brilliant mentors during my graduate career at the University of California, Berkeley. Barrie Thorne, Raka Ray, Dawne Moon, Nancy Chodorow, Arlie Hochschild, Kim Voss, and Michael Burowoy all guided me through the Berkeley graduate program and the writing of this book in one way or another. From the initial stages of my research, Barrie Thorne encouraged me to think about this project as a book. While I worked on this manuscript she served as a sociological mentor, a feminist role model, and an academic mother. Her expertise in feminist theory, theories of interaction, and theories of childhood largely influenced my approach to the youth of River High. I am forever grateful that she encouraged me to both build on and challenge her own approaches to the social world.

Countless other scholars have informally mentored me as I crafted this manuscript. Warm thanks to Michael Messner, Michael Kimmel, Karin Martin, Amy Best, and Neill Korobov for reading various portions of this manuscript and providing invaluable comments on my analysis of gender, youth, and sexuality. I also thank Naomi Schneider, my editor at UC Press, for her guidance and enthusiasm about this project.

Colleagues, students, and dear friends have shaped my thinking, my research, and my analysis of teenagers' experiences of gender and sexuality. Youyenn Teo, Orit Avishai-Bentovim, Marianne Cooper, Beth Popp, and Mark Harris all listened to various incarnations of this project, acting as much-needed sounding boards. My students in the courses "The Sociology of Gender," "Gender and Education," "Masculinities," and "Sociology of Sexualities" gave me invaluable feedback as I crafted this project, asking insightful questions and keeping me up to date on teen culture.

David Tremblay, Rebeca Burciaga, Sarah Stickle, Joanne Chao, Libby Heckman, and Scott Tipping always asked about how the manuscript was coming along, even though it must have seemed that I was working on it for an inordinately long time! Thankfully, in various ways, they all reminded me that I was a whole person and not just a researcher or author. Brooke Warner helped me navigate the world of publishing. Special thanks to Gabriella and Antonio for keeping a smile on my face as I wrote the final stages of this manuscript.

Two writing groups provided intellectual, emotional, and nutritional sustenance as I wrote this book. The members of Thursday Night Writing Group—Teresa Sharpe, Rita Gaber, and Chris Neidt—not only provided tasty meals but also helped shape the final form of this manuscript. Teresa Sharpe's close readings and Google searches for answers to pressing, yet random questions improved both my writing and the writing process.

The D-Group sustained me during my often emotionally trying research, encouraged me as I wrote, and provided much-needed critique at all stages of writing. Members of the D-Group—Natalie Boero, Leslie Bell, and Meg Jay—read draft after draft of various chapters in this manuscript. Both Leslie and Meg, trained psychotherapists, encouraged me to pay attention to my subjects' emotions and internal conflicts about gender and sexuality. Natalie has the dubious distinction of having read and commented on every version of every chapter in this manuscript. Without her insights this book would certainly not be as comprehensive, as engaging, or as insightful.

I'm so happy to thank my partner, Megan Sheppard, for her role in bringing up this book. I can't put here all the ways she made this manuscript possible. Megan kept me grounded, reminded me that fun and relaxation are important parts of the creative process, and, because of her job as a teacher and mentor to youth much like those at River High, constantly challenged me to think in new ways about my material.

Finally, I'd like to thank the youth at River High for putting up with my constant lurking and questioning. You were all just trying to have a good time in high school, and there I was, sticking my nose in the middle of it. I will be forever inspired by some of you—Ricky, Lacy, Genevieve, Riley, Jessie, Rebeca, Michelle, and Valerie. This book is dedicated to you. Thank you for working to make this world a better place for all of us.

CHAPTER ONE

Making Masculinity

Adolescence, Identity, and High School

REVENGE OF THE NERDS

Cheering students filled River High's gymnasium. Packed tightly in the bleachers, they sang, hollered, and danced to loud hip-hop music. Over their heads hung banners celebrating fifty years of River High's sports victories. The yearly assembly in which the student body voted for the most popular senior boy in the school to be crowned Mr. Cougar was under way, featuring six candidates performing a series of skits to earn student votes.

Two candidates, Brent and Greg, both handsome, blond, "all-American" water polo players, entered the stage dressed like "nerds" to perform their skit, "Revenge of the Nerds." They wore matching outfits: yellow button-down shirts; tight brown pants about five inches too short, with the waistbands pulled up clownishly high by black suspenders; black shoes with white kneesocks; and thick black-rimmed glasses held together with white tape. As music played, the boys started dancing, flailing around comically in bad renditions of outdated dance moves like the Running Man and the Roger Rabbit. The crowd roared in laughter when Brent and Greg rubbed their rear ends together in time to the music. Two girls with long straight hair and matching miniskirts and black tank tops, presumably the nerds' girlfriends, ran out to dance with Brent and Greg.

Suddenly a group of white male "gangstas" sporting bandannas, baggy pants, sports jerseys, and oversized gold jewelry walked, or, more correctly, gangsta-limped, onto the stage. They proceeded to shove Brent and Greg, who looked at them fearfully and fled the stage without their girlfriends. The gangstas encircled the two girls, then "kidnapped" them by forcing them off the stage. After peering timidly around the corner of the stage, Brent and Greg reentered. The crowd roared as Brent opened his mouth and, in a high-pitched feminine voice, cried, "We have to get our women!"

Soon a girl dressed in a sweat suit and wearing a whistle around her neck carried barbells and weight benches onto the stage. Greg and Brent emerged from behind a screen, having replaced their nerd gear with matching black and white sweat pants and T-shirts. The female coach tossed the barbells around with ease, lifting one with a single hand. The audience hooted in laughter as the nerds struggled to lift even the smallest weight. Brent and Greg continued to work out until they could finally lift the weights. They ran up to the crowd to flex their newfound muscles as the audience cheered. To underscore how strong they had become, Brent and Greg ripped off their pants. The crowd was in hysterics as the boys revealed, not muscled legs, but matching red miniskirts. At first Greg and Brent looked embarrassed; then they triumphantly dropped the skirts, revealing matching shorts, and the audience cheered.

Brent and Greg ran off stage as stagehands unfurled a large cloth sign reading "Gangstas' Hideout." Some of the gangstas who had kidnapped the girlfriends sat around a table playing poker, while other gangstas gambled with dice. The nerds, who had changed into black suits accented with ties and fedoras, strode confidently into the hideout. They threw the card table in the air, causing the gangstas to jump back as the cards and chips scattered. Looking frightened at the nerds' newfound strength, the gangstas scrambled out of their hideout. After the gangstas had fled, the two miniskirted girlfriends ran up to Brent and Greg, hugging them gratefully. Several African American boys, also dressed in suits and fedoras, ran onto the stage, dancing while the former nerds stood behind them with their arms folded. After the dance, the victorious nerds walked off stage hand in hand with their rescued girlfriends.

I open with this scene to highlight the themes of masculinity I saw during a year and a half of fieldwork at River High School. The Mr. Cougar competition clearly illuminates the intersecting dynamics of sexuality, gender, social class, race, bodies, and institutional practices that constitute adolescent masculinity in this setting. Craig and Brent are transformed from unmasculine nerds who cannot protect their girlfriends into heterosexual, muscular men. This masculinizing process happens through a transformation of bodies, the assertion of racial privilege, and a shoring up of heterosexuality.

The story line of the skit—Brent and Craig's quest to confirm their heterosexuality by rescuing their girlfriends—posits heterosexuality as central to masculinity. Brent and Craig's inability to protect "their women" marks their physical inadequacy. Their appearance—tight, ill-fitting, outdated clothes—codes them as unmasculine. Their weakness and their high-pitched voices cast them as feminine. Their homoerotic dance moves position them as homosexual. By working out, the boys shed their weak, effeminate, and possibly homosexual identities. Just in case they didn't get their message across by bench-pressing heavy weights, the boys shed their last remnants of femininity by ripping off their matching miniskirts. They become so physically imposing that they don't even have to fight the gangstas, who flee in terror at the mere hint of the nerds' strength.

This skit lays bare the ways racialized notions of masculinity may be enacted through sexualized tropes. The gangstas symbolize failed and at the same time wildly successful men in their heterosexual claim on the nerds' women. Their "do-rags," baggy pants, shirts bearing sports team insignias, and limping walks are designed to invoke a hardened inner-city gangsta style, one portrayed on television and in movies, as a specifically black cultural style. In representing black men, the gangstas symbolize hypersexuality and invoke a thinly veiled imagery of the black rapist (A. Davis 1981), who threatens white men's control over white women. But in the end, the gangstas are vanquished by the white, middle-class legitimacy of the nerds, turned masculine with their newfound strength. The skit also portrays black men as slightly feminized in that they act as cheerleaders and relieve the white heroes of the unmasculine practice of dancing.

Markers of femininity such as high voices and skirts symbolize emasculation when associated with male bodies. The girlfriends also signal a relationship between femininity and helplessness, since they are unable to save themselves from the gangstas. However, the female coach symbolizes strength, a sign of masculinity the nerds initially lack. The students in the audience cheer her as she engages in a masculinized practice, lifting weights with ease, and they laugh at the boys who can't do this. Male femininity, in this instance, is coded as humorous, while female masculinity is cheered.

Drawing on phenomena at River High such as the Mr. Cougar Assembly, the goal of this study is to explain how teenagers, teachers, and the institutional logics of schooling construct adolescent masculinity through idioms of sexuality. This book investigates the relationships between gender and sexuality as embedded in a major socializing institution of modern youth: high school. I ask how heteronormative and homophobic discourses, practices, and interactions in an American high school produce masculine identities. To examine the construction of masculinity in adolescence, I follow the deployment of, resistance to, and practices surrounding sexuality and gender in high school. I focus on the gender and sexuality practices of students, teachers, and administrators, with an emphasis on school rituals.

My findings illustrate that masculinity is not a homogenous category that any boy possesses by virtue of being male. Rather, masculinity—as constituted and understood in the social world I studied—is a configuration of practices and discourses that different youths (boys and girls) may embody in different ways and to different degrees. Masculinity, in this sense, is associated with, but not reduced or solely equivalent to, the male body. I argue that adolescent masculinity is understood in this setting as a form of dominance usually expressed through sexualized discourses.[1]

Through extensive fieldwork and interviewing I discovered that, for boys, achieving a masculine identity entails the repeated repudiation of the specter of failed masculinity. Boys lay claim to masculine identities by lobbing homophobic epithets at one another. They also assert masculine selves by engaging in heterosexist discussions of girls' bodies and their own sexual experiences. Both of these phenomena intersect with racialized identities in that they are organized somewhat differently by and for African American boys and white boys. From what I saw during my research, African American boys were more likely to be punished by school authorities for engaging in these masculinizing practices. Though homophobic taunts and assertion of heterosexuality shore up a masculine identity for boys, the relationship between sexuality and masculinity looks different when masculinity occurs outside male bodies. For girls, challenging heterosexual identities often solidifies a more masculine identity. These gendering processes are encoded at multiple levels: institutional, interactional, and individual.

To explore and theorize these patterns, this book integrates queer theory, feminist theory, and sociological research on masculinities. In this chapter I address the current state of sociological research on masculinity. Then, using feminist theories and theories of sexuality, I rework some of the insights of the sociology of masculinity literature. I conclude by suggesting that close attention to sexuality highlights masculinity as a process rather than a social identity associated with specific bodies.

WHAT DO WE MEAN BY MASCULINITY?

Sociologists have approached masculinity as a multiplicity of gender practices (regardless of their content) enacted by men whose bodies are assumed to be biologically male. Early in the twentieth century, when fears of feminization pervaded just about every sphere of social life, psychologists became increasingly concerned with differentiating men from women (Kimmel 1996). As a result, part of the definition of a psychologically "normal" adult came to involve proper adjustment to one's "gender role" (Pleck 1987). Talcott Parsons (1954), the first sociologist to really address masculinity as such, argued that men's "instrumental" role and women's "expressive" role were central to the functioning of a well-ordered society. Deviations from women's role as maternal caretakers or men's role as breadwinners would result in "role strain" and "role competition," weakening families and ultimately society.

With the advent of the women's movement, feminist gender theorists examined how power is embedded in these seemingly neutral (not to mention natural) "gender roles" (Hartmann 1976; Jaggar 1983; Rosaldo and Lamphere 1974; Rubin 1984). Psychoanalytic feminist theorists explicitly addressed masculinity as an identity formation constituted by inequality. Both Dorothy Dinnerstein (1976) and Nancy Chodorow (1978) argued that masculinity, as we recognize it, is the result of a family system in which women mother. Identification with a mother as the primary caregiver proves much more problematic in the formation of a gender identity for a boy than for a girl child, producing a self we understand as masculine characterized by defensive ego boundaries and repudiation of femininity. Feminist psychoanalytic theorists equate contemporary masculinity with a quest for autonomy and separation, an approach that influences my own analysis of masculinity.

Recognizing the changes wrought for women by feminist movements, sociologists of masculinity realized that feminism had radical implications for men (Carrigan, Connell, and Lee 1987). Frustrated with the paucity of non-normative approaches to masculinity, and what they saw (a bit defensively) as feminist characterizations of masculinity as "un-relieved villainy and all men as agents of the patriarchy in more or less the same degree" (64), these sociologists attempted to carve out new models of gendered analysis in which individual men or men collectively were not all framed as equal agents of patriarchal oppression.

The emergent sociology of masculinity became a "critical study of men, their behaviors, practices, values and perspectives" (Whitehead and Barrett 2001, 14). These new sociologists of masculinity positioned themselves in opposition to earlier Parsonian theories of masculinity, proffering, not a single masculine "role," but rather the idea that masculinity is understandable only in a model of "multiple masculinities" (Connell 1995). Instead of focusing on masculinity as the male role, this model asserts that there are a variety of masculinities, which make sense only in hierarchical and contested relations with one another. R. W. Connell argues that men enact and embody different configurations of masculinity depending on their positions within a social hierarchy of power. *Hegemonic masculinity*, the type of gender practice that, in a given space and time, supports gender inequality, is at the top of this hierarchy. *Complicit masculinity* describes men who benefit from hegemonic masculinity but do not enact it; *subordinated masculinity* describes men who are oppressed by definitions of hegemonic masculinity, primarily gay men; *marginalized masculinity* describes men who may be positioned powerfully in terms of gender but not in terms of class or race. Connell, importantly, emphasizes that the content of these configurations of gender practice is not always and everywhere the same. Very few men, if any, are actually hegemonically masculine, but all men do benefit, to different extents, from this sort of definition of masculinity, a form of benefit Connell (1995) calls the "patriarchal dividend" (41).

This model of multiple masculinities has been enormously influential, inspiring countless studies that detail the ways different configurations of masculinity are promoted, challenged, or reinforced in given social situations. This research on how men do masculinity has provided insight into practices of masculinity in a wide range of social institutions, such as families (Coltrane 2001), schools (Francis and Skelton 2001; Gilbert 1998; Mac an Ghaill 1996; Parker 1996), the workplace (Connell 1998; Cooper 2000), the media (Craig 1992; Davies 1995), and sports (Curry 2004; Edley and Wetherell 1997; Majors 2001; Messner 2002). This focus on masculinity as what men do has spawned an industry of cataloguing "types" of masculinity: gay, black, Chicano, working class, middle class, Asian, gay black, gay Chicano, white working class, militarized, transnational business, New Man, negotiated, versatile, healthy, toxic, counter, and cool masculinities, among others (Messner 2004b).

While Connell intends this model of masculinities to be understood as fluid and conflictual, the multiple masculinities model is more often used to construct static and reified typologies such as the ones listed by Michael Messner. These descriptions of masculinity are intended to highlight patterns of practice in which structure meets with identity and action, but they have the effect of slotting men into masculinity categories: a hegemonic man, a complicit man, a resistant man (or the multitude of ever-increasing types of masculinities catalogued above). While these masculinities may be posited as ideal types, they are sometimes difficult to use analytically without lapsing into a simplistic categorical analysis. Because of the emphasis on masculinities in the plural, a set of types some men can seemingly step in and out of at will, this model runs the risk of collapsing into an analysis of styles of masculinity, thereby deflecting attention from structural inequalities between men and women. In other words, we must always pay attention to power relations when we think in pluralities and diversities; otherwise we are simply left with a list of differences (Zinn and Dill 1996). Additionally, the category of "hegemonic masculinity" is so rife with contradictions it is small wonder that no man actually embodies it (Donaldson 1993). According to this model both a rich, slim, soft-spoken businessman and a poor, muscular, violent gang member might be described as hegemonically masculine. At the same time neither of them would really be hegemonically masculine, since the businessman would not be physically powerful and the poor gang member would lack claims on institutional gendered power. Because of some of these deployment problems, those studying masculinities have for some time called for a more sophisticated analysis of masculinity (Messner 1993; Morgan 1992).

To refine approaches to masculinity, researchers need to think more clearly about the implications of defining masculinity as what men or boys do. This definition conflates masculinity with the actions of those who have male bodies. Defining masculinity as "what men do" reifies biologized categories of male and female that are problematic and not necessarily discrete categories to begin with (Fausto-Sterling 1995). In the end, masculinity is framed as a social category based on an assumed biological difference that in itself is constituted by the very social category it purports to underlie. This is not to say that sociologists of masculinity are biological determinists, but by assuming that the male body is the location of masculinity their theories reify the assumed biological basis of gender. Recognizing that masculinizing discourses and practices extend beyond male bodies, this book traces the various ways masculinity is produced and manifested in relation to a multiplicity of bodies, spaces, and objects. That is, this book looks at masculinity as a variety of practices and discourses that can be mobilized by and applied to both boys and girls.

BRINGING IN SEXUALITY

Heeding the admonition of Carrigan, Connell, and Lee (1987) that "analysis of masculinity needs to be related as well to other currents in feminism" (64), I turn to interdisciplinary theorizing about the role of sexuality in the construction of gender identities. Building on studies of sexuality that demonstrate that sexuality is an organizing principle of social life, this book highlights intersections of masculinizing and sexualizing practices and discourses at River High.

Thinking about sexuality as an organizing principle of social life means that it is not just the property of individuals. Sexuality, in this sense, doesn't just indicate a person's sexual identity, whether he or she is gay or straight. Rather, sexuality is itself a form of power that exists regardless of an individual's sexual identity. Thinking about sexuality this way can be initially quite jarring. After all, usually we discuss sexuality as a personal identity or a set of private practices. However, researchers and theorists have increasingly argued that sexuality is a quite public part of social life (Foucault 1990). Though sexuality was initially studied as a set of private acts, and eventually identities, by physicians and other medical professionals intent on discerning normal from abnormal sexuality, social theorists are now documenting the ways institutions, identities, and discourses interact with, are regulated by, and produce sexual meanings.

In this sense, *sexuality* refers to sex acts and sexual identities, but it also encompasses a range of meanings associated with these acts and identities. The meanings that vary by social class, location, and gender identity (Mahay, Laumann, and Michaels 2005) may be more important than the acts themselves (Weeks 1996). A good example of this is heterosexuality. While heterosexual desires or identities might feel private and personal, contemporary meanings of heterosexuality also confer upon heterosexual individuals all sorts of citizenship rights, so that heterosexuality is not just a private matter but one that links a person to certain state benefits. Similarly contemporary meanings of sexuality, particularly heterosexuality, for instance, eroticize male dominance and female submission (Jeffreys 1996, 75). In this way what seems like a private desire is part of the mechanisms through which the microprocesses of daily life actually foster inequality.

Interdisciplinary theorizing about sexuality has primarily taken the form of "queer theory." Like sociology, queer theory destabilizes the assumed naturalness of the social order (Lemert 1996). Queer theory moves the deconstructive project of sociology into new areas by examining much of what sociology sometimes takes for granted: "deviant" sexualities, sexual identities, sexual practices, sexual discourses, and sexual norms (Seidman 1996). In making the taken-for-granted explicit, queer theorists examine sexual power as it is embedded in different areas of social life and interrogate areas of the social world not usually seen as sex-

uality—such as the ways heterosexuality confers upon an individual a variety of citizenship rights (A. Stein and Plummer 1994). The logic of sexuality not only regulates intimate relations but also infuses social relations and social structures (S. Epstein 1994; Warner 1993).

This book uses queer theory to frame bodies, desires, sexualities, and
identities in a way that isn't necessarily or solely about the oppression or
liberation of the homosexual subject but rather about how institutional
and interactional practices organize sexual life and produce sexual knowledge (Seidman 1996). Queer theory draws on a postmodern approach to
studying society that moves beyond traditional categories such as
male/female, masculine/feminine, and straight/gay to focus instead on
the instability of these categories. That is, we might think of "heterosexual" and "homosexual" as stable, opposing, and discrete identities, but really they are fraught with internal contradictions (Halley 1993). To this
end, queer theory emphasizes multiple identities and multiplicity in general. Instead of creating knowledge about categories of sexual identity,
queer theorists look to see how those categories themselves are created,
sustained, and undone.

One of the ways a queer theory approach can bring studies of masculinity in line with other feminist theorizing is to uncouple the male
body from definitions of masculinity. The masculinities literature, while
attending to very real inequalities between gay and straight men, tends
to look at sexuality as inherent in static identities attached to male bodies, not as a major organizing principle of social life (S. Epstein 1994;
Warner 1993). As part of its deconstructive project, queer theory often
points to disjunctures between pairings thought of as natural and inevitable. In doing so queer theorists may implicitly question some of the
assumptions of the multiple masculinities model—specifically the assumption that masculinity is defined by the bodily practices of boys and
men—by placing sexuality at the center of analysis. Eve Sedgwick (1995),
one of the few theorists to address the problematic assumption of the
centrality of the male body to academic discussions of masculinity, argues
that sometimes masculinity has nothing to do with men and that men

don't necessarily have anything to do with masculinity. As a result "it is important to drive a wedge in, early and often and if possible conclusively, between the two topics, masculinity and men, whose relation to one another it is so difficult not to presume" (12).

Assuming that masculinity is only about men weakens inquiries into masculinity. Therefore it is important to look at masculinizing processes outside the male body, not to catalogue a new type of masculinity, but to identify practices, rituals, and discourses that constitute masculinity. Doing so indicates the centrality of sexualized meanings to masculinity in relation to both male and female bodies.

Dislodging masculinity from a biological location is a productive way to highlight the social constructedness of masculinity and may even expose a latent sexism within the sociological literature in its assumption that masculinity, as a powerful social identity, is only the domain of men. Judith Kegan Gardiner (2003) points out in her review of gender and masculinity textbooks "the very different investments that men, including masculinity scholars, appear to have in preserving masculinity as some intelligible and coherent grounding of identity in comparison to the skepticism and distance shown by feminists towards femininity" (153). Indeed, gender scholars who study women have not been nearly as interested in femininity as scholars of men have been in masculinity.

It is not that bodies are unimportant. They are. Bodies are the vehicles through which we express gendered selves; they are also the matter through which social norms are made concrete. What is problematic is the unreflexive assumption of an embodied location for gender that echoes throughout the masculinities literature. Looking at masculinity as discourses and practices that can be mobilized by female bodies undermines the conflation of masculinity with an embodied state of maleness (Califia 1994; Halberstam 1998; Paechter 2006). Instead, this approach looks at masculinity as a recognizable configuration of gender practices and discourses.

Placing sexuality at the center of analysis highlights the "routinely unquestioned heteronormative expectations and proscriptions that exist as background context in contemporary U.S. culture," assumptions that "emerge when traditional normative gender boundaries are crossed" (Neilsen, Walden, and Kunkel 2000, 292). Examining these heteronormative structures and how masculine girls and feminine boys challenge them gets at contemporary constructions of masculinity in adolescence. Studying gender transgressions in adolescence provides empirical evidence to bolster and extend some of the claims of queer theory, an approach that often relies on literary or artistic examples for its data (Gamson and Moon 2004, 49).

RETHINKING MASCULINITY, SEXUALITY, AND BODIES

Attending to sexuality and its centrality to gendered identities opens insight into masculinity both as a process (Bederman 1995) and as a field through which power is articulated (Scott 1999) rather than as a never-ending list of configurations of practice enacted by specific bodies. My research indicates that masculinity is an identity that respondents think of as related to the male body but as not necessarily specific to the male body. Interviews with and observations of students at River High indicate that they recognize masculinity as an identity expressed through sexual discourses and practices that indicate dominance and control.[2]

As scholars of gender have demonstrated, gender is accomplished through day-to-day interactions (G. Fine 1989; Hochschild 1989; Thorne 2002; West and Zimmerman 1991). In this sense gender is the "activity of managing situated conduct in light of normative conceptions of attitudes and activities appropriate for one's sex category" (West and Zimmerman 1991, 127). People are supposed to act in ways that line up with their presumed sex. That is, we expect people we think are females to act like women and males to act like men. People hold other people accountable for "doing gender" correctly.

The queer theorist Judith Butler (1999) builds on this interactionist approach to gender, arguing that gender is something people accomplish through "a set of repeated acts within a highly rigid regulatory frame that congeal over time to produce the appearance of substance, of a natural sort of being" (43). That is, gender is not just natural, or something one is, but rather something we all produce through our actions. By repeatedly acting "feminine" or "masculine" we actually create those categories. Becoming gendered, becoming masculine or feminine, is a process.

Butler argues that gendered beings are created through processes of repeated invocation and repudiation. People constantly reference or invoke a gendered norm, thus making the norm seem like a timeless truth. Similarly, people continually repudiate a "constitutive outside" (Butler 1993, 3) in which is contained all that is cast out of a socially recognizable gender category. The "constitutive outside" is inhabited by what she calls "abject identities," unrecognizably and unacceptably gendered selves. The interactional accomplishment of gender in a Butlerian model consists, in part, of the continual iteration and repudiation of an abject identity. The abject identity must be constantly named to remind individuals of its power. Similarly, it must be constantly repudiated by individuals or groups so that they can continually affirm their identities as normal and as culturally intelligible. Gender, in this sense, is "constituted through the force of exclusion and abjection, one which produces a constitutive outside to the subject, an abjected outside, which is, after all, 'inside' the subject as its own founding repudiation" (Butler 1993, 3). This repudiation creates and reaffirms a "threatening specter" (3) of failed gender, the existence of which must be continually repudiated through interactional processes.

Informed by this interactionist approach to gender, in which gender is not just a quality of an individual but the result of interactional processes, this study examines masculinity as sexualized processes of confirmation and repudiation through which individuals demonstrate mastery over others. Building on the insights of the multiple masculinities literature, I emphasize that this definition of masculinity is not universal but local, age limited, and institutional and that other definitions of masculinity may be found in different locales and different times. Examining masculinity using Butler's theory of interactional accomplishment of gender indicates that the "fag" position is an "abject" position and, as such, is a "threatening specter" constituting contemporary American adolescent masculinity at River High. Similarly, drawing on Butler's concept of the constitution of gender through "repeated acts within a highly rigid regulatory frame" elucidates how seemingly "normal" daily interactions of male adolescence are actually ritualized interactions constituting masculinity. These repeated acts involve demonstrating sexual mastery and the denial of girls' subjectivity. The school itself sets the groundwork for boys' interactional rituals of repudiation and confirmation, like those illustrated in the opening vignette.

Butler also suggests ways to challenge an unequal gender order. Individuals who deliberately engage in gender practices that render them culturally unintelligible, such as practices that are at odds with their apparent sex category, challenge the naturalness and inevitability of a rigid gender order. Some girls at River High engage in precisely this sort of resistance by engaging in masculinizing processes. While challenging an unequal gender order at the level of interactions does not necessarily address larger structural inequalities, it is an important component of social change. That said, doing gender differently by engaging in gender practices not "appropriate" for one's sex category, such as drag, also runs the risk of reifying binary categories of gender. Resistance, in this model, is fraught with danger, since it is both an investment in gender norms and a subversion of them. Sometimes it challenges the gender order and sometimes it seems to bolster it.

METHODOLOGY
Adolescence as a Social Category

Because of the intense identity work that occurs during adolescence, it is a particularly fruitful site for illuminating and developing these theoretical issues. In contemporary Western societies the teenage years are often ones in which youths explore and consolidate identity (Erikson 1959/1980).

The issue of whether adolescence is a universal developmental stage or a creation of modernity has been debated in historical, psychological, and sociological literatures (Suransky 1982; Tait 2000). Regardless of its universal, timeless, localized, or temporal features, adolescence is currently constructed as a time in which teenagers work to create identity and make the transition from childhood to adulthood. It is also constructed as a turbulent time psychologically, biologically, and socially.

Since the "invention" of the adolescent in the United States in the early twentieth century (Ben-Amos 1995), teen cultures have emerged as a unique cultural formation where varied forms are characterized by gender differentiation and sexuality. In fact, G. Stanley Hall, the psychologist who created and popularized the concept of adolescence, described it as a time when boys engage in masculinizing activities that set them apart from girls (Kimmel 1996). One of the primary ways teen cultures evolved was through heterosexual rituals such as courtship, which became enshrined and ritualized through the emergence of large public high schools (Modell 1989). Such rituals began with the popularization of the private automobile and continued to be set up as a cultural norm through school yearbooks, school newspapers, and the organization of school activities encouraging heterosexual pairings, such as dances and proms. Given the historical tie between adolescence, sexuality, and gender, it seems a fitting life phase in which to study the formation of gendered identities.

Levels of Analysis

To explore masculinity as a process, I attend to multiple levels of analysis, including individual investments in and experiences of gendered and sexualized identities, institutional discourses, and collective gender practices.

Social processes can be understood through the experiences of individuals who live them (Chodorow 2000). Social processes and cultural categories are also instantiated at the level of personal meanings, which are created in a "tangle of experience" (Briggs 1998, 2). Although gendered meanings are often contradictory, gender is also experienced and talked about as a real and stable category. Gender is personally created, understood, and negotiated through individual biography, fantasy, and projection (Chodorow 1995). To get at individual meanings of masculinity, I pay attention to teens' voices in one-on-one interviews where they discuss the role of masculinity in their lives.

However, looking at masculinity in adolescence without paying attention to larger structural patterns results in overly individualized and psychologized analyses that distort larger issues of inequality. Recently a spate of psychological books have called for more attention to be paid to the "real" victims of the so-called "gender wars." These authors claim that boys are forced by families, peer groups, schools, and the media to hide their "true" emotions and develop a hard emotional shell that is what we know as masculinity (Kindlon and Thompson 1999; Pollack 1998; Sommers 2000). William Pollack's book rightly encourages parents and other caregivers to listen to the "boy code" in order to hear boys' emotions and struggles. Sommers and Kindlon and Thompson, among others, either overtly or tacitly treat gender as a zero-sum game in which gains for girls must equal losses for boys, an assumption that has been critiqued by gender researchers (American Association of University Women [AAUW] 2001; Kimmel 1999). None of these volumes address larger issues of gender and power in adolescence and childhood; instead, they focus on the idea that boys and girls are naturally different and that boys are the ones suffering from discrimination, not girls.

To avoid this sort of emphasis on individual and idiosyncratic experiences, I examine relational and institutional gender processes, emphasizing how gender happens in groups. Friendships, peer groups, and cliques are exceedingly important to the formation of identity in adolescence (Bettie 2003; Hallinan and Williams 1990; Kinney 1993). Attending to gender as a relational process is important, since peer cultures trump or at least compete with parental influence in terms of setting up conceptions of gender (Risman and Myers 1997). As a result, masculinity processes look very different in groups than they do when teens discuss their own experiences around masculinity.

At the level of the institution, schools are a primary institution for identity formation, development, and solidification for contemporary American youth. They are important sites for the construction of race, class, and gender inequalities as well as pivotal locations of social change in challenging these inequalities (Tyack and Hansot 1990). Social groups in schools, such as cliques, provide one of the ways that youth begin to identify and position themselves by social class (Eckert 1989; Willis 1981), gender (AAUW 2001; Adler, Kless, and Adler 1992; Eder, Evans, and Parker 1995; Thorne 1993), and race (Eckert 1989; Eder, Evans, and Parker 1995; Perry 2002; Price 1999). The categories most salient to students have varied historically and regionally—cowboys and preps may be salient in one school, whereas jocks and goths may be organizing groups in another. Furthermore, schools play a part in structuring adolescent selves through the setting up of institutional gender orders, or the totality of gender arrangements in a given school—including relations of power, labor, emotion, and symbolism (Connell 1996; Heward 1990; Skelton 1996; Spade 2001). This book examines the way gendered and sexualized identifications and the institutional ordering of these identifications in a California high school both reinforce and challenge inequality among students.

Research Site

I conducted fieldwork at a suburban high school that I call River High. (Names of places and people have been changed.) River High is a suburban, working-class, fifty-year-old high school in a town I call Riverton in north central California. With the exception of median household income and racial diversity (both of which are higher than the national average due to Riverton's location in California), the town mirrors national averages in the proportion of those who have attended college, marriage rates, and age distribution. Riverton's approximately one hundred thousand residents are over half white and about a quarter Latino or Hispanic. The rest identify in relatively equal numbers as African American or Asian (U.S. Bureau of the Census 2000). It is a moderate to conservative religious community. Most of the churches are Baptist, Pentecostal, Evangelical, or nondenominational. Many residents commute to surrounding cities for work. The major employers in Riverton are the school district, the city itself, medical centers, and large discount retailers such as Wal-Mart or Target.

On average Riverton is a middle-class community. However, residents are likely to refer to the town as two communities: "Old Riverton" and "New Riverton." A busy highway and railroad tracks bisect the town into these two sections. River High is literally on the "wrong side of the tracks," in Old Riverton. Exiting the freeway and heading north into Old Riverton, one sees a mix of old ranch-style homes, their yards strewn with various car parts, lawn chairs, appliances, and sometimes chickens surrounded by chain-link fences. Old Riverton is visually bounded on the west and east by smoke-puffing factories. While effort has clearly been made to revitalize the downtown, as revealed by recently repainted storefronts, it appears sad and forlorn, with half of its shops sitting empty.

Driving south under the freeway and over a rise, one encounters New Riverton. The streets widen and sidewalks appear. Instead of a backdrop of smokestacks, a forested mountain rises majestically in the background. Instead of old run-down single-story houses with sheets hanging in the windows for curtains, either side of the street is lined with walled-off new home developments composed of identical stucco two-story homes with perfectly manicured lawns. The teens from these homes attend Hillside High School, the other high school in the Riverton district.

River High looks like many American high schools. It is made up of several one-story buildings connected by open-air walkways, though the students cram into closed hallways to find their lockers in between classes. Like many schools unable to afford new buildings to accommodate their burgeoning student populations, River relies on mobile classrooms, which are continually encroaching on the basketball courts. It is an open campus where students can come and go as they please, though they can't get far in this suburban community without a car. Many of the students stay on campus to eat and socialize in one of the two main "quads" made up of grass, concrete, and benches, or in the noisy and overcrowded cafeteria.

Roughly two thousand students attended River High during my time there. Its racial/ethnic breakdown roughly represented California at large: 49 percent white, 28 percent Latino, 10 percent African American, and 6 percent Asian (as compared to California's 59, 32, 7, and 11 percents respectively) (U.S. Bureau of the Census 2000). The students at River High were primarily working class, though there were middle-class and poor students.³ Lauren Carter, the guidance counselor, described it as an archetypical American high school emphasizing tradition, sports, and community. She illustrated this focus by telling me of the centrality of football to the social life of both Riverton and River High. "There's all these old-timers who come out to the football games. Which I think is pretty funny. It's like Iowa. This school could be straight out of Iowa." The principal, Mr. Hobart, had played on the football team when he had attended River. Lauren told me that Mr. Hobart's career path was a common one: "You go to River. You go to Carrington State for college. You come back to River and teach." She also told me that the historically industry-based economy of Riverton (which had manufactured a variety of chemical, oil, metal, and paper products) was faltering and that consequently poverty rates were rising. In fact, only one of the factories that had historically provided jobs for residents was still in operation.

Research

I gathered data using the qualitative method of ethnographic research. I spent a year and a half conducting fieldwork in the school and connected sites; I formally interviewed fifty students (forty-nine from River High and one from Hillside), and I informally interviewed countless students, faculty, and administrators.

I recruited students for interviews through formal classroom presentations and through informal networks among students. I conducted presentations in a range of classes (English, auto shop, drama, history, social studies, weight lifting, stagecraft, bowling, and economics) and clubs (Asian Club, the Gay/Straight Alliance, and Student Government). I also hung around at lunch, before school, after school, and at various school events talking to various students about my research, which I presented as "writing a book about guys." The Appendix includes a detailed discussion of my experiences conducting research at River High.

The interviews usually took place at school, either after school hours or during class time. Students with a car sometimes met me at one of the local fast-food restaurants, where I treated them to a meal. The interviews usually lasted forty-five minutes to an hour and a half. I tape-recorded them.

The initial interviews I conducted helped me map a gendered and sexualized geography of the school from which I chose my observation sites. In the tradition of Michael Messner (2004a) and Barrie Thorne (1993), I focused on highly salient gendered moments by attending major school rituals such as Winter Ball, school rallies, plays, dances, and lunches. In addition to these schoolwide rituals I conducted most of my research in three areas: a gender-"neutral" site (a senior government classroom, where sexualized meanings were subdued); three sites that students marked as fag (drama classes and the Gay/Straight Alliance); and two normatively "masculine" sites (auto shop and weight lifting). I took daily field notes focusing on how students, faculty, and administrators negotiated, regulated, and resisted particular meanings of gender and sexuality. I would also occasionally ride along with Mr. Johnson (Mr. J.), the head of the school's disciplinary system, in his battery-powered golf cart to watch which and how and when students were disciplined.

Given the importance of appearance in high school, I gave some thought to how I would present myself to the students at River High. I wore my standard graduate student gear—comfortable, baggy cargo pants, a black T-shirt or sweater, and tennis shoes. I carried a messenger bag instead of a backpack. I didn't wear makeup. Because I look young, both students and faculty sometimes asked me if I was a new student.

More than a few times teachers or security personnel whom I hadn't yet met reprimanded me for walking around the halls during class time. I did not try to pass as or fit in with the students in my interactional style. I spoke differently than the students, using just enough slang so that I didn't seem like a teacher but asking them to explain themselves frequently enough to indicate that I was not one of them. See the Appendix for a more extensive discussion of the unique difficulties of conducting research in a high school as well as the challenges and benefits of being a woman conducting research on male and female adolescents.

ORGANIZATION OF THE BOOK

Analyzing interactions between teachers, school rules, and students, chapter 2 continues to draw upon the Mr. Cougar competition as a metaphor for masculinity at River High. This chapter begins to paint a picture of River High—its flavor, traditions, students, teachers, and administration. It focuses on how sexuality is embedded in the daily life of the school and how sexual discourses interact with definitions of masculinity. Heteronormative practices, those that affirm that boy-girl pairings are natural and preferable to same-sex pairings, are entrenched in official and unofficial school rules, school rituals, and pedagogical practices.

In chapter 3, I continue to link meanings of sexuality to definitions of masculinity. Specifically I examine how a fag identity is continually used to discipline boys into heterosexually masculine positions. The *fag* epithet has both sexual and nonsexual meanings that always draw on notions of gender. Examining the use of the word *fag* as a trope reveals that it is not necessarily a static identity that attaches permanently to a certain (gay) boy's body; rather, it is a fluid identity that boys struggle to avoid, often by lobbing the insult at others. I conclude by showing that the fag identity is, in part, racialized, taking on different meanings and salience in various social groups.

Chapter 4 discusses complicated relationships between heterosexuality and masculinity in adolescence. Discussions about teenage boys are riddled with clichés concerning hormone-driven behavior. This chapter moves beyond these trite characterizations of testosterone-fueled locker-room talk by reframing it as "compulsive heterosexuality," in which these sorts of practices are ritualized demonstrations of mastery over girls' bodies, not necessarily indicators of sexual desire. Compulsive heterosexuality plays a central role in boys' thoughts, actions, and discussions at River High. Through rituals of "getting girls," cross-gender touching, and engaging in "sex talk" with one another, some boys continually demonstrate to themselves and others that they are indeed masculine. Defining masculinity as mastery builds on the definitions of masculinity elaborated in chapter 3, in which boys make it clear that the most unmasculine position is a fag position, in which a boy is weak, penetrated, and lacking in mastery over his and others' bodies. In the Appendix, I discuss how these masculinizing processes in adolescence don't just take place among peers but also happen between a female researcher and (primarily) male respondents. I focus particularly on the ways the boys infused our interactions with sexual content and the ways I managed these interactions so as to maintain rapport while simultaneously enforcing a professional distance and preserving my dignity.

Chapter 5 challenges the dominant mode of thinking in the sociology of masculinity literature that treats masculinity as, more or less, whatever male bodies do. Three cases of girls who act like guys reveal the different ways non-normative sexual identities interact with gender identity and social status. These case studies indicate that masculine girls occupy higher-status social positions than do feminine boys. They also indicate that doing gender differently can, but doesn't always, challenge gender inequality.

The concluding chapter revisits topics discussed in the substantive chapters and lays out the theoretical significance of the project. It raises questions about how adolescent gender and sexual identities can be reconfigured to be less homophobic and sexist. In this discussion I make

connections between homophobia, sexuality, and inequality. I conceptu-
alize the teasing and bullying that goes on in adolescence as a socialization process in which all youth—boys and girls, straight and gay, feminine
and masculine—suffer. This chapter provides specific recommendations
about the creation of antihomophobia programs and structural support
for gay and non-normatively gendered students.

CHAPTER TWO

Becoming Mr. Cougar

Institutionalizing Heterosexuality and
Masculinity at River High

Before Brent and Greg took the stage to perform their "Revenge of the Nerds" sketch, they, like the other Mr. Cougar candidates, paraded around the gym while students cheered in what looked a lot like a marriage ceremony. As Brent's name was announced, a female student emerged from the back of the gym holding up a poster board sign decorated with his name and his water polo number. Behind her, Brent, dressed in a tuxedo and flanked by his mother and a formally attired female escort, stepped out into the auditorium of raucous students. The quartet proceeded around the gym, pausing at each of three sets of bleachers so the students could applaud as Brent and his escort waved to their friends. His mother beamed as she held tightly to his arm. Brent stopped at the third set of bleachers to deposit her in a row of chairs specially designated for the mothers of the Mr. Cougar candidates (no seats were provided for fathers or other relatives, who presumably sat behind them in the bleachers). Brent planted a kiss on her cheek and proceeded around the remainder of the gym with his teenage escort. After all members of the "Top Six" (the six candidates who had received the most votes in the Mr. Cougar contest) had engaged in this procession, they disappeared behind a screen to ready themselves for their skits.

Like a wedding, this popularity ritual marks a transition to adulthood (Modell 1989). The Top Six are handed off from an opposite-sex parent to an age- and gender-appropriate escort. In this case, the mother's relinquishing of her son to a female date while receiving a chaste but sexualized sign of goodbye, the kiss, symbolizes the way certain heterosexual practices denote adulthood. As in a wedding ritual, the starring couple is dressed up in costume, cheered by others, and posed for pictures so that the two remain linked in students' minds for years to come.

Though teenagers and sexuality are almost redundant concepts, schools are not necessarily thought of as sexual institutions. Rather, teens themselves are seen as hypersexual and adults are charged with containing this sexuality. Life markers such as a teen's first kiss, "going steady," and loss of virginity all function as recognizable tropes of adolescent sexuality. Teen sexuality occupies an ambivalent cultural space, marking a maturation process and denoting danger and chaos because teens' sexual practices are seen as unsafe and out of control (Tait 2000). Researchers tend to focus on dangerous aspects of teen sexual activity such as sexually transmitted diseases, date rape, and pregnancy (Medrano 1994; Strunin 1994). Researchers who do examine sexualized adolescent identities rather than practices tend to focus on non-normative identities such as gay and lesbian teenagers (Kulkin, Chauvin, and Percle 2000; Waldner-Haugrud and Magruder 1996).

This chapter takes a slightly different approach to teenage sexuality. Rather than address individual sexual practices or identities of teenagers, I look at the school itself as an organizer of sexual practices, identities, and meanings. Beginning in elementary school, students participate in a "heterosexualizing process" (Renold 2000) in which children present themselves as "normal" girls or boys through discourses of heterosexuality (see also Kehily 2000; K. Robinson 2005). Schools that convey and regulate sexual meanings are often organized in ways that are heteronormative and homophobic (Walford 2000; Walters and Hayes 1998; Wood 1984). The ordering of sexuality from elementary school through high school is inseparable from the institutional ordering of gendered identities. The heterosexualizing process organized by educational institutions cannot be separated from, and in fact is central to, the development of masculine identities.

While school rituals such as Mr. Cougar are a prime site for the affirmation and definition of normative sexual and gender identities, seemingly neutral areas of academic instruction also draw upon and reinforce normative definitions of heterosexuality (Letts and Sears 1999). For instance, at one elementary school a teacher invoked imagery of a heterosexual wedding to teach children rules of grammar (Ingraham 1999). The class put on a mock wedding between the letters "Q" (the groom) and "U" (the bride), to illustrate the common coupling of the two letters. Similar heteronormative discourses permeate sex education curricula, which often feature a heterosexual married couple as the model for teen sexuality (Moran 2000; Trudell 1993), and biology classes, in which gendered metaphors are used to explain the fertilization process (E. Martin 1997).[1]

Building on this insight that schools are sexualized and gendered institutions, this chapter investigates River High's "informal sexuality curriculum" (Trudell 1993),[2] or the way sexuality is constructed at the level of the institution through disciplinary practices, student-teacher relationships, and school events. Looking at the structure of sexuality at school is important because masculinity and femininity are forged through a "heterosexual matrix" (Butler 1995) that involves the public ordering of masculinity and femininity through meanings and practices of sexuality. Both the formal and informal sexuality curricula at River High encouraged students to craft normative sexual and gendered identities, in which masculinity and femininity were defined by heterosexuality (Neilsen, Walden, and Kunkel 2000). Through these institutional practices of heterosexuality River High provided the scaffolding for an adolescent masculinity constituted by interactional rituals of heterosexism and homophobia. Through school rituals, pedagogical practices, and disciplinary procedures, River High set up formal and informal sexual practices that reflected definitions of masculinity and femininity as opposite, complementary, unequal, and heterosexual (Butler 1993). Thus sexuality, in this sense, cannot be looked at as separate from gender. Heterosexuality both depends upon and produces gendered identities, meanings, and practices. This informal and formal institutional ordering of gender and sexuality sets the stage for the rest of the book, in which I document how boys and girls engage in interactional rituals to achieve masculine identities, which are, in large part, based in similar homophobic and heterosexualizing processes.

RIVER HIGH'S GENDER
AND SEXUALITY CURRICULUM

River High's official policies about sexual matters reflected an ambivalence about adolescent sexuality. Administrators strove to protect students from exposure to sexualized topics and at the same time were exceedingly interested in students' sexual practices, expressions, and identities. While River High's administration was wary of any official discussion of sexuality, informal discussions happened all the time, many of them instigated by or occurring within earshot of teachers or other school officials.

I first experienced River High's ambivalent stance about students and sexuality when I was trying to secure the school as a research site. Following the instructions of Mr. Hobart, the principal of River High, I wrote a letter to the school district office outlining my research plans and requesting permission to conduct interviews with students. In the letter I outlined eight interview topics I planned to cover: families, self-image, adolescence, friends, pastimes, the future, and gender. When Principal Hobart e-mailed me to discuss the project he told me that the school board was concerned with the "gender" subheading and questions I might ask about "sexual identity development."[3] None of the other proposed topics concerned them. Lauren Carter, River High's guidance specialist, underscored this point when she later told me that the school had recently been contacted to participate in a survey of students' "at-risk" behavior. The organization sponsoring the study had offered the school a much-needed $10,000 for participating. Lauren laughed as she explained that there was "no way" the school would allow people to ask students about sex. Her comment and the school board's wariness echoed larger social anxieties about kids and sexual behavior. Because, in the United States, adults interpret adolescent sexuality as problematic and disruptive, as opposed to a normal part of the life course, they try to avoid inspiring sexual behavior by refusing to talk about it (Schalet 2000). American schools' reliance on abstinence-only sex education programs (Trudell 1993) and River High's suspicion of researchers reflect this sort of approach to teen sexuality. They reflect the twin assumptions that American teens are too innocent to know about sexuality and too sexual to be trusted with information.

River High's administrators, while concerned with researchers talking to students about sex, were keenly interested in students' sexual behaviors. During a meeting with Lauren on my first day of research, she talked about a recent incident in which several football players had raped a female student. She explained that this scandal was one of the reasons the administration found my research so interesting. While administrators didn't want adults actually talking to students about sex, they did want to know about students' sexual behavior, and they understood that a focus on teen sex and sexuality would address some very serious social problems, like rape. As a result administrators at River High found themselves in an odd position in which they both regulated and encouraged discussions of sex, sexuality, and sexual practices.

Official policies about sexuality were also policies about gender. River High's dress code emphasized gender difference through its clothing policies. At the beginning of each year a dress code published in a student planner was distributed to students during fall registration. The year I was there, it detailed that girls were not allowed to wear clothes that showed their midriff or tank tops with thin straps.[4] Boys were not allowed to wear what students referred to as "beaters," short for "wife beaters." These are thin, white, ribbed tank tops usually worn underneath an unbuttoned, oversized button-down shirt. Girls, much to the consternation of many boys, were allowed to wear these, though most opted not to. The principal published an article in the school paper outlining the school's dress code:

> For the young women of River High, that means you should dress in clothes that cover your bodies ensuring that personal portions of your torso are not exposed. This includes ensuring that belly buttons are covered. For the gentlemen of RHS you need to ensure that your pants remain at the waistline and that your underclothes and/or skin are not exposed.

The dress code clearly prevented both boys and girls from revealing certain parts of their bodies. However, the genders were charged with slightly different prohibitions. Even though the school dress code prohibited both boys and girls from showing certain parts of bare skin, Principal Hobart emphasized gender differentiation. According to this dress code a boy could show a belly button and a girl could wear pants below her waistline. In a similar spirit of gender differentiation through dress, boys and girls were assigned different-colored graduation robes. In fact, each year River held an assembly to display the yellow and black graduation robes, modeled by a girl and a boy respectively. Accompanied by loud music and an emcee, a boy wearing a black robe and a girl wearing a yellow robe strutted across the gym floor in front of throngs of screaming seniors, who were encouraged to order their robes as soon as possible.

In addition to emphasizing gender difference, official school policies encouraged sexual abstinence and discouraged homosexuality.[5] River Unified School District policies dictated that in sex education courses, which were given from sixth to twelfth grade, abstinence be taught as the best practice. However, River High, like many schools in California, expressed some official, if reluctant, tolerance for "alternative" sexualities and gender expressions. Students were not suspended for wearing opposite-gender clothing (assuming it stayed within the boundaries dictated by the dress code). The administration (after a student threatened a lawsuit) allowed the formation of a Gay/Straight Alliance (although, to be fair, it also allowed the formation of a White Heritage Club, a thinly veiled racist group). While the sex education standards did emphasize abstinence, they also emphasized recognition of different lifestyles as part of the curriculum. In the end, the school's official sexuality curriculum, while somewhat problematic, also indicated a willingness to change if that change was initiated by persistent students. Given the conservative area of California in which River High is located, this sort of flexibility about moral issues was impressive.

PEDAGOGY: THE UNOFFICIAL GENDER
AND SEXUALITY CURRICULUM

The junior and senior social science classroom belonging to Ms. Macallister (whom students affectionately called Ms. Mac) was a shrine to heterosexuality. Ms. Mac was one of the most popular and effective teachers at River High. Short in stature, sporting high heels and an enormous personality, Ms. Mac infused the learning process with life and laughter. During my research at River, I always enjoyed my time in her classroom because she reminded me of some of my favorite high school teachers. River graduates often returned to visit her, and current students frequently popped their heads in her colorful classroom just to say "hi." Walking into her room, students saw a row of floor-to-ceiling cabinets decorated with long laminated ribbons designed to look like film from a movie reel. Down the center of these film rolls ran pictures of River students from proms and Winter Balls of years past. While a senior picture or two occasionally interrupted the parade of formal dresses and tuxes, the vast majority of the pictures showed boy-girl pairs dressed in their formal best. This had the effect of creating an environment in which a gender-differentiated heterosexuality was celebrated and made a focal point.

Ms. Mac established a comfortable rapport with her students through lighthearted teasing. Much of this teasing revolved around students' romantic relationships. One morning, as usual, friends Jeremy and Angela walked in late, chatting amiably. Ms. Mac looked at them and shook her head, sighing, "Ah, the couple of the year coming in late." Jeremy and Angela rolled their eyes and laughed as they took their seats. Ms. Mac's comment effectively transformed a cross-gender friendship into a het-erosexualized pairing. In commenting on Jeremy and Angela this way, she turned them into a pair who would fit right in with the normative im-ages on her wall.

Like other teachers, Ms. Mac frequently drew on and reinforced con-cepts of heterosexuality in her teaching. One day, she was trying to ex-plain to the students the "full faith and credit clause" of the Constitution, which states that one state has to honor another state's laws. Using mar-riage as an example, Ms. Mac explained, "If a state makes a law that twelve-year-olds can get married without their parents' permission . . . " Cathy interrupted her, shouting, "That's disgusting! Does that mean a twelve-year-old can marry a thirty-year-old?" Calvin and Rich yelled, "Oooh, gross!" Ignoring them, Ms. Mac continued to teach: "We have different state laws about marriage. If something happened they decided to live elsewhere and they had children . . . " Again several students yelled, "Eewww!" Brett helpfully added, "It would be damn near impos-sible for a twelve-year-old to do his deed."

Ms. Mac presumably used marriage as an example to which all the stu-dents could relate because of its assumed universality and ahistorical na-ture. However, she could have drawn on timely, social justice–oriented examples such as the Defense of Marriage Act and movements for gay marriage. She instead reinforced, with the help of the students, a narra-tive of heterosexuality that depends on a similar age of the two partners, involves the state sanction of that relationship, and encourages procre-ation as central to such a relationship. Brett built on this discourse by stat-ing that it would "be damn near impossible for a twelve-year-old to do his deed." By saying this he linked sexual development and masculinity and referenced a definition of sexuality predicated on a man's ejaculatory abilities. This comment drew on narratives of masculinity that see sexu-ality as an important part of a movement from boyhood into manhood.

Like the administrators, teachers at River High often felt the need to control a potentially out-of-control sexuality in the classroom, even though they drew on imagery of this same sexuality in their pedagogical practices. Invoking sexual examples and metaphors was a useful pedagogical tool that allowed teachers to communicate with students and hold their attention; but because teen sexuality was perceived as potentially explosive teachers constantly sought to corral these same discussions. In doing so, teachers directed their energies primarily at the boys. Ms. Mac, for instance, walked this delicate line as she managed a class project in which the students were supposed to create a political party. The students needed to outline a platform, design campaign goals, and develop fundraising strategies. Student groups created parties ranging from those that addressed serious issues, such as the Civil Rights Party and the Environmental Party, to fanciful parties such as the Party Party (devoted to what else—partying) or the Man Party, dedicated to ending women's suffrage. The boys told me with relish, and the girls with anger, how the members of this party walked around school with clipboards to gather signatures from students supporting the termination of women's suffrage. The boys laughed as they explained that most of the girls thought that *suffrage* meant suffering.

The members of the Safer Sex Party, Jenni, Stephanie, and Arturo, planned to encourage condom use by handing out free condoms they had picked up at the local Planned Parenthood office. Jenny, to illustrate their point, held up a paper bag from which she withdrew a handful of multicolored condoms to show me. When the Safer Sex Party presented their project the next day, Ms. Mac panicked as they began to pass out condoms taped to pieces of paper with their party's slogan on them. Ms. Mac cried, "Oh, my goodness!" and looked at me, wide eyed. I said, "I knew this was coming." She responded, half seriously, half joking, "I could have used a warning!" Arturo read their statement of purpose, saying they had formed their party to "prevent HIV and AIDS." Chaos swept the class as students laughed and made jokes about the condoms. Ms. Mac sighed dramatically and repeatedly, muttering, "No, no no no no." Alan, mocking her, started repeating, "No no no no." Chad asked, "Can we have an example of safe sex?" Students laughed. Ms. Mac announced, with a note of pain, "Ladies and gentlemen, I'm just a little bit shocked by this. I could get fired. School board policy prevents distribution of them. I'm going to have to collect these afterwards." Alan, trying to keep his condom, challenged, "What if when you get them back one is missing?" Ms. Mac, starting to collect them, responded, "All you guys who put them in your wallets, give them back." After she had collected the condoms, the class had settled down, and other groups had presented, Ms. Mac looked over at Brett's bag and saw a condom in it. She picked it up and slipped it in her pocket. Alan, seeing that his friend was caught, reluctantly handed over the condom he had hidden earlier. Then Alan looked at Arturo, one of the Safer Sex Party members, and nodded at him with a knowing look, motioning that he'd get more from Arturo later. This incident so rattled Ms. Mac that for weeks afterward she teased me about not warning her.

In this instance the condom served as a symbol around which social anxieties about teen sexuality cohered. The condom was a "cultural object," or something that tells a story about the culture in which it is found (Griswold 1994). It represented students' real or potential sexual practices. While Ms. Mac certainly followed the school board's edict in her concern about the condom distribution, the panic in her voice belied a concern about students' sexual behavior and reflected the River High administration's general anxiety about it. This panic around the condom was ironic, as the students were acting, in this instance, as responsible sexual agents. Their political party was dedicated to promoting safer sex practices and stemming the spread of sexually transmitted diseases. With this goal they challenged River High's orthodoxy that students were not responsible enough to control their own sexual behavior by asserting that, in spite of their sex education curriculum, they did know about condoms and actually cared about their and other students' sexual health.

The condom, as a cultural object, also illustrated the importance of heterosexual activity to masculine identities. While the girls tittered and laughed, it was the boys in the class for whom the link with sexual activity was important. For boys the condoms served as evidence of masculinity in that they were a proxy for heterosexual success. The boys were the ones who held on to the condoms instead of handing them back, made sure other students knew they held on to them, and attempted to gather more condoms. Chad also demonstrated his heterosexuality, in a way that no girl did, by requesting an example of "safe sex." Even Ms. Mac acknowledged the importance of condoms as symbols of virility when she specifically addressed the boys in the classroom as she tried to manage condom distribution frenzy—"so all you guys who put them in your wallets, give them back." The condoms became concrete symbols of masculinity through their signification of heterosexual activity. The condoms both threatened the stability of the classroom (in the minds of the teachers and the school administrators) and symbolized masculinity by indicating sexual activity.

In addition to teaching practices built on shared understandings of heterosexuality, mild discourses of homophobia permeated student-teacher interactions. Homophobic jokes between teachers and students, usually boys, figured prominently in River High's unofficial sexuality curriculum. Such interactions were especially frequent in mostly male spaces such as the weight room or the auto shop classroom. While Ms. Mac worried about the potential sexual activity of the boys in her class (and seemingly ignored the sexism of the boys who formed the Man Party), other teachers teased boys for an obvious lack of heterosexual experience. Huey, a large, white junior who sported an outdated high-top haircut and walked with an oafish loping gate, was a regular recipient of these sorts of homophobic taunts. His unfashionable clothing and sluggish interactional style marked him as an outcast. He wore his pants high on his waist, as opposed to the low-slung style favored by most boys, and tight-fitting shirts tucked into his pants, cinched by a belt. Other boys usually wore oversized shirts and certainly didn't tuck them neatly into their pants. Looking for approval from the other boys in auto shop, Huey continually pulled stunts of stunning stupidity, usually at the urging of other boys. One day when I walked into auto shop, the entire class was in an uproar, screaming about how Huey had run and dived headfirst into the hood of the old Volvo that sat in the center of the room. The boys frequently joked about Huey's hypothetical girlfriend.

Mr. Ford, the art teacher, and Mr. Kellogg, the auto shop teacher, also teased Huey about his lack of heterosexual success. One afternoon, after school let out, Mr. Ford walked across the quad from the art room to stand with Mr. Kellogg in front of the auto shop room. He pointed across the quad at Huey, who was slowly loping toward them. Mr. Ford turned to Mr. Kellogg, saying, "I had to teach him a lesson. I turned around and caught Huey flipping me off. I said, 'You should be doing that to girls, not to me.' " Both Mr. Kellogg and Mr. Ford laughed as Mr. Kellogg said, "I don't even know if Huey knows what that is yet! But I'm sure somebody has told him." Although, like most gestures, flipping someone off or giving someone "the finger" has multiple meanings and generally means one is simply disregarding another, in this instance Mr. Ford invoked its literal meaning—"fuck you." In doing so Mr. Ford invoked commonsense notions of masculinity in which, because Huey was a boy, he should be "fucking" girls, not Mr. Ford. This sort of interaction reaffirmed that, as a boy, Huey should be participating in masculine behavior such as engaging in sexual activities with girls. The comment also drew on a mild homophobia by reminding Huey that he should be "fucking" girls, not men.

Teachers commonly turned a deaf ear to boys' homophobic and sexist comments. Ignoring or passively watching boys' sexist and homophobic comments often occurred in primarily male spaces where, if a teacher were to address every offensive comment students uttered, very little learning would take place. Mr. Kellogg, the auto shop teacher who had teased Huey, primarily ignored the boys' off-color comments about sexuality. One hot afternoon he sent the students out to disassemble lawn mowers as a way to practice dismantling car engines. A group of boys grabbed rubber mallets and began pounding away at the tires and other parts of the mowers instead of quietly dismantling them with screw-drivers the way they had been instructed to do the previous week. Presumably this wouldn't be the way they would actually dismantle car engines. I laughed along with the boys, who had formed a circle around those who were ferociously beating a lawn mower. Colin, standing next to me in the circle, said, "We have a whole class of retards who hit like girls." Surprisingly, this was one of the few times I heard a boy insult another by comparing him to a girl (or to someone who was developmentally disabled). Before each hit, the boy wielding the mallet yelled out in a deep affected voice, "One time!" to indicate that he would remove a given piece of the lawn mower by hitting it only one time instead of requiring multiple tries. Sufficient destruction with one hit indicated a given boy's strength and competence. As Jayden positioned himself to swing the mallet, Mr. Kellogg, who stood next to me and rolled his eyes, gently reminded Jayden to move his ankle away from the mallet so that he wouldn't shatter it. After yelling "One time!" Jayden hit the lawn mower, but apparently not to his satisfaction. So he turned around, switched hitting hands, and cried in a high-pitched voice, "I'm a switch hitter." The circled audience laughed and chanted, "Switch hitter! Switch hitter!" Swishing his hips and lisping, Jayden continued, "I'll show you a switch hitter!" Josh yelled, "I bet you will!" The session concluded as Josh, disgusted and surprised, yelled, "Dude, you hit like a girl!" The boys in auto shop drew on images of both femininity—"you hit like a girl"—and bisexuality—"I'll show you a switch hitter." (A bisexual man was often referred to as a "switch hitter" or as someone who "played for both teams.") Mr. Kellogg not only ignored these comments but seemingly wrote them off to "boys will be boys" behavior, for he shook his head and laughed at their antics.

None of this is to say that Mr. Kellogg meant to be homophobic. Rather, this sort of collective affirmation of masculinity provided one of the few ways teachers could build rapport with their students, though it replicated definitions of masculinity as homophobic and sexist. Joking about sexuality was a way for teachers to cross generational boundaries, illustrating to their students that they were not rendered completely irrelevant by their age. In this way teachers in both mixed and single-sex classrooms curried boys' favor by catering to their senses of humor, often at the expense of girls' dignity.

While teachers must have heard students use derogatory words such as *fag, gay, dyke*, or, as in the previous instance, *switch hitter*, with one exception I never heard any reprimands. Mr. McNally, the drama teacher and the exception, instructed his students not to call things they thought were stupid "gay," comparing it to calling a pair of shoes they didn't like "Mexican." When I was explaining my research to his class, they asked me what sorts of things I took notes about. Among other things, I said that I took notes on situations in which it looked like "guys were being not guy enough." A slight male sophomore to my left asked, "You mean gay, like homosexual?" Mr. McNally piped in with

> That's something we haven't talked about in this class yet. You guys have been really good and I haven't seen the need to talk about this, but we might as well, since we're on the subject. You know how people use the word *gay* and they're usually calling something stupid, right? Well I have a lot of friends who are gay and they aren't stupid. So when you call something gay and mean stupid, you're really calling my friends stupid! It's not like I go around saying, "Oh, that's so Italian" or "Oh, that's so Mexican" or "Oh, that's so people-who-wear-blue-shirts!" So that sort of language is really not acceptable in this class, okay?

The students laughed at Mr. McNally's comparisons and seemed to receive this admonition seriously. Mr. McNally was the only teacher I saw specifically address this issue in or out of the classroom.

But even Mr. McNally, who prided himself on creating a classroom environment in which homophobic slurs were not tolerated, let pass boys' sexualized insults and sometimes participated in these jokes. Consider Mr. McNally's interaction with Rob during his advanced drama class. Rob walked to the stage preparing to perform that day's assignment, a dramatic enactment of a song. He wore a black tank top, jeans, and black wrap-around glasses. His hair was cropped short and spiked up.

He looked as if he had just stepped off the set of the movie *The Matrix*. Mr. McNally commented, "Rob's lookin' sharp with those glasses." This comment was followed by a short pause as the class grew silent. Then Mr. McNally asked, raising his eyebrows suggestively, "What are you doing after class, Rob?" The class cracked up. "It was on everybody else's mind!" Mr. McNally defended himself, laughing along with them. Although Mr. McNally had previously lectured the class on the inappropriateness of homophobic insults, he easily participated in a masculinized homophobic ritual in which he pretended to hit on Rob in order to make the class laugh, as if to remind them they should laugh at men who hit on other men.

Heterosexist and homophobic discourses about masculinity permeated the educational process at River High. Heterosexual discourses were embedded in the physical environment of the classroom, teachers' instructional practices, and students' classroom behavior. Teachers used these discourses to illustrate instructional concepts in ways that presumably resonated with male students. The same sort of balancing act maintained by the administration between knowing about student sexual practices and discouraging any acknowledgment of such practices was reflected in these interactions between teachers and students, in which teachers used sexually loaded discussions to relate to students while simultaneously discouraging sexual activity. These sorts of practices primarily centered on boys; thus messages about sexuality were simultaneously messages about gender.

SCHOOL RITUALS: PERFORMING
AND POLICING GENDER AND SEXUALITY

As most students at River High would report, the major rituals of the school year were the Homecoming Assembly and football game, the Winter Ball, the Mr. Cougar Assembly, and prom. Whether students loved them, hated them, or professed indifference, these rituals shaped and organized much of their school-based social lives. The centrality of ritual to social life in high school is little different from the centrality of ritual to social life in general. Sociologists and anthropologists have long noted that ritual is key to the formation and continuation of society (Durkheim 1995; Turner 1966). Through rituals members of a society reaffirm shared morality and values. School rituals are symbolic, bodily performances that affirm in- and out-groups, the normal and the abnormal (Light 2000; Quantz 1999), reproducing dominant understandings of race, gender, and class (Foley 1990). School rituals don't just reflect heteronormative gender difference; they actually affirm its value and centrality to social life.

At River High the majority of the important school rituals involved upperclassmen, especially seniors. Because part of the function of ritual is to contain anxiety and foster the transition from one social state to another, it makes sense that the most important school rituals would focus on seniors' transitions from adolescence to adulthood. The senior photographs in the yearbook provide a telling example of the ways sexuality and gender intersected as students undertook this transition. Unlike the sophomores and juniors, who could wear whatever they liked for their yearbook photos, seniors at River High wore prescribed costumes. The senior boys wore tuxedos and the girls wore off-the-shoulder, strapless, black wraps, some accented with a feather boa. The girls' pictures were cropped suggestively just below the top of the black wrap, often revealing a bit of cleavage. Boys were not only covered but excessively covered, with their tuxedo collars reaching high up their necks. It was as if students graduating into adulthood also moved into more highly dichotomized and sexualized gender difference. The time for individual gender expression had been in childhood, when the ninth, tenth, and eleventh graders chose their own outfits. But as seniors, they were pressed by outside conventions to emphasize sexualized gender difference.

The yearbook was an important social document in that it provided visual representations of the cultural and social life of River High. In this way the "superlatives" sections throughout the book emphasized male-female pairings as natural and necessary. Each grade featured a superlatives section that highlighted "best of" categories for girls and boys in each grade. Pictured here were boy-girl pairings for categories like "best dressed," "biggest flake," "best smile," "best looking," and "best couple." These pairings framed the heterosexual coupling as an important way of organizing students, reflecting larger understandings of the heterosexual dyad as a fundamental human pairing (Warner 1993).

Other school rituals at River High also highlighted gender difference and naturalized heterosexual pairings. Dances and student assemblies, the main rituals at River, were talked about for months in advance, covered in the school newspaper, and talked about for years afterward as the stories about assembly content, after-dance parties, and who drank how much grew larger and more outrageous with the passing of time. Students saved up money, bought special clothes, and had formal pictures taken of these events.

Dances were one of the few school events where students were not differentiated by grade. As in the senior yearbook photos, girls were usually excessively uncovered for these events, wearing short skirts, tight pants, or slinky dresses. Boys, on the other hand, sported baggy pants and equally baggy shirts. Generally dance sound tracks were filled with popular hip-hop songs featuring sexist lyrics about women's bodies. The students, especially the female students, eagerly sang along with these lyrics. At the Winter Ball the DJ played a song by the popular rap artist Nelly. Nelly rapped the chorus of the song, "It's gettin' hot in here / So take off all your clothes." The girls screamed along with the all-female chorus, "I am gettin' so hot / I wanna take my clothes off." This song was followed with a tune by the now-deceased Tupac Shakur that included the chorus "No matter where I go / I see the same ho." When the chorus reached the word *ho* the DJ turned down the speaker volume so that all the students could scream "ho" at the top of their lungs. While the school administrators and teachers tried to contain students' sexual behavior, there were instances, such as at dances, where students were able to behave in more sexually explicit ways. These sexually explicit lyrics centered on girls' sexual availability—such as girls taking off their clothes, being sexually promiscuous, or being instructed by men to get naked.

These school rituals were a time of emphasized heterosexuality and also a time of increased school control of sexual activity. Dances were especially charged with sexual meanings. As bodily school rituals, they mobilized adult concern about controlling students' desires and practices. A campus supervisor, Betty, a thirtyish white woman with bleached blonde hair and copious makeup, expressed concern about students' dancing habits when I asked her about the Halloween Dance. She rolled her eyes and looked at me slowly, shaking her head: "I wouldn't even call it dancing, what those kids do. Mr. J. told us ahead of time to keep our eyes on the chairs." Surprised, I asked her, "Why the chairs?" She explained, "Boys like to sit on the chairs and then the girls stand up and dance for them." Betty made motions indicating that the girls were doing something like lap dancing. "We were pulling chairs out of the middle of the dance floor all night long." While girls could scream that they wanted to take their clothes off and boys and girls alike could refer to women as "hos," the administration drew the line at lap-dance simulations. It appears that the administrators weren't as concerned with sexism or the creation of a hostile environment as they were about the potential for sexual activity.

Before each dance, students were warned about dancing inappropriately, although what constituted inappropriate dancing was up for debate. The first rule listed on a sheet detailing the dance rules handed to students when they bought their tickets read: "Inappropriate dancing or unruly behavior will result in your removal from the dance and parents will be called." Only one teacher, Mr. Hoffman, told me that he had actually escorted a student from the dance for dancing inappropriately. He went out of his way one day in the hallway to ask me, "What did you think of the dancing at the dance? Can you believe the way they dance?" Without really waiting for an answer, he told me that last year a girl had pinned a boy against a wall, backed up into him, and bent all the way over, rubbing her behind into the boy's groin. He demonstrated this himself in the middle of the student-filled hallway. He said that after the girl had performed this same dance move three times, he finally asked her to leave the dance.

While school administrators worried about students' potential for sexual activity, they also encouraged students' heterosexual relationships with each other, especially at these sexually charged events. For instance, when two students, a boy and a girl, were leaving Winter Ball early, two of the vice principals joked with them, "You two going to a hotel or what?" The two students turned around and laughed. So, while the staff were concerned with students' sexuality, they also, to some extent, encouraged it through sponsoring these types of rituals and joking with students about sexual activity. The gender inequality fostered by such heterosexuality never seemed to be of concern to school officials.

Performing Masculinity and Heterosexuality: Mr. Cougar

Years in advance, Mr. Cougar hopefuls talked about the election. John, a junior, spoke with me extensively about becoming Mr. Cougar. "It's neat," he told me with a smile on his face. "You wait for it all through high school. When you are a freshman you wait till you are a senior just to do it." Eric emphasized that Mr. Cougar was a "popularity contest." He expressed his frustration that he didn't qualify for the "Top Six," saying, "People want to be Mr. Cougar. Yeah, I wanted to be Mr. Cougar. But all it is is a popularity contest based on sports figures." This dual attitude toward the ritual echoed most boys' approaches to Mr. Cougar. They both wanted to become Mr. Cougar and rejected the whole endeavor because of its impossible standards.

The Mr. Cougar ritual began toward the end of the basketball season when each student received a list including the names of every senior boy. Over the next few weeks through a series of votes the list was whittled down to the six candidates referred to as the Top Six. From their freshman year on, students talked about the Top Six. Many set achieving membership in the Top Six as a goal early on in high school. During the weeks before the Mr. Cougar Assembly, candidates were featured prominently around school, with the Mr. Cougar nominees competing in lunchtime games. The day of the final election an assembly was held in which all the candidates participated in skits in front of the entire student body. A panel of four teachers judged the skits. After the assembly the students voted for Mr. Cougar. That night the winning skit and the winner of the Mr. Cougar title were revealed at the basketball game.

Mr. Cougar skits, such as the "Revenge of the Nerds" skit that opened the book, illustrate the relationships between heterosexuality and masculinity, with girls often framed as a reward for masculine feats of strength. Randy Green and Freddy Martinez squared off in a similarly masculinized contest in their skit, "Wrestling World."[6] The skit began with two boys carrying out a sign reading "Wrestling World, River High School 7:00 November 5." Loud music blared and four boys emerged, sparring, onto the stage. Randy mouthed as a deep voice boomed over the speakers, "You ready to do this?" Freddy answered with an equally deep voice, "I'm totally ready." Two other wrestlers, wearing turquoise and white to indicate that they were from River's rival high school, Hillside, responded in high-pitched female voices, "Let's do this!" The student body laughed at the whiny "girl" voices. As in the "Revenge of the Nerds" skit, male imitations of seemingly female behavior drew laughter and derision from the audience.

Twenty girls ran out on stage to dance a choreographed routine while the wrestlers changed offstage. The girls' shirts indicated which team they supported, with the River supporters in gold and the Hillside supporters in turquoise. Freddy and Randy emerged in loose-fitting white T-shirts and gym shorts. They warmed up by jumping rope, performing push-ups, and sparring with each other. Their Hillside opponents appeared, not in workout clothes, but in red long johns, cowboy boots, and cowboy hats, riding broomstick "ponies." They performed "girl" push-ups from their knees rather than their feet and made a big show of not being able to jump rope, instead tangling themselves up in the short rope. They concluded this fantastic display of incompetence and femininity by slapping each other in a manner students referred to as "girl-fighting," rather than sparring with each other like real boxers, as Freddy and Randy did.

As soon as the boys finished their warm-ups, the chorus to the disco hit "It's Raining Men" played over the speakers. Presumably leaving their competition aside, the boys from each team threw their arms over each other's shoulders and proceeded to high-kick together like a line of Rockettes. The crowd roared in laughter at this imitation of femininity. Suddenly the music switched to the theme song from the movie *Rocky* as stagehands set up a wrestling ring. The wrestlers ran behind a screen to change into their outfits. Freddy and Randy emerged in sweats stuffed to make them appear huge and well-muscled. As the music changed from the Rocky anthem to the "Oompah Loompah" chorus from the movie *Willy Wonka and the Chocolate Factory*, the Hillside team emerged skipping instead of strutting, and wearing bathrobes instead of sweat suits. They soon dropped the bathrobes, revealing tiny tight spandex wrestling singlets, at which point the audience laughed.

As the match began, surprisingly, the weaklings from Hillside High began to beat the River team. The crowd laughed hysterically as the supposed underdogs started to win the match. However, the River team soon recovered, and the match ended as Freddy picked up the skinniest Hillside wrestler and swung him around before tossing him out of the ring. After this sound defeat, Queen's "We Are the Champions" started to play. The dancing girls reappeared, and those wearing turquoise shirts ripped them off revealing gold shirts, thus indicating that they were now aligned with the winning team from River. They ran up to Freddy and danced around him to a song repeating the lyric "What does it take to be number one?"

Much like the "Revenge of the Nerds" skit, "Wrestling World" tells a story of masculinity and heterosexuality at River High. The skit fostered and encouraged masculinity as heterosexual, with women as rewards for a job well done. Like Brent and Craig, Freddy and Randy showed that they were men deserving of the Mr. Cougar crown through their deep voices, their physical strength, and their rejection of femininity. More importantly, "hicks" from Hillside were held up as an object lesson. The audience was supposed to, and did, laugh at them for their "hick" (read poor) clothing, their lack of physical strength, and their high-pitched voices. Additionally the audience was encouraged to laugh at all displays of male femininity when the boys threw their arms over one another's shoulders to perform high kicks as if they were Rockettes. School officials vetted these skits, so presumably they encouraged, agreed with, or at least saw as unproblematic these definitions of masculinity. By providing the space and institutional support for such rituals, the school, in effect, endorsed normative masculinity as heterosexual and dominant.

Policing Gender and Sexuality

While, in dealing with the Mr. Cougar skits, the school administrators seemingly turned a blind eye to overt displays of heterosexuality, they didn't do this in all situations. While expressions of sexuality were often encouraged or at least tolerated for white boys, for certain groups of students, especially African American boys, they were especially discouraged. Later in the book I will talk about how the administrators policed sexuality by punishing public and political endorsements of homosexuality.

At River High African American students, both boys and girls, were disproportionately visible and the boys were disproportionately popular. This in-school status conflicted with their social status in the outside world, in which black men are disproportionately poor, jobless, and homeless. As James Earl Davis (1999) describes this seeming contradiction, "Black males are both adored and loathed in American schools. They are on the vanguard of hip-hop culture and set the standards of athleticism. On the other hand, they experience disproportionate levels of punishment and academic marginality" (49). African American boys move from the unjust disciplinary system of high school to a racist social and economic system. They are frequently under stricter disciplinary scrutiny than their white counterparts (Ferguson 2000; Majors 2001; Price 1999). Black men in America are consistently seen as hypersexual and hypermasculine (Ross 1998). Accordingly at River High differential treatment often coalesced around African American boys' sexualized behaviors. The reclaiming of white women from the clutches of the gangstas in the Mr. Cougar sketch illustrates the assumed destructive potential of black male sexuality. This fear of black male heterosexuality is also revealed in the informal disciplinary regimes deployed around school rituals.

Each year River High School put on a dance show. During my fieldwork the show "Music Brings the People All Together," consisted of twenty-four different dance routines, some by individuals, most by groups, and a grand finale featuring the entire cast. Many of the dances were rather sexual. The dance show started off with a "cancan" routine in which a line of girls dressed in period costume rapidly and repeatedly flipped up their skirts in the front and back, showing their underwear. It seemed that the entire point of the routine was to show their underwear as many times as possible.

The last routine was an ensemble piece (one of seven mixed-gender dance routines) to "I've Had the Time of My Life," the theme song to the movie *Dirty Dancing*. The routine drew from the story line of the movie, in which teenagers at an upscale resort in the 1950s are prohibited from dancing "dirty." Dancing in such a way that one's pelvis meets with another's in a grinding motion is forbidden. In the end of the movie the teenagers triumph at the resort's annual talent show in which the male lead, Johnny, and female lead, Baby, rebel against their parents' stodgy ways to dance "dirty" to the song "I've Had the Time of My Life."

In the beginning of this routine, Ricky and Samantha stood in the middle of the stage facing each other and staring intently into each other's eyes, as do Baby and Johnny in the movie. Also, as in the movie, Ricky's[7] hands ran seductively up and down Samantha's arms and sides as they began to gyrate their hips simultaneously in time to the music. The two continued to perform sexually evocative moves accompanied by sexually charged looks. Several minutes into the song all of the performers joined them to execute a final group dance, spilling out onto the floor of the theater in a celebration of "dirty dancing."

However, not all students were given free reign to dance this seductively. The eighteenth dance number was put on by the Pep Club, the name given to a group of primarily African American students, much to their frustration, by the school administration. The Pep Club, or Bomb Squad,[8] as they renamed themselves, had formed to give black students a presence at school assemblies and games. The cheerleading squads, as at other schools, were primarily composed of white girls (Adams and Bettis 2003). There were no African American members during my time there. African American girls at River were keenly aware of this, frequently noting the whiteness of the cheer squad as they performed at assemblies. One particular group of African American girls, many of whom were on the Bomb Squad, danced and sang through many of the assemblies. As the mostly white cheerleading team took the floor at the Fall Sports Assembly, one of these girls, Trisha, yelled out, "I don't see no black cheerleaders!" She was right, there were no black cheerleaders. They were mostly white and Asian, and a smattering of Latina girls. At another time I heard a white cheerleader make a similar comment when Sarah told me that African American girls who were talented dancers tried out for cheerleading but never made the squad.

The Bomb Squad had similar problems appearing on stage at school events. According to the Bomb Squad members, they often had trouble getting the school administration to let them perform at rallies and assemblies, even though the student body went wild as they performed their high-energy dance, step, and chanting routines.

The Bomb Squad's performance to an initially slow hip-hop song that picked up tempo as it continued opened with the six boys sitting in chairs and the girls dancing in front of them, gyrating their bottoms in front of the boys' faces. The boys eventually stood up to dance behind the girls, rotating their hips, but never touching the girls. At the end of the song the group ran off the stage, the boys high-fiving and hugging each other, each yelling over the others, "I didn't touch her!" "I didn't either!" K. J. stopped to explain to me, "We'd get suspended if we touched the girls."

The next day in weight lifting, several of the boys explained to me that before the dance show several of the vice principals had come to watch the dances in order to give them official approval. While three of the dances were relatively sexual—the cancan, the "dirty dancing" finale, and this routine—only the African American boys were singled out and given strict instructions not to touch the girls. The dancers in the finale were white, and in the cancan there were no boys. So while sexuality was certainly on display and approved of in the dance show, it was the relationship between race, gender, and sexuality that rendered black boys so potentially dangerous to the delicate balance of the (hetero)sexual order established by the school.

The problem here is not heterosexuality but a particularly racialized and gendered heterosexuality. Teenagers are seen as inherently sexual and black men are seen as extremely sexual. So the sexual behavior of African American teenage boys is taken much more seriously than that of white boys. In her study of sixth-grade African American boys, Ann Ferguson (2000) argued that teachers and administrators attributed an intentionality to African American boys' misbehavior that they did not attribute to white boys' misdeeds. When white boys misbehaved, teachers excused them with a resigned "boys will be boys" response. However, when African American boys joked, spoke out, or otherwise misbehaved in the classroom or schoolyard, adults at the school Ferguson studied assumed that they were doing so on purpose. This assumption of an adult intentionality results in harsher punishments for African American boys. By setting up a logic of institutionalized racism, this sort of treatment stunts their educational development. When white boys danced sexually with (usually white) girls, the administration didn't take note of it, possibly regarding it as a normal teenage behavior. It is likely that, much like the adults at the school Ferguson studied, the administrators at River saw African American boys' sexual behavior as adult and intentional. African American boys embodied contradictions in that they were both profoundly threatening and profoundly disempowered in the world of River High.

GENDER AND SEXUALITY REGIMES

The social space of River High was a complex cultural arena in which students, teachers, and administrators invested in and reproduced larger cultural meanings around gender and sexuality.[9] Because of that, River High's structuring of gender and sexuality was, in the end, unremarkable but important because it provided the context in which boys and girls forged gendered and sexual identities. As teachers and administrators told me when I first entered the school, it indeed felt like a school out of middle America. It wasn't just that the school was objectively average, it was that the students and administrators saw it that way. Students often spoke of "Cougar Pride" or "tradition" without embarrassment. I expected to hear sarcasm, but instead I heard an earnest passion in their voices as they talked about what they liked about River. Some even talked about returning to teach at River like Mr. McNally, the drama teacher, or Mr. Hobart, the principal. Their ordering of the heterosexual matrix was interesting precisely because it was the stuff of everyday life. In time-honored high school rituals, masculinity and femininity were produced as opposite and unequal identities primarily through heterosexual practices, metaphors, and jokes.

River High's administrators, like many parents and policy makers, were wary of teens' burgeoning sexuality. They feared that too much information or too much discussion of sex might encourage the students to engage in all sorts of irresponsible behaviors. In a nation that views teenage pregnancy rates as a sign of its moral worth, refuses to provide single and unemployed mothers with sufficient financial support, and is deeply divided about abortion, sex is indeed a scary subject. Ms. Mac's terror about the loss of her job in the face of students' distribution of condoms illustrates how seriously school boards, parents, and some teachers take the issue of teen sex. However, teachers must also navigate the everyday educational process. They somehow must engage students in learning about things that seem foreign to their own lives, such as the Interstate Commerce Act or the Fourteenth Amendment. To this end, Ms.

Mac took a path several other teachers do: she used examples about sex. That way she could forge rapport with students by catching their attention (wow—my teacher is talking about sex!) and relating a seemingly esoteric subject to topics that permeated much of student life—sex and romantic relationships. But the way she deployed sexual talk in her pedagogy was not neutral. That is, her sex talk was directed primarily at boys—assuming, for instance, that they were the ones interested in condoms. It seemed that girls' subjectivity was tangential to course work—as when a group of boys formed the Man Party, literally dedicated to rolling back women's citizenship rights, with no repercussions. Similarly male teachers curried boys' attention by allowing sexist and homophobic conversations and practices to go unchecked.

River High's school rituals mirrored society's expectations of a dominant, white heterosexual masculinity and a sexually available femininity. Boys were represented in these rituals as heterosexually successful and physically dominant over girls and over weaker boys. They repeatedly emphasized their masculinity by losing their feminine voices, beating other boys into submission, and validating their heterosexuality by "winning" girls. Girls, conversely, were represented as sexually available in both the yearbook pictures and the homecoming skits. The administration, for all of its fear about teen sexuality, organized and funded school rituals that fostered a sexist heterosexuality, with girls as sexual objects or rewards.

It seemed that the administrators, the teachers, and the kids were trying to accomplish the task of education and socialization in the best way they knew. This task and the way these students were taught to become adult men and women illustrate not just the particularities at River High but the ambivalence and anxieties we, as a society, feel about issues of gender, sexuality, and race. In the next chapter I continue to explore the centrality of sexuality to definitions of masculinity at River High by focusing on a particular sort of interactional process through which boys affirm to themselves and each other that they are straight: engaging with the threatening specter of the faggot.

CHAPTER THREE

Dude, You're a Fag

Adolescent Male Homophobia

The sun shone bright and clear over River High's annual Creative and Performing Arts Happening, or CAPA. During CAPA the school's various art programs displayed students' work in a fairlike atmosphere. The front quad sported student-generated computer programs. Colorful and ornate chalk art covered the cement sidewalks. Tables lined with student-crafted pottery were set up on the grass. Tall displays of students' paintings divided the rear quad. To the left of the paintings a television blared student-directed music videos. At the rear of the back quad, a square, roped-off area of cement served as a makeshift stage for drama, choir, and dance performances. Teachers released students from class to wander around the quads, watch performances, and look at the art. This freedom from class time lent the day an air of excitement because students were rarely allowed to roam the campus without a hall pass, an office summons, or a parent/faculty escort. In honor of CAPA, the school district bussed in elementary school students from the surrounding grammar schools to participate in the day's festivities.

Running through the rear quad, Brian, a senior, yelled to a group of boys visiting from the elementary schools, "There's a faggot over there! There's a faggot over there! Come look!" Following Brian, the ten-year-olds dashed down a hallway. At the end of the hallway Brian's friend Dan pursed his lips and began sashaying toward the little boys. As he minced, he swung his hips exaggeratedly and wildly waved his arms. To the boys Brian yelled, "Look at the faggot! Watch out! He'll get you!" In response, the ten-year-olds raced back down the hallway screaming in terror. Brian and Dan repeated this drama throughout the following half hour, each time with a new group of young boys.

Making jokes like these about faggots was central to social life at River High. Indeed, boys learned long before adolescence that faggots were simultaneously predatory and passive and that they were, at all costs, to be avoided. Older boys repeatedly impressed upon younger ones through these types of homophobic rituals that whatever they did, whatever they became, however they talked, they had to avoid becoming a faggot.

Feminist scholars of masculinity have documented the centrality of homophobic insults and attitudes to masculinity (Kimmel 2001; Lehne 1998), especially in school settings (Burn 2000; Kimmel 2003; Messner 2005; Plummer 2001; G. Smith 1998; Wood 1984). They argue that homophobic teasing often characterizes masculinity in adolescence and early adulthood and that antigay slurs tend to be directed primarily at gay boys. This chapter both expands on and challenges these accounts of relationships between homophobia and masculinity. Homophobia is indeed a central mechanism in the making of contemporary American adolescent masculinity. A close analysis of the way boys at River High invoke the faggot as a disciplinary mechanism makes clear that something more than simple homophobia is at play in adolescent masculinity. The use of the word *fag* by boys at River High points to the limits of an argument that focuses centrally on homophobia. Fag is not only an identity linked to homosexual boys but an identity that can temporarily adhere to heterosexual boys as well. The fag trope is also a racialized disciplinary mechanism.

Homophobia is too facile a term with which to describe the deployment of *fag* as an epithet. By calling the use of the word *fag* homophobia—and letting the argument stop there—previous research has obscured the gendered nature of sexualized insults (Plummer 2001). Invoking homophobia to describe the ways boys aggressively tease each other overlooks the powerful relationship between masculinity and this sort of insult. Instead, it seems incidental, in this conventional line of argument, that girls do not harass each other and are not harassed in this same manner. This framing naturalizes the relationship between masculinity and homophobia, thus obscuring that such harassment is central to the formation of a gendered identity for boys in a way that it is not for girls.

Fag is not necessarily a static identity attached to a particular (homosexual) boy. Fag talk and fag imitations serve as a discourse with which boys discipline themselves and each other through joking relationships. Any boy can temporarily become a fag in a given social space or interaction. This does not mean that boys who identify as or are perceived to be homosexual aren't subject to intense harassment. Many are. But becoming a fag has as much to do with failing at the masculine tasks of competence, heterosexual prowess, and strength or in any way revealing weakness or femininity as it does with a sexual identity. This fluidity of the fag identity is what makes the specter of the fag such a powerful disciplinary mechanism. It is fluid enough that boys police their behaviors out of fear of having the fag identity permanently adhere and definitive enough so that boys recognize a fag behavior and strive to avoid it.

An analysis of the fag discourse also indicates ways in which gendered power works through racialized selves. The fag discourse is invoked differently by and in relation to white boys' bodies than it is by and in relation to African American boys' bodies. While certain behaviors put all boys at risk for becoming temporarily a fag, some behaviors can be enacted by African American boys without putting them at risk of receiving the label. The racialized meanings of the fag discourse suggest that something more than simple homophobia is involved in these sorts of interactions. It is not that gendered homophobia does not exist in African American communities. Indeed, making fun of "negro faggotry seems to be a rite of passage among contemporary black male rappers and filmmakers" (Riggs 1991, 253). However, the fact that "white women and men, gay and straight, have more or less colonized cultural debates about sexual representation" (Julien and Mercer 1991, 167) obscures varied systems of sexualized meanings among different racialized ethnic groups (Almaguer 1991). Thus far male homophobia has primarily been written about as a racially neutral phenomenon. However, as D. L. King's (2004) recent work on African American men and same-sex desire pointed out, homophobia is characterized by racial identities as well as sexual and gendered ones.

WHAT IS A FAG? GENDERED MEANINGS

"Since you were little boys you've been told, 'Hey, don't be a little faggot,'" explained Darnell, a football player of mixed African American and white heritage, as we sat on a bench next to the athletic field. Indeed, both the boys and girls I interviewed told me that *fag* was the worst epithet one guy could direct at another. Jeff, a slight white sophomore, explained to me that boys call each other fag because "gay people aren't really liked over here and stuff." Jeremy, a Latino junior, told me that this insult literally reduced a boy to nothing, "To call someone *gay* or *fag* is like the lowest thing you can call someone. Because that's like saying that you're nothing."

Most guys explained their or others' dislike of fags by claiming that homophobia was synonymous with being a guy. For instance, Keith, a white soccer-playing senior, explained, "I think guys are just homophobic." However, boys were not equal-opportunity homophobes. Several students told me that these homophobic insults applied only to boys and not to girls. For example, while Jake, a handsome white senior, told me that he didn't like gay people, he quickly added, "Lesbians, okay, that's *good*." Similarly Cathy, a popular white cheerleader, told me, "Being a lesbian is accepted because guys think, 'Oh that's cool.'" Darnell, after telling me that boys were warned about becoming faggots, said, "They [guys] are fine with girls. I think it's the guy part that they're like ewwww." In this sense it was not strictly homophobia but a gendered homophobia that constituted adolescent masculinity in the culture of River

High. It is clear, according to these comments, that lesbians were "good" because of their place in heterosexual male fantasy, not necessarily because of some enlightened approach to same-sex relationships. A popular trope in heterosexual pornography depicts two women engaging in sexual acts for the purpose of male titillation. The boys at River High are not unique in making this distinction; adolescent boys in general dislike gay men more than they dislike lesbians (Baker and Fishbein 1998). The fetishizing of sex acts between women indicates that using only the term *homophobia* to describe boys' repeated use of the word *fag* might be a bit simplistic and misleading.

Girls at River High rarely deployed the word *fag* and were never called fags. I recorded girls uttering *fag* only three times during my research. In one instance, Angela, a Latina cheerleader, teased Jeremy, a well-liked white senior involved in student government, for not ditching school with her: "You wouldn't 'cause you're a faggot." However, girls did not use this word as part of their regular lexicon. The sort of gendered homophobia that constituted adolescent masculinity did not constitute adolescent femininity. Girls were not called dykes or lesbians in any sort of regular or systematic way. Students did tell me that *slut* was the worst thing a girl could be called. However, my field notes indicate that the word *slut* (or its synonym *ho*) appeared one time for every eight times the word *fag* appeared.

Highlighting the difference between the deployment of *gay* and *fag* as insults brings the gendered nature of this homophobia into focus. For boys and girls at River High *gay* was a fairly common synonym for "stupid." While this word shared the sexual origins of *fag*, it didn't *consistently* have the skew of gender-loaded meaning. Girls and boys often used *gay* as an adjective referring to inanimate objects and male or female people, whereas they used *fag* as a noun that denoted only unmasculine males. Students used *gay* to describe anything from someone's clothes to a new school rule that they didn't like. For instance, one day in auto shop, Arnie pulled out a large older version of a black laptop computer and placed it on his desk. Behind him Nick cried, "That's a gay laptop! It's five inches thick!" The rest of the boys in the class laughed at Arnie's outdated laptop. A laptop can be gay, a movie can be gay, or a group of people can be gay. Boys used *gay* and *fag* interchangeably when they referred to other boys, but *fag* didn't have the gender-neutral attributes that *gay* frequently invoked.

Surprisingly, some boys took pains to say that the term *fag* did not imply sexuality. Darnell told me, "It doesn't even have anything to do with being gay." Similarly, J. L., a white sophomore at Hillside High (River High's cross-town rival), asserted, "*Fag*, seriously, it has nothing to do with sexual preference at all. You could just be calling somebody an idiot, you know?" I asked Ben, a quiet, white sophomore who wore heavy-metal T-shirts to auto shop each day, "What kind of things do guys get called a fag for?" Ben answered, "Anything . . . literally, anything. Like you were trying to turn a wrench the wrong way, 'Dude, you're a fag.' Even if a piece of meat drops out of your sandwich, 'You fag!' " Each time Ben said, "You fag," his voice deepened as if he were imitating a more masculine boy. While Ben might rightly *feel* that a guy could be called a fag for "anything . . . literally, anything," there were actually specific behaviors that, when enacted by most boys, could render them more vulnerable to a *fag* epithet. In this instance Ben's comment highlights the use of *fag* as a generic insult for incompetence, which in the world of River High, was central to a masculine identity. A boy could get called a fag for exhibiting any sort of behavior defined as unmasculine (although not necessarily behaviors aligned with femininity): being stupid or incompetent, dancing, caring too much about clothing, being too emotional, or expressing interest (sexual or platonic) in other guys. However, given the extent of its deployment and the laundry list of behaviors that could get a boy in trouble, it is no wonder that Ben felt a boy could be called fag for "anything." These nonsexual meanings didn't replace sexual meanings but rather existed alongside them.

One-third (thirteen) of the boys I interviewed told me that, while they might liberally insult each other with the term, they would not direct it at a homosexual peer. Jabes, a Filipino senior, told me, "I actually say it *[fag]* quite a lot, except for when I'm in the company of an actual homosexual person. Then I try not to say it at all. But when I'm just hanging out with my friends I'll be like, 'Shut up, I don't want you hear you any more, you stupid fag.' " Similarly J. L. compared homosexuality to a disability, saying there was "no way" he'd call an actually gay guy a fag because "there's people who are the retarded people who nobody wants to associate with. I'll be so nice to those guys, and I hate it when people make fun of them. It's like, 'Bro do you realize that they can't help that?' And then there's gay people. They were born that way." According to this group of boys, gay was a legitimate, or at least biological, identity.

There was a possibility, however slight, that a boy could be gay and masculine (Connell 1995). David, a handsome white senior dressed smartly in khaki pants and a white button-down shirt, told me, "Being gay is just a lifestyle. It's someone you choose to sleep with. You can still throw around a football and be gay." It was as if David was justifying the use of the word *fag* by arguing that gay men could be men if they tried but that if they failed at it (i.e., if they couldn't throw a football) then they deserved to be called a fag. In other words, to be a fag was, by definition, the opposite of masculine, whether the word was deployed with sexualized or nonsexualized meanings. In explaining this to me, Jamaal, an African American junior, cited the explanation of the popular rap artist Eminem: "Although I don't like Eminem, he had a good definition of it. It's like taking away your title. In an interview they were like, 'You're always capping on gays, but then you sing with Elton John.' He was like 'I don't mean gay as in gay.' " This is what Riki Wilchins (2003) calls the "Eminem Exception. Eminem explains that he doesn't call people 'faggot' because of their sexual orientation but because they're weak and unmanly" (72). This is precisely the way boys at River High used the term *faggot*. While it was not necessarily acceptable to be gay, at least a man who was gay could do other things that would render him acceptably masculine. A fag, by the very definition of the word, could not be masculine.

This distinction between fag as an unmasculine and problematic identity and gay as a possibly masculine, although marginalized, sexual identity is not limited to a teenage lexicon; it is reflected in both psychological discourses and gay and lesbian activism. Eve Sedgwick (1995) argues that in contemporary psychological literature homosexuality is no longer a problem for men so long as the homosexual man is of the right age and gender orientation. In this literature a homosexual male must be an adult and must be masculine. Male homosexuality is not pathologized, but gay male *effeminacy* is. The lack of masculinity is the problem, not the sexual practice or orientation. Indeed, the edition of the *Diagnostic and Statistical Manual of Mental Disorders* (a key document in the mental health field) that erased homosexuality as a diagnosis in the 1970s added a new diagnosis in its wake: Gender Identity Disorder. According to Sedgwick, the criteria for diagnosis are different for girls and boys. A girl has to actually assert that she is a boy, indicating a psychotic disconnection with reality, whereas a boy need only display a preoccupation with female activities. The policing of boys' gender orientation and of a strict masculine identity for gay men is also reflected in gay culture itself. The war against fags as the specter of unmasculine manhood appears in gay male personal ads in which men look for "straight-appearing, straight-acting men." This concern with both straight and gay men's masculinity not only reflects teenage boys' obsession with hypermasculinity but also points to the conflict at the heart of the contemporary "crisis of masculinity" being played out in popular, scientific, and educational arenas.

BECOMING A FAG: FAG FLUIDITY

"The ubiquity of the word *faggot* speaks to the reach of its discrediting capacity" (Corbett 2001, 4). It's almost as if boys cannot help shouting it out on a regular basis—in the hallway, in class, or across campus as a greeting. In my fieldwork I was amazed by the way the word seemed to pop uncontrollably out of boys' mouths in all kinds of situations.[1] To quote just one of many instances from my field notes: two boys walked out of the PE locker room, and one yelled, "Fucking faggot!" at no one in particular. None of the other students paid them any mind, since this sort of thing happened so frequently. Similar spontaneous yelling of some variation of the word *fag*, seemingly apropos of nothing, happened repeatedly among boys throughout the school. This and repeated imitations of fags constitute what I refer to as a "fag discourse."

Fag discourse is central to boys' joking relationships. Joking cements relationships among boys (Kehily and Nayak 1997; Lyman 1998) and helps to manage anxiety and discomfort (Freud 1905). Boys both connect with one another and manage the anxiety around this sort of relationship through joking about fags. Boys invoked the specter of the fag in two ways: through humorous imitation and through lobbing the epithet at one another. Boys at River High imitated the fag by acting out an exaggerated "femininity" and/or by pretending to sexually desire other boys. As indicated by the introductory vignette in which an older boy imitated a predatory fag to threaten little boys, male students at River High linked these performative scenarios with a fag identity. They also lobbed the *fag* epithet at each other in a verbal game of hot potato, each careful to deflect the insult quickly by hurling it toward someone else. These games and imitations made up a fag discourse that highlighted the fag not as a static but rather as a fluid identity that boys constantly struggled to avoid.

In imitative performances the fag discourse functioned as a constant reiteration of the fag's existence, affirming that the fag was out there; boys reminded themselves and each other that at any moment they could become fags if they were not sufficiently masculine. At the same time these performances demonstrated that the boy who was invoking the fag was *not* a fag. Emir, a tall, thin African American boy, frequently imitated fags to draw laughs from other students in his introductory drama class. One day Mr. McNally, the drama teacher, disturbed by the noise outside the classroom, turned to the open door, saying, "We'll shut this unless anyone really wants to watch sweaty boys playing basketball." Emir lisped, "I wanna watch the boys play!" The rest of the class cracked up at his imitation. No one in the class actually thought Emir was gay, as he purposefully mocked both same-sex sexual desire (through pretending to admire the boys playing basketball) and an effeminate gender identity (through speaking with a lisp and in a high-pitched voice). Had he said this in all seriousness, the class most likely would have responded in stunned silence. Instead, Emir reminded them he was masculine by immediately dropping the fag act. After imitating a fag, boys assure others that they are not a fag by instantly becoming masculine again after the performance. They mock their own performed femininity and/or same-sex desire, assuring themselves and others that such an identity deserves derisive laughter.

Boys consistently tried to force others into the fag position by lobbing the *fag* epithet at each other. One day in auto shop, Jay was rummaging through a junk-filled car in the parking lot. He poked his head out of the trunk and asked, "Where are Craig and Brian?" Neil responded with "I think they're over there," pointing, then thrusting his hips and pulling his arms back and forth to indicate that Craig and Brian might be having sex. The boys in auto shop laughed. This sort of joke temporarily labeled both Craig and Brian as faggots. Because the fag discourse was so familiar, the other boys immediately understood that Neil was indicating that Craig and Brian were having sex. However, these were not necessarily identities that stuck. Nobody actually thought Craig and Brian were homosexuals. Rather, the fag identity was fluid—certainly an identity that no boy wanted but that most boys could escape, usually by engaging in some sort of discursive contest to turn another boy into a fag.

In this way the fag became a hot potato that no boy wanted to be left holding. One of the best ways to move out of the fag position was to thrust another boy into that position. For instance, soon after Neil made the joke about Brian having sex with Craig, Brian lobbed the *fag* epithet at someone else, deflecting it from himself, by initiating a round of a favorite game in auto shop, the "cock game." Brain said quietly, looking at Josh, "Josh loves the cock," then slightly louder, "Josh loves the cock." He continued saying this until he was yelling, "JOSH LOVES THE COCK!" The rest of the boys laughed hysterically as Josh slunk away, saying, "I have a bigger dick than all you motherfuckers!" These two instances show how the fag could be mapped, for a moment, onto one boy's body and how he, in turn, could attach it to another boy, thus deflecting it from himself. In the first instance Neil made fun of Craig and Brian for simply hanging out together. In the second instance Brian went from being a fag to making Josh into a fag through the "cock game." Through joking interactions boys moved in and out of the fag identity by discursively creating another as a fag.

Given the pervasiveness of fag jokes and the fluidity of the fag identity, it is difficult for boys to consistently avoid the brand. As Ben stated, it almost seemed that a boy could get called a fag for "anything." But most readily acknowledged that there were spaces, behaviors, and bodily comportments that made one more likely to be subject to the fag discourse, such as bodily practices involving clothing and dancing.

According to boys at River, fags cared about the style of their clothes, wore tighter clothes, and cared about cleanliness. Nils explained to me that he could tell that a guy was a fag by the way he dressed: "Most guys wear loose-fitting clothing, just kind of baggy. They [fags] wear more tight clothes. More fashionable, I guess." Similarly, nonfags were not supposed to care about dirtying their clothes. Auto shop was a telling example of this. Given that the boys spent two hours working with greasy car parts, they frequently ended up smudged and rumpled by the end of class. While in the front of the classroom there was a room boys could change in, most of them opted not to change out of their school clothes, with a few modifying their outfits by taking their shirts off and walking around in their "beaters." These tank tops were banned at River High because of their association with gang membership. Auto shop was the one place on campus where boys could wear them with impunity. Like most of the boys in auto shop, Ben never changed out of his jeans or heavy-metal T-shirts. After working on a particularly oily engine he walked in to the classroom with grease stains covering his pants. He looked down at them, made a face, and walked toward me laughing, waving his hands around with limp wrists, and lisping in a high-pitched singsong voice, "I got my good panths all dirty!" Ben's imitation indicated that only a fag would actually care about getting his clothes dirty. "Real" guys didn't care about their appearance; thus it didn't matter if they were covered in grease stains. Of course, to not care about one's clothes, or to make fun of those who care about their clothes, ironically, is to also care about one's appearance. In this sense, masculinity became the carefully crafted appearance of not caring about appearance.

Indeed, the boys' approach to clothing and cleanliness mirrored trends in larger society and the ascendance of the "metrosexual." *Metrosexual* is the recently coined label for straight men who care about their appearance, meticulously piecing together outfits, using product in their hair, and even making manicure appointments (for clear polish, of course). Because these sorts of grooming practices are associated with gay men, straight men developed a new moniker to differentiate themselves from other straight men and from gay men.

Dancing was another practice that put a boy at risk of being labeled a fag. Often boys would jokingly dance together to diffuse the sexualized and feminized meanings embedded in dancing. At dances white boys frequently held their female dates tightly, locking their hips together. The boys never danced with one another unless they were joking or trying to embarrass one another. The examples of boys jokingly dancing together are too numerous to discuss, but the following example was particularly memorable. Lindy danced behind her date, Chris. Chris's friend Matt walked up and nudged Lindy aside, imitating her dance moves behind Chris. As Matt rubbed his hands up and down Chris's back, Chris turned around and jumped back, startled to see Matt there instead of Lindy. Matt cracked up as Chris turned red and swore at his friend.

A similar thing happened at CAPA as two of the boys from the band listened to another band play swing music. These two boys walked toward each other and began to ballroom-dance. Within a second or two they keeled over in laughter, hitting each other and moving away. This ritualized dance, moving closer and then apart, happened again and again when music played at River High. Boys participated in this ritualized exchange to emphasize that indeed they weren't fags.

When boys were forced to dance with one another, as in classroom activities, this sort of joking escalated. In the drama class Mr. McNally walked the students through an exercise that required them to stand so close to each other that most parts of their bodies touched. He instructed the students to stand in two circles on the stage, with each person on the outer circle directly behind someone in the inner circle. He began to play a haunting instrumental song with no vocals. As the song continued Mr. McNally told the students in the inner circle to close their eyes and let their bodies go limp, while still standing. He instructed the students in the outer circle to move the person in front through an interpretive dance, following his lead as he moved the student in front of him. As the music continued, most of the students in the outer circle watched Mr. McNally's movements intently, trying their best to mirror his actions. The result was an intimate and beautiful puppet-and-puppeteer–like dance with the student in back moving the student in front through slow, fluid poses. Instead of following Mr. McNally's movements like the rest of the class, one pair of white sophomores, Liam and Jacob, barely touched. Jacob stood in back of Liam and, instead of gently holding Liam's wrist with their full arms touching as the other students did, picked up Liam's wrist with two fingers as if picking up something repulsive and flung Liam's hand to its destination. He made jokes with Liam's arm, repeatedly flinging it up against Liam's chest in a movement that indicated Liam was "retarded." The jokes continued as the students switched places, so that the inner circle became the outer circle, with Liam now "in control" of Jacob. Liam placed Jacob's hand against his forehead as if saluting, made his arms flap like birds, and used Jacob's finger to poke at his eyes, all the while, unlike the other students, never letting the majority of his body touch Jacob's. At the end of the exercise Mr. McNally asked for the students' feedback. One of the girls said, a little embarrassed, "I hate to say it, but it was almost sexual." To which Mr. McNally responded, "Yeah, it's full physical contact," at which point Liam and Jacob took two steps apart from one another. Even though the entire class was assigned to touch one another simultaneously, Jacob and

Liam had a hard time following the instructions because it was so dangerous to actually "dance" together like this. Even in a class situation, in the most nonsuspect of interactions, the fag discourse ran deep, forbidding boys to touch one another.

The constant threat of the fag regulated boys' attitudes toward their bodies in terms of clothing, dancing, and touching. Boys constantly engaged in repudiatory rituals to avoid permanently inhabiting the fag position. Boys' interactions were composed of competitive joking through which they interactionally created the constitutive outside and affirmed their positions as subjects.

EMBODYING THE FAG: RICKY'S STORY

Through verbal jockeying, most boys at River continually moved in and out of the fag position. For the one boy who permanently inhabited the fag position, life at River High was not easy. I heard about Ricky long before I met him. As soon as I talked to any student involved with drama, the choir, or the Gay/Straight Alliance, they told me I had to meet Ricky. Ricky, a lithe, white junior with a shy smile and downcast eyes, frequently sported multicolored hair extensions, mascara, and sometimes a skirt. An extremely talented dancer, he often starred in the school's dance shows and choreographed assemblies. In fact, he was the male lead in "I've Had the Time of My Life," the final number in the dance show. Given how important other students thought it was that I speak to him, I was surprised that I had to wait for nearly a year before he granted me an interview. His friends had warned me that he was "heterophobic" and as a result was reluctant to talk to authority figures he perceived were heterosexual. After I heard his stories of past and present abuse at the hands of negligent adults, cruel teenagers, and indifferent school administrators, I understood why he would be leery of folks asking questions about his feelings, experiences, and opinions. While other boys at River High engaged in continual repudiatory rituals around the fag identity, Ricky embodied the fag because of his homosexuality and his less normative gender identification and self-presentation.

Ricky assumed (rightly so in this context) that other people immediately identified him with his sexuality. He told me that when he first met people, "they'll be like, 'Can I ask you a personal question?' And I'm like, 'Sure.' And they say, 'Are you gay?' And I'm like, 'Yeeeaahh.' 'Okay, can I ask you another question?' And I'm like, 'Sure.' And they'll go, 'Does it hurt?' It always goes . . . " He rolled his eyes dismissively, telling me, "They go straight up to the most personal question! They skip everything else. They go straight to that. Sometimes I'll get the occasional 'Well, how did you know that you were [gay]?' " He answered with "For me it's just always been there. I knew from the time I could think for myself on. It was pretty obvious," he concluded gesturing to his thin frame and tight-fitting tank top with a flourish.

Ricky lived at the margins of school, student social life, and society in general. His mother died when he was young. After her death, he moved around California and Nevada, alternately living with his drug-addicted father, a boyfriend's family, his aunt, his sister, and his homophobic grandmother (who forbade him to wear nail polish or makeup). The resulting discontinuities in his education proved difficult in terms of both academics and socialization:

> It's really hard to go to a school for a period of time and get used to their system and everything's okay. Then when all of a sudden you have to pick up and move the next week, get into a new environment you have no idea about, you don't know how the kids are gonna react to you. You don't know what the teachers are like and you don't know what their system is. So this entire time I have not been able to get used to their system and get used to the environment at all. That's why I had to say, "Fuck it," cause for so long I've been going back and going back and reviewing things I did in like fifth grade. I'm at a fourth-grade math level. I am math illiterate, let me tell you.

In addition to the continual educational disruptions, Ricky had to contend with intense harassment. Figuring out the social map of the school was central to Ricky's survival. Homophobic harassment at the hands of teachers and students characterized his educational experience. When he was beat up in a middle school PE class, the teacher didn't help but rather fostered this sort of treatment:

> They gave them a two-day suspension and they kind of kept an eye on me. That's all they could do. The PE coach was very racist and very homophobic. He was just like "faggot this" and "faggot that." I did not feel comfortable in the locker room and I asked him if I could go somewhere else to change, and he said, "No, you can change here."

Sadly, by the time Ricky had reached River High he had become accustomed to the violence.

> In a weird sense, in a weird way, I'm comfortable with it because it's just what I've known for as long as I can remember. I mean, in elementary school, I'm talking like sixth grade, I started being called a fag. Fifth grade I was called a fag. Third grade I was called a fag. I have the paperwork, 'cause my mom kept everything, I still have them, of kids harassing me, saying "Gaylord," at that time it was "Gaylord."

Contrary to the protestations of boys earlier in the chapter that they would never call someone who was gay a fag, Ricky experienced this harassment on a regular basis, probably because he couldn't draw on identifiably masculine markers such as athletic ability or other forms of dominance to bolster some sort of claim on masculinity.

Hypermasculine environments such as sporting events continued to be venues of intense harassment at River High. "I've had water balloons thrown at me at a football game. Like, we [his friends Genevieve and Lacy] couldn't have stayed at the homecoming game. We had to go." The persecution began immediately at the biggest football game of the year. When he entered with his friend Lacy, "Two guys that started walking up to get tickets said, 'There's the fucking fag.'" When Ricky responded with "Excuse me?" the boy shot back, "Don't talk to me like you know me." The boy and his friends started to threaten Ricky. Ricky said, "He started getting into my face, and his friends started saying, 'Come on, man, come on, man'" as if they were about to hit Ricky. Ricky felt frustrated that "the ticket people are sitting there not doing a damn thing.

This is right in front of them!" He found Ms. Chesney, the vice principal, after the boys finally left. While Ms. Chesney told him, "We'll take care of it," Ricky said he never heard about the incident again. Later at the game he and Lacy had water bottles thrown at them by young boys yelling, "Oh look, it's a fag!" He said that this sentiment echoed as they tried to sit in the bleachers to watch the half-time show, which he had choreographed: "Left and right, 'What the fuck is that fag doing here?' 'That fag has no right to be here.' Blah blah blah. That's all I heard. I tried to ignore it. And after a while I couldn't take it and then we just went home." While many of the boys I interviewed said they would not actually harass a gay boy, that was not Ricky's experience. He was driven out of the event he had choreographed because of the intense homophobic harassment.

Ricky endured similar torment at CAPA, the event at which Brian and Dan socialized the young boys to fear faggots by chasing them. Boys reacted with revulsion to Ricky's dance performances while simultaneously objectifying the girls dancing on the stage. The rear quad served as the stage for CAPA's dancers. The student body clustered around the stage to watch the all-female beginning jazz dance class perform. Mitch, a white senior, whose shirt read, "One of us is thinking about sex. It must be me," muttered, "This is so gay" and began to walk away. Jackson yelled after him, "Where are you going, *fag?*" As Mitch walked away, Jackson turned back to the dancing girls, who now had their backs to the boys, gyrating their behinds in time to the music, and shouted, "Shake that ass!" Jackson reached in his pocket to grab his glasses. Pablo commented, "He's putting on his glasses so he can see her shake her ass better." Watching the girls' behinds, Jackson replied, as he pointed to one of them, "She's got a *huge* ass." Mitch turned to Pablo and asked, seriously, "Why are there no guys?" Pablo responded, "You're such a fag."

The advanced dance troupe took the stage with Ricky in the center. Again, all the dancers sported black outfits, but this time the pants were baggy and the shirts fitted. Ricky wore the same outfit as the girls. He danced in the "lead" position, in the front and the center of the dance formation. He executed the same dance moves as the girls, which is un-common in mixed-gender dance troupes. Usually the boys in a mixed-gender dance troupe perform the more "physical" moves such as flips, holding up the girls, and spinning them around. Ricky, instead, per-formed all the sexually suggestive hip swivels, leg lifts, arm flares, and spins that the girls did.

Nils and his group of white male friends made faces and giggled as they stared at Ricky. Soon Nils turned to Malcolm and said, "It's like a car wreck, you just can't look away." Both shook their heads in dismay as they continued to watch the "car wreck" with what can only be described as morbid absorption. Other boys around the stage reacted visibly, re-coiling at Ricky's performance. One of them, J. R., a hulking junior and captain of the football team, shook his head and muttered under his breath, "That's disgusting." I asked him, "What?" J. R. turned to me with his nose wrinkled in revulsion and responded, "That guy dancing, it's just disgusting! Disgusting!" He again shook his head as he walked off. Soon afterward an African American boy turned to his friend and admiringly said of Ricky, "He's a better dancer than all the girls! That takes talent!" He turned to me and said, "Can I wiggle my hips that fast?" and laughed as he tried. The white boys' revulsion bordering on violence was com-mon for boys when talking about Ricky and his dancing. More surpris-ing was the African American boys' admiration, if tinged with humor, of these skills. In these moments boys faced a terrifying, embodied abject, not just some specter of a fag.

Even though dancing was the most important thing in his life, Ricky told me he didn't attend school dances because he didn't like to "watch my back" the whole time. Meanings of sexuality and masculinity were deeply embedded in dancing and high school dances. Several boys at the school told me that they wouldn't even attend a dance if they knew Ricky was going to be there. In auto shop, Brad, a white sophomore, said, "I heard Ricky is going in a skirt. It's a hella short one!" Chad responded, "I wouldn't even go if he's there." Topping Chad's response, Brad claimed, "I'd probably beat him up outside." K. J. agreed: "He'd probably get jumped by a bunch of kids who don't like him." Chad said, "If I were a gay guy I wouldn't go around telling everyone." All of them agreed on this. Surprised and somewhat disturbed by this discussion, I asked incredulously, "Would you really not go to prom because a gay guy would be in the same room as you all?" They looked at me like I had two heads and said again that of course they wouldn't. Ricky's presentation of both sexual preference and gender identity was so profoundly threatening that boys claimed they would be driven to violence.

Ricky developed different strategies to deal with the fag discourse, given that he was not just *a* fag but *the* fag. While other boys lobbed the epithet at one another with implied threats of violence (you are not a man and I am, so watch out), for Ricky that violence was more a reality than a threat. As a result, learning the unwritten rules of a particular school and mapping out its social and physical landscape was literally a matter of survival. He found River High to be one of the most homophobic schools he had attended: "It's the most violent school I think that I've seen so far. With all the schools the verbal part about, you know the slang, 'the fag,' the 'fuckin' freak,' 'fucking fag,' all that stuff is all the same. But this is the only school that throws water bottles, throws rocks, and throws food, ketchup, sandwiches, anything of that nature."[2]

While there is a law in California protecting students from discrimination based on sexual identity, when Ricky requested help from school authorities he was ignored, much as in his interaction with the vice principal at the homecoming game. Ricky responded to this sort of treatment with several evasion strategies. He walked with his eyes downcast to avoid meeting other guys' eyes, fearing that they would regard eye contact as a challenge or an invitation to a fight. Similarly he varied his route to and from school:

> I had to change paths about three different times walking to school. The same people who drive the same route know, 'cause I guess they leave at the same time, so they're always checking something out. But I'm always prepared with a rock just in case. I have a rock in my hand so if anything happens I just chuck one back. I always walk with something like that.

Indeed, when I was driving him home from the interview that day, boys on the sidewalk glared at him and made comments I couldn't hear. He also, with the exception of the homecoming football game, avoided highly sexualized or masculinized school events where he might be subject to violence.

Soon after my research ended, Ricky dropped out of River High and moved to a nearby city to perform in local drag shows. While other boys moved in and out of the fag position, Ricky's gendered practices and sexual orientation forced him to bear all that the other boys cast out of masculinity. His double transgression of sexual and gender identity made his position at River High simply unlivable. The lack of protection from the administration meant facing torture on a daily basis. The abuse that was heaped on him was more than one person, certainly more than one parentless, undereducated, sweet, artistic adolescent, could bear.[3]

RACIALIZING THE FAG

While all groups of boys, with the exception of the Mormon boys, used the word *fag* or fag imagery in their interactions, the fag discourse was not deployed consistently or identically across social groups at River High. Differences between white boys' and African American boys' meaning making, particularly around appearance and dancing, reveal ways the specter of the fag was racialized. The specter of the fag, these invocations reveal, was consistently white. Additionally, African American boys simply did not deploy it with the same frequency as white boys. For both groups of boys, the *fag* insult entailed meanings of emasculation, as evidenced by Darnell's earlier comment. However, African American boys were much more likely to tease one another for being white than for being a fag. Precisely because African American men are so hypersexualized in the United States, white men are, by default, feminized, so *white* was a stand-in for *fag* among many of the African American boys at River High. Two of the behaviors that put a white boy at risk for being labeled a fag didn't function in the same way for African American boys.

Perhaps because they are, by necessity, more invested in symbolic forms of power related to appearance (much like adolescent girls), a given African American boy's status is not lowered but enhanced by paying attention to clothing or dancing. Clean, oversized, carefully put together clothing is central to a hip-hop identity for African American boys who identify with hip-hop culture. Richard Majors (2001) calls this presentation of self a "cool pose" consisting of "unique, expressive and conspicuous styles of demeanor, speech, gesture, clothing, hairstyle, walk, stance and handshake," developed by African American men as a symbolic response to institutionalized racism (211). Pants are usually several sizes too big, hanging low on the hips, often revealing a pair of boxers beneath. Shirts and sweaters are similarly oversized, sometimes hanging down to a boy's knees. Tags are frequently left on baseball hats worn slightly askew and perched high on the head. Meticulously clean, unlaced athletic shoes with rolled-up socks under the tongue complete a typical hip-hop outfit. In fact, African American men can, without risking a fag identity, sport styles of self and interaction frequently associated with femininity for whites, such as wearing curlers (Kelley 2004). These symbols, at River High, constituted a "cool pose."

The amount of attention and care given to clothing for white boys not identified with hip-hop culture (that is, most of the white boys at River High) would certainly cast them into an abject, fag position, as Ben indicated when he cried, jokingly, "I got my good panths all dirty!" White boys were not supposed to appear to care about their clothes or appearance because only fags cared about how they looked. However African American boys involved in hip-hop culture talked frequently about whether their clothes, specifically their shoes, were dirty. In drama class both Darnell and Marc compared their white Adidas basketball shoes. Darnell mocked Marc because black scuff marks covered his shoes, asking incredulously, "Yours are a week old and they're dirty, I've had mine for a month and they're not dirty!" Both laughed. Monte, River High's star football player, echoed this concern about dirty shoes. Looking at the fancy red shoes he had lent to his cousin the week before, he told me he was frustrated because after his cousin used them the "shoes are hella scuffed up." Clothing, for these boys, did not indicate a fag position but rather defined membership in a certain cultural and racial group (Perry 2002). Especially for poor African American boys (as most were at River High), clean clothing was an indicator of class status. If one had enough money to have clean shoes one was not "ghetto," in the parlance of the students at River.

As in many places in the United States, racial divisions in Riverton line up relatively easily with class divisions. Darnell grabbed me at lunch one day to point this out to me, using school geography as an example. He sauntered up and whispered in my ear, "Notice the separation? There's the people who hang out in there (pointing toward the cafeteria), the people who hang out in the quad. And then the people who leave." He smashed one hand against the other in frustration: "I talk to these people in class. Outside we all separate into our groups. We don't talk to each other. Rich people are not here. They got cars and they go out." He told me that the "ball players" sat in the cafeteria. And he was right: there were two tables at the rear of the cafeteria populated by African American boys on the basketball and football teams, the guys whom Darnell described to me as his "friends." He said there were "people who leave, people who stay and the people over there [in the quad]. The people who stay are ghetto." He added, "*Ghetto* come to mean 'niggerish.' That reflects people who are poor or urban."

Carl and his friend James, both African American basketball players, were also clear about the ways race lined up with class at River: "White people always take us to lunch cause black people don't have cars." Because African American boys lacked other indicators of class such as cars and the ability to leave campus during lunch, clean expensive basketball shoes took on added symbolic status.

Dancing was another arena that carried distinctly fag-associated meanings for white boys but masculine meanings for African American boys who participated in hip-hop culture. White boys often associated dancing with fags. However, dancing did not carry this sort of sexualized gender meaning for all boys at River High. For African American boys dancing demonstrates membership in a cultural community (Best 2000). At River, African American boys frequently danced together in single-sex groups, teaching each other the latest dance moves, showing off a particularly difficult move, or making each other laugh with humorous dance moves. In fact, while in drama class Liam and Jacob hit each other and joked through the entire dancing exercise, Darnell and Marc seemed very comfortable touching one another. They stood close to one another, heel to toe, as they were supposed to. Their bodies touched, and they gently and gracefully moved the other's arms and head in a way that was tender, not at all like the flailing of the two white boys.

Dancing ability actually increased an African American boy's social status. Students recognized K. J., along with Ricky, as the most talented dancer at the school. K. J. was a sophomore of mixed racial descent, originally from the Philippines, who participated in the hip-hop culture of River High. He continually wore the latest hip-hop fashions. His dark complexion and identification with hip-hop culture aligned him with many of the African American boys at River High. Girls hollered his name as they walked down the hall and thrust love notes folded in complicated designs into his hands as he sauntered to class. For the past two years K. J. had won first place in the talent show for dancing. When he danced at assemblies the auditorium reverberated with screamed chants of "Go K. J.! Go K. J! Go K. J.!" Because dancing for boys of color, especially African American boys, placed them within a tradition of masculinity, they were not at risk of being labeled a fag for engaging in this particular gendered practice. Nobody called K. J. a fag. In fact, in several of my interviews boys of multiple racial/ethnic backgrounds spoke admiringly of K. J.'s dancing abilities. Marco, a troublemaking white senior, said of K. J., "Did you know he invented the Harlem Shake?" referring to a popular and difficult dance move. Like Ricky, K. J. often choreographed assembly dance routines. But unlike Ricky, he frequently starred in them at the homecoming and Mr. Cougar rallies.

None of this is to say that participation in dancing made boys less homophobic. K. J. himself was deeply homophobic. But like the other boys, it was a gendered homophobia that had to do with masculine gender transgressions as much as sexuality. His sister, for instance, identified as a lesbian, and he looked up to and liked her. But he loathed Ricky. Because of their involvement with dance, the two came into contact relatively frequently. Stylistically, they mirrored one another. Both sported long hair: K. J.'s in cornrows and Ricky's lengthened with highlighted extensions. Both wore elaborate outfits. K. J. favored oversized matching red and white checked shorts and a button-down shirt over a white tank top, while Ricky sported baggy black pants, combat boots, and a white tank top. Both were thin with delicate facial features and little facial hair. But the meanings associated with what might seem like gender transgressions by both of them were mediated by their racial and sexual identities, leading to K. J.'s popularity and Ricky's debasement. K. J.'s appearance identified his style as hip-hop, a black, masculine cultural style, whereas Ricky's style identified him as gender transgressive and feminine.

Not surprisingly, K. J. and Ricky were the stars of the dance show at River High. As the day of the show arrived, K. J. asked me for what must have been the hundredth time if I was planning to attend. He said, "Everyone is sayin' that Ricky is my competition, but I don't think so. He's not my competition." K. J. continued to tell me that he was very upset with Ricky because the night before at the dress rehearsal Ricky had walked up to him, saying, "Hey, K. J., awesome dance." Ricky had put his hand on K. J.'s back when he said this. Angry and red, K. J. said to me, "I wanted to hit him hella bad! Then he came up *again*. I was like 'Oh My God!' Ugh!" Trying to identify exactly who Ricky was, another boy said, "I think that's the same guy who is in our history class. The guy who looks like a girl?" K. J., wanting to make sure the other boys knew how repulsive Ricky was, said, "You know how you look at girls like they are hella fine? That's how he looks at guys, dude! He could be looking at you!" All the boys groaned. K. J. expressed relief that he was "safe," saying Ricky "only checks out white guys." K. J. took pains to differentiate himself from Ricky by saying that Ricky wasn't his competition and that Ricky didn't even look at him as a sexual object because of his race. The respect K. J. commanded at River was certainly different from the treatment Ricky received because the meanings associated with African American boys and dancing were not the same as the ones associated with white boys and dancing. K. J.'s dancing ability and carefully crafted outfits bolstered his popularity with both boys and girls, while Ricky's similar ability and just as carefully chosen outfits placed him, permanently, in a fag position.

None of this is to say that the sexuality of boys of color wasn't policed. In fact, because African American boys were regarded as so hypersexual, in the few instances I documented in which boys were punished for engaging in the fag discourse, African American boys were policed more stringently than white boys. It was as if when they engaged in the fag discourse the gendered insult took on actual combative overtones, unlike the harmless sparring associated with white boys' deployments. The intentionality attributed to African American boys in their sexual interactions with girls seemed to occur as well in their deployment of the fag discourse. One morning as I waited with the boys on the asphalt outside the weight room for Coach Ramirez to arrive, I chatted with Kevin and Darrell. The all-male, all-white wrestling team walked by, wearing gold and black singlets. Kevin, an African American sophomore, yelled out, "Why are you wearing those faggot outfits? Do you wear those tights with your balls hanging out?" The weight-lifting students stopped their fidgeting and turned to watch the scene unfold. The eight or so members of the wrestling team stopped at their SUV and turned to Kevin. A small redhead whipped around and yelled aggressively, "Who said that?!" Fingers from wrestling team members quickly pointed toward Kevin. Kevin, angrily jumping around, yelled back as he thrust his chest out, "Talk about jumping me, nigger?" He strutted over, advancing toward the small redhead. A large wrestler sporting a cowboy hat tried to block Kevin's approach. The redhead meanwhile began to jump up and down, as if warming up for a fight. Finally the boy in the cowboy hat pushed Kevin away from the team and they climbed in the truck, while Kevin strutted back to his classmates, muttering, "All they know how to do is pick somebody up. Talk about jumping me . . . weak-ass wrestling team. My little bro could wrestle better than any of those motherfuckers."

It would seem, based on the fag discourse scenarios I've described thus far, that this was, in a sense, a fairly routine deployment of the sexualized and gendered epithet. However, at no other time did I see this insult almost cause a fight. Members of the white wrestling team presumably took it so seriously that they reported the incident to school authorities. This in itself is stunning. Boys called each other fag so frequently in everyday discussion that if it were always reported most boys in the school would be suspended or at least in detention on a regular basis. This was the only time I saw school authorities take action based on what they saw as a sexualized insult. As a result Mr. J. explained that somebody from the wrestling team told him that Kevin was "harassing" them. Mr. J. pulled Kevin out of weight-lifting class to discuss the incident. According to him, Kevin "kept mouthing off" and it wasn't the first time he had been in trouble, so they decided to expel him and send him to Hillside.

While Kevin apparently had multiple disciplinary problems and this interaction was part of a larger picture, it is important that this was the only time that I heard any boy (apart from Ricky) tattle on another boy for calling him gay or fag. Similarly it was the only time I saw punishment meted out by the administration. So it seems that, much as in the instance of the Bomb Squad at the Dance Show, intentionality was more frequently attributed to African American boys. They weren't just engaging in the homophobic bantering to which teachers like Mr. Kellogg turned a blind eye or in which Mr. McNally participated. Rather, they were seen as engaging in actual struggles for dominance by attacking others. Because they were in a precarious economic and social position, the ramifications for African American boys for engaging in the fag discourse were more serious. Precisely because some of them were supposed to be attending, not River High, but the "bad" school, Chicago, in the neighboring school district, when they did encounter trouble their punishment was more severe.

WHERE THE FAG DISAPPEARS:
DRAMA PERFORMANCES

While, for the most part, a boy's day at River entailed running a gauntlet of competitive and ritualized sexual insults, there were two spaces of escape—the Gay/Straight Alliance and drama performances. Theater productions were not the same as the drama classroom, where I have already indicated that Mr. McNally sometimes drew upon the fag discourse for laughs and to forge rapport with male students. Drama performances typically didn't involve all of the students in drama classes. Rather, students who were involved were ones who identified as drama students and cared about the theater; some of them envisioned trying to make a career out of it. Drama is notoriously a fag space in high schools. The ironic result of this connection is that the insult disappears. Not only does the insult disappear, but drama becomes a space where male students can enact a variety of gender practices.

The opening night of the yearly spring musical illustrates how the *fag* insult disappeared and male students enacted a variety of gender practices without negative ramifications. Drama students ran around in various stages of costuming and undress in the backstage area of the River High auditorium as they prepared for the opening night of the spring musical, *Carousel*. As the balmy spring air blew through the stage door, I smiled as I thought back to my high school days and felt that same nervous energy as we prepped for choir concerts and musicals like *Fiddler on the Roof*. Squealing, giggling, and singing, students frantically searched for spare props, costume parts, and makeup. Students flew past me in clouds of hairspray, carrying parasols or sailor paraphernalia as they readied themselves to perform this relatively dark musical about romantic betrayal, domestic violence, and murder.

I leaned against the wall outside the dressing rooms as students costumed themselves and each other. Girls quickly and carefully applied makeup under the bright yellow bulbs. Boys lined up waiting for an available girl to apply makeup. I waited for the inevitable fag comment as the girls plastered rouge, lip gloss, and eye shadow on the boys' faces. Surprisingly, even though all but one of the boys (Brady) participating in this musical were straight, I heard not a one. Instead Trevor, the handsome blond lead, and the other boys checked out the girls' handiwork in the surrounding mirrors, suggesting slight changes or thanking them for their help. Squealing with delight at their new look, the boys ran back into the beehive of noise and activity that constituted the backstage area outside the dressing rooms. That reaction and their impromptu singing surprised me as much their pride in sporting makeup. The normally tough and competitive exterior that they displayed in the rest of the school disappeared, and the boys showed as much excitement as the girls did, smiling and giggling as they anticipated their performance.

Soon the backstage area quieted down as students took their marks and the orchestra, really a group of four musicians, played the opening bars. Students danced around the stage, depicting a picnic, a fair, and other tableaus of small-town American life in the 1900s. Remarkably, all the students watched or sang a musical number entitled "You're a Queer One, Julie Jordan" without cracking a single joke about fags or homosexuality. This refusal to engage in insults, homophobic comments, or sexist joking continued throughout the evening. Conditioned as I was at this point to hearing the fag discourse, I was stunned at the myriad opportunities to levy the epithet and the seeming refusal by all of these boys, gay and straight, to invoke it.

The most striking example of this refusal occurred midway through the play as eight boys dressed as sailors tumbled over each other as they prepared to go on stage. They joked about their lack of "sailorness" as they waited excitedly in the wings. Brady, surveying his fellow soldiers, admonished the boys laughingly to "act like sailors, men!" Jake laughed back in a loud whisper, "Oh yeah, right!" Randy sarcastically said, "We look sooo much like sailors," puffing out his chest and mock-strutting across the stage. The boys all giggled at this performance. They soon gathered around Brady, who, as part of his effort to appear like a tough sailor, had had his friend draw a temporary tattoo on his hairy bicep. It was a truly sailorlike tattoo, a mermaid. But this mermaid was more a visual pun than anything else because she was not a sultry, buxom siren but Ariel from the Disney movie *The Little Mermaid*. Brady beamed as he showed it off to everyone. The other boys admired the artwork and remarked, with a tinge of jealousy, that it was a great tattoo. They heard their cue and strutted on stage, eventually forming a semicircle and singing: "Blow high, blow low / Away then we will go / We'll go away in the sailin' away / Away we'll go / Blow me high an' low." During the song, boys took their turns performing a short solo dance. Some performed typically masculine moves such as flips or swaggers, while others performed pirouettes or delicate twirls.

Sailors, in the contemporary United States, are already laden with all sorts of gay innuendo. From the sailor member of the famous gay disco group the Village People to actual sailors stuck on ships with all-male crews, to jokes about "sea men," sailors represent a subtext of same-sex desire. So a bunch of sailors jumping around singing a song that relies upon the repeated lyrics "blow me" is pretty funny. However, the boys took an approach to this that was, more than anything, simply playful.

Watching this scene unfold, I was surprised that given all of the fag iconography in this moment—sailors, dancing, Disney cartoons, and the repeated singing of the word *blow* (which by itself can get boys joking for hours)—I didn't hear a single invocation of the fag discourse. At the end of the night I turned to David and asked why no one uttered the word *fag* the entire night. He explained, "That's cause we're drama freaks." In a sense, because these boys were near the bottom of the social hierarchy at River High, they were, by default, fags. But I think the lack of the fag discourse during that evening was a more complicated story.

The boys had fun with the double entendres and played with masculinity. Brady's tattoo functioned as a sort of queering of masculinity in which he visually punned by drawing a mermaid who was not so much sexy as a singing heroine for little girls. The theater is a place for all sorts of experimentation, so why not a metaphorical and physical space for gender and sexual experimentation? After watching what boys endured daily at River High, I found this dramatic performance a space of liberation and relaxation. The boys were able to try on gender identities, integrating masculine and feminine gender practices, without fear of being teased. Instead of constantly policing their own and others' gender displays, they were able to be playful, emotional, and creative. It was as if, because they were in a space where they were all coded as fags anyway and couldn't be any lower socially, it didn't matter what they did. Such is the liberatory potential of the theater. These boys had nothing left to lose socially, which meant that, ironically, they were free from the pressures of adolescent masculinity, at least temporarily (though it should be noted here that the boys involved in drama productions weren't among the most ardent users of the fag discourse, even outside dramatic performances). What they weren't able to do, however, was to engage in these sorts of playful practices around gender outside the drama performance space.

REFRAMING HOMOPHOBIA

Homophobia is central to contemporary definitions of adolescent masculinity. Unpacking multilayered meanings that boys deploy through their uses of homophobic language and joking rituals makes clear that it is not just homophobia but a gendered and racialized homophobia. By attending to these meanings, I reframe the discussion as a fag discourse rather than simply labeling it as homophobia. The fag is an "abject" (Butler 1993) position, a position outside masculinity that actually constitutes masculinity. Thus masculinity, in part, becomes the daily interactional work of repudiating the threatening specter of the fag.

The fag extends beyond a static sexual identity attached to a gay boy. Few boys are permanently identified as fags; most move in and out of fag positions. Looking at fag as a discourse in addition to a static identity reveals that the term can be invested with different meanings in different social spaces. *Fag* may be used as a weapon with which to temporarily assert one's masculinity by denying it to others. Thus the fag becomes a symbol around which contests of masculinity take place.

Researchers who look at the intersection of sexuality and masculinity need to attend to how racialized identities may affect how *fag* is deployed and what it means in various social situations. While researchers have addressed the ways in which masculine identities are racialized (Bucholtz 1999; Connell 1995; J. Davis 1999; Ferguson 2000; Majors 2001; Price 1999; Ross 1998), they have not paid equal attention to the ways *fag* might be a racialized epithet. Looking at when, where, and with what meaning *fag* is deployed provides insight into the processes through which masculinity is defined, contested, and invested in among adolescent boys.

Ricky demonstrates that the fag identity can, but doesn't have to, inhere in a single body. But it seems that he needed to meet two criteria— breaking both gendered and sexual norms—to be constituted as a fag. He was simultaneously the penetrated fag who threatened psychic chaos (Bersani 1987) and the man who couldn't "throw a football around." Not only could he not "throw a football," but he actively flaunted his unmasculine gender identification by dancing provocatively at school events and wearing cross-gendered clothing. Through his gender practices Ricky embodied the threatening specter of the fag. He bore the weight of the fears and anxieties of the boys in the school who frantically lobbed the *fag* epithet at one another.

The *fag* epithet, when hurled at other boys, may or may not have explicit sexual meanings, but it always has gendered meanings. When a boy calls another boy a fag, it means he is not a man but not necessarily that he is a homosexual. The boys at River High knew that they were not supposed to call homosexual boys fags because that was mean. This, then, has been the limited success of the mainstream gay rights movement. The message absorbed by some of these teenage boys was that "gay men can be masculine, just like you." Instead of challenging gender inequality, this particular discourse of gay rights has reinscribed it. Thus we need to begin to think about how gay men may be in a unique position to challenge gendered as well as sexual norms. The boys in the drama performances show an alternative way to be teenage boys, which is about playing with gender, not just enforcing gender duality based on sexual meanings.

CHAPTER FOUR

Compulsive Heterosexuality

Masculinity and Dominance

The weight room, a freestanding module by the football field, stank with a familiar musty smell of old sweat, metal, and rubber. Colorful diagrams of deltoids, biceps, quads, and other muscle groups adorned the walls. Each day Coach Ramirez, a gentle, soft-spoken man, called roll and told the (mostly male) students to run a lap or two as he entered the module to place his folders in his office and turn on the stereo. After running their laps, the sweaty boys filed in as loud hip-hop music blared from the stereo. Dressed in regulation black gym shorts and T-shirts, boys milled about, picking up weights, completing a few sets, and then moving on to other machines. Some of the African American boys danced to the music, while, inevitably, Josh and his white friends asked for country music.

One fall morning, as some of the boys grew tired of lifting, they gathered around a set of benches in the front of the weight room. Reggie, a white rugby-playing junior, asked the gathering group, "Did you hear about the three 'B's?' " Before anyone had a chance to respond, Reggie announced triumphantly, "Blow job, back massage, and breakfast in bed!" Rich asked skeptically, "Shouldn't the back massage come first?" The conversation soon turned to the upcoming Winter Ball and their prospects for sex with their dates. Jerome complained that he was not "gonna get laid at Winter Ball." Josh admonished, "That's why you gotta go for the younger ones, fool! Like twelve years old!" Reggie, Rich, and Pedro laughed at Josh's advice. Pedro, never quiet for long, told the rest, "If you can put their legs behind their head and eat them out they'll have the fattest orgasm." The conversation quickly evolved into a game of sexual one-upmanship as Reggie, Rich, Jerome, and Josh began talking over each other, each with a more fantastic story. Josh claimed he was "so good" that he couldn't "control the girl from thrashing around on the bed and hurting herself on the headboard." In response Jerome advised, "That's why you gotta start out at the headboard!" Reggie shouted, "My girlfriend's bed broke!" Rich jumped in with "One time my girlfriend's dad came home while we were doing it and I had to hide in the closet." Josh, not to be outdone, replied, "Hey man, try getting a b.j. [blow job] while you are driving home!" This challenge was answered by a chorus of groans and "I've done that!"

This sort of locker-room talk is what one expects to find when researching teenage boys and masculinity. Indeed, the public face of male adolescence is filled with representations of masculinity in which boys brag about sexual exploits by showing off a girl's underwear (as in the 1980s film *Pretty in Pink*), spend the end of their senior year talking about how they plan to lose their virginity (*American Pie*), or make cruel bets about who can bed the ugliest girl in the school (*She's All That*). In many ways, the boys at River High seemed much like their celluloid representatives. As this scene in the weight room indicates, heterosexual innuendoes, sexual bravado, and sexual one-upmanship permeated these primarily male spaces. This chapter looks at these gender practices and, instead of taking them at face value as testosterone-fueled verbal jockeying, pays attention to the meanings of masculinity embedded in them. In these sorts of interactions and gendered spaces, masculinity, in spite of boys' talk about the gay boys' ability to be masculine as discussed in the previous chapter, is assumed to be synonymous with heterosexuality. But, as they do when invoking the fag discourse, boys talking about heterosexuality are and are not talking about sex. Their talk about heterosexuality reveals less about sexual orientation and desire than it does about the centrality of the ability to exercise mastery and dominance literally or figuratively over girls' bodies (Wood 1984). These heterosexually based gender practices serve to defend boys against emasculating insults like those in the fag discourse (Hird and Jackson 2001). Engaging in very public practices of heterosexuality, boys affirm much more than just masculinity; they affirm subjecthood and personhood through sexualized interactions in which they indicate to themselves and others that they have the ability to work their will upon the world around them. Imposing one's will and demonstrating dominance in this way aligns boys with personhood and subjectivity, historically coded as masculine (Jaggar 1983; Mackinnon 1982). Demonstrating dominance in a variety of ways is a central part of contemporary American masculinity (Peirce 1995).

Compulsive heterosexuality[1] is the name I give to this constellation of sexualized practices, discourses, and interactions. This term builds on Adrienne Rich's (1986) influential concept of "compulsory heterosexuality."[2] Rich argues that heterosexuality not only describes sexual desires, practices and orientations but is a "political institution" (23). The "enforcement of heterosexuality for women as a means of assuring male right of physical, economic and emotional access" (50) is a central component of gender inequality. The microprocesses of heterosexuality as an institution are so embedded in daily life that, while heterosexuality may be personally meaningful, it can simultaneously function as an oppressive social institution. While compulsory heterosexuality may regulate both men and women, "their experiences of it and the power and privilege that accompany it are different" (V. Robinson 1996, 120).

Practices of "compulsive heterosexuality" exemplify what Butler (1995) calls "gender performativity," in which gender "is produced as a ritualized repetition of conventions, and . . . this ritual is socially compelled in part by the force of a compulsory heterosexuality" (31). Compulsive heterosexuality is not about desire for sexual pleasure per se, or just about desire to be "one of the guys"; rather, it is "an excitement felt as sexuality in a male supremacist culture which eroticizes male dominance and female submission" (Jeffreys 1998, 75). Indeed, ensuring positions of power entails boys' constant "recreation of masculinity and femininity" through rituals of eroticized dominance (Jeffreys 1998, 77). Looking at boys' ritualistic sex talk, patterns of touch, and games of "getting girls" indicates how this gender inequality is reinforced through everyday interactions. Taken together, these ritualized interactions continually affirm masculinity as mastery and dominance. By symbolically or physically mastering girls' bodies and sexuality, boys at River High claim masculine identities.

A STUD WITH THE LADIES

Not surprisingly, the most popular boys at River High are heterosexual. Expressing heterosexual desire establishes a sort of baseline masculinity. Bradley, a charming blond, blue-eyed sophomore who could hardly contain his excitement about being interviewed, explained, "To be the coolest guy? If you're just like a stud at sports and you're a stud with the ladies." If anyone at River High was a "stud at sports" and a "stud with the ladies," it was Chad, a tall, well-muscled, strikingly good-looking senior football player of mixed white and Latino heritage. Chad spent much of his interview describing how he was *"that guy"* on campus: "I'm Chad Rodgers. I play football. I'm going to college. All that kind of shit. Badass, you know?" He said that because of this, other guys were envious of him. When I asked him why this was the case, he answered confidently, with a bit of a sneer, "Probably 'cause they can't get girls. I work out. I got muscles and a nice body." In her interview, Cathy confirmed Chad's view of himself, saying, with admiration, "Chad? He's a big, cocky man. But he deserves the right to be cocky. He is *really* hot. But he knows it. That's just Chad. He just thinks the world revolves around him." Indeed, after interviewing him, I received the same impression of Chad.

Chad told me that he, along with some of his football teammates, frequently teased another teammate: "This dude, Dax Reynolds, he gets made fun of a lot 'cause he's always holding his girlfriend's hand. To the other guys it's funny. We just make fun of him." According to Chad, a successful sex life was more important than public displays of affection. If a guy wasn't having sex, "he's no one. He's nobody." Chad explained that some guys tried to look cool by lying about sex, but they "look like a clown, [they get] made fun of." He assured me, however, that he was not one of those "clowns" forced to lie about sex, bragging, "When I was growin' up *I* started having sex in the eighth grade." However, his description of these sexual adventures sounded scarily close to date rape. He told me, "The majority of the girls in eighth and ninth grade were just stupid. We already knew what we were doing. They didn't know what they were doing, you know?" When I asked him to explain this, he continued, "Like say, comin' over to our house like past 12:00. What else do you do past 12:00? Say we had a bottle of alcohol or something. I'm not saying we forced it upon them. I'm sayin' . . . " He trailed off here as he tried to explain that he didn't need to actually rape girls, though his friends did: "Kevin Goldsmith and uh, Calvin Johnson, they got charged with rape." Chad assured me that in spite of his statement that he had used alcohol with underage girls he had never had to force a girl to have sex: "I'll never [be in] that predicament, you know. I've never had a hard time, or had to, you know, alter their thinking."

Other boys echoed Chad's assertions about the importance of sex, saying that they felt the pressure to have sex, or at least act like they were having sex. Connor, a white junior who frequently wore Harley Davidson insignia T-shirts and a black leather jacket, suggested that sex was important to maintain one's image:

> If his friends are talking about it [sex] and they got some and this guy is like "oh man, they're cool and I wanna be cool." So they go and do whatever as far as prostitution or actually drugging a girl or whatever. As far as image goes—yeah, they think it's [sex] important.

Angela told me that one of her male friends was so desperate to be seen as sexually experienced that he lied about it:

> They brag about it. They lie about it. I noticed a lot of guys lie about it. Like that guy I like. He's my best friend now, one of them. And he

messed around with one of my friends before me and him started talking. He told people at football camp that they had sex. But he told me he was still a virgin. He was like, bragging about it. I asked him, "Are you still a virgin?" All of his other close friends were like, "Yeah. He's still a virgin." I said, "Why did you lie about it?" He was like, "I just wanted people to think I was cool."

Ben concurred with this analysis: "Of course they lie about it . . . It's like, tell your friends, 'Last night it was good.' And then the girl walks up and they talk about something else. You know how it is."

The way boys talked about heterosexual practices and orientations in their interviews reveals that their public sexuality was as much about securing a masculine social position as it was about expressions of desire or emotion. David explicitly talked about this "image" problem as one of "peer pressure," saying, "If you haven't scored with someone, then you are not adequate to anyone else, you know?"

In this sense, Chad was both an exemplar and an arbiter of heterosexuality. Like other boys, he recognized only specific expressions of heterosexuality as masculine. In groups boys act as a sort of "sexual police" (Hird and Jackson 2001), deriding each other's expressions of love, romance, or emotional desire, such as Dax's holding of his girlfriend's hand. Chad also had the ability to discern whether other guys were lying about their sexual activities. It seems that lying about it might actually make one less masculine than simply not engaging in it! Finally, as noted by Cathy and Chad himself, Chad was the paragon of masculinity at River High. He was "really hot" and "muscular" and could "get girls" when other guys couldn't.

If boys couldn't actually bed a girl, they had to at least act as if they were sexually attracted to girls. Jace told me that guys who weren't interested in girls were "all gay guys." Indeed, Gary confirmed that having a girlfriend served as proof of heterosexuality. I asked Gary, a white senior with spiky burgundy hair and a smartly assembled Abercrombie and Fitch outfit who was involved in drama and choir, "Is it important that guys have girlfriends?" He explained,

Probably. Yeah. It shows you're a man. I think it's important. Let's say the top actor guy who everybody thought was gay had a really nice girlfriend. That might happen just for a cover-up so that guy can be left alone from the stereotypes and the teasing. I think it may be important to some people just so they can go through high school without worrying about anybody talking about them.

Girlfriends both protected boys from the specter of the fag and bolstered their masculinity. In fact, in the "Revenge of the Nerds" skit discussed in the introduction, the deciding factor in the nerds' ascendance to masculinity was their ability to reclaim "their" girlfriends.

Not surprisingly, given Chad's comment that if a guy hadn't had sex he was no one, boys felt pressured to make sure others knew that they thought about sex. In fact, thinking about sex was so important that boys often named it (much like homophobia) as a defining facet of adolescent masculinity. Connor explained this in response to my question "How would you describe teenage guys?"

I *do* think it's true for 99.9 percent of the guys that they think about girls every 5.2 seconds . . . Every time they think of a girl they think of something sexually. Like every time they see a girl they look at her ass or whatever. Guys are into girls.

Connor's comments reflected what many boys at River told me, that teenage guys think about sex all of the time. What Connor left out was that boys not only thought about girls "every 5.2 seconds" but constantly, compulsively expressed this thought process. Like Connor, Tal, a slim white underclassman, also positioned thinking about sex as a defining aspect of teen masculinity. As we walked out of the weight room one day, I asked if there was anything he'd like me to include in my notes. He replied, "I got something for you! All guys think about is eating pussy twenty-four-seven!"

At River High, sex, thinking about sex, and talking about sex were framed repeatedly as specifically masculine concerns, even in the classroom. In drama class Mr. McNally was walking the class through the different components of a story—the introduction, the buildup, and then the climax. A boy in the back of the class yelled out, "Climax! Every guy knows what that is!" The class laughed. While girls might have thought about it, enjoyed it, and even desired it, sex tended to be marked as a male domain.

Heath, a tall, white attractive junior involved in the drama program who was known for his unique clothing style, told me that this sort of behavior was expected of boys; teenage guys were supposed to be "more outspoken about sexual stuff and hollering at girls and all that stuff." Darren identified auto shop as a particularly masculine arena rife with sexual discussions, explaining, "Auto shop class is a stereotype. Very typical teenage guys. All they ever talk about is sex and cars . . . it seems like sex always comes up." Jose told me something similar: "Most guys want a girl for a night and that's it. That's all it is over here. They're just looking for a girl and then they'll just forget about it the next day and then go onto something else." He told me that his friend was one of those guys:

> Some guys kind of put it in their [girls'] minds that they're going to be with them and then the next day they won't call them. Like I know a guy [who is] especially good at that. He's one of my best friends. He can pull out a phone book and be like, "Who do I want to talk to tonight?" Then he'll be with them for the night. He's just a guy and he just wants as many girls as he can. Just wants girls, I guess.

For the most part boys seemed to be proud of this stereotypical "love 'em and leave 'em" behavior. While seemingly promiscuous girls were quickly and shamefully labeled *slut*, boys proudly donned the moniker of *male whore*. One of my interviewees, John, laughingly described his friend as "a male whore. Guys just don't care! Like my friend, Jeff—a male whore. I swear to God, that guy!" I asked, surprised, "He's proud?" John answered, "Oh yeah! He's proud!" Similarly Heath told me that "double standards" applied to girl and boy sexual behaviors: if a "guy sleeps around, he's the man. Girl sleeps around, oh, she's a slut. It's weird. I don't know why."

Sadly, it seems that for all the feminist activism of the past several decades little has changed in the day-to-day public sexual practices and discourses of adolescent boys. Boys still look to "score," and girls' bodies still serve as proof of masculinity. Girls who have sex are still labeled sluts, and boys who have sex are still vaulted to popularity.

GETTING GIRLS

Chad sneered at boys who, unlike him, couldn't "get girls." Getting girls, like the "girl watching" documented by Beth Quinn (2002), "functions as a game men play to build shared masculine identities and social relations" (387). Boys who couldn't engage in this game of "getting girls" lost masculine capital. School rituals such as the homecoming assembly mirrored Chad's derision of boys who failed to play at "getting girls." At the Homecoming Assembly two boys, Lamar and Tonio, stood in front of the cheering student body, lip-synching a comedy routine between Chris Rock and Michael Jackson.[3] Leering and pointing at two attractive girls clad in hip-high leather boots, black miniskirts, and white tank tops walking across the stage, the two boys pulled each other aside. Lamar, as Chris Rock, dared Tonio, as Jackson, to "get a girl." They paced back and forth in front of the girls, "Chris Rock" saying, "That girl! Oh man!" "Michael Jackson" responded in a high-pitched voice, "Goodness gracious! She is too fine!" "Rock" agreed, "She sho' is fine!" "Rock" turned to "Jackson," challenging him, "You can't get that girl!" "Jackson" responded defensively, in a high voice, "I *can* get her!" Again "Rock" challenged him, "I *bet* you can't get that girl! Michael, you are going to Neverland again!" The students roared in laughter as the two boys strutted back to "get" the girls.

The ritual of "getting girls" played out in this homecoming skit illustrates one of the ways compulsive heterosexuality becomes a part of boys' friendships and interactional styles. "Rock" and "Jackson," like boys at River High, jokingly challenged each other to dominate—or, in their words, to "get"—a girl. In these rituals girls' bodies functioned as a symbol of male heterosexuality and tangible evidence of repudiation of same sex-desire (Butler 1999). That is, if boys desired girls, then they couldn't possibly desire each other.

Both of the Mr. Cougar sketches I have outlined thus far involved stories of getting girls. In each one the victorious pair of boys was rewarded with girls as confirmation of their dominance. When Brent and Greg defeated the "gangstas," they were rewarded with "their girls," and when Freddy and Randy, as River High wrestlers, defeated their wrestling foes, the "dancing girls" ripped off their shirts to reveal a color pattern that symbolically linked them to Freddy and Randy. Rituals of getting girls allowed boys to find common ground in affirming each other's masculinity and positioned them as subjects who had a right to control what girls did with their bodies. A close examination indicates that rituals of "getting girls" relied on a threat of sexualized violence that reaffirmed a sexualized inequality central to the gender order at River High.

On Halloween, Heath arrived at school dressed as an elf carrying a sprig of mistletoe and engaged in a fairly typical ritual of getting girls. He told anyone who would listen that an elf costume was a brilliant idea for Halloween because "it's the wrong holiday!" We stood by his friends at the "water polo" table who tried to sell greeting cards as a fundraiser for the team. Heath attempted to "help" by yelling at girls who passed by, "Ten dollars for a card and a kiss from the elf! Girls only!" Girls made faces and rolled their eyes as they walked past. Graham walked up and Heath yelled to him, arms outstretched, "Come here, baby!" Graham walked toward him with his hips thrust forward and his arms open, saying, "I'm coming!" and quickly both of them backed away laughing. Graham challenged Heath's kissing strategy, saying that the mistletoe sticking out of his green shorts wouldn't work because it wasn't Christmas. Heath, to prove his point that mistletoe worked at any time of the year, lifted the mistletoe above his head and, moving from behind the table, walked up to a group of girls. They looked at him with a bit of trepidation and tried to ignore his presence. Finally one acquiesced, giving him a peck on the cheek. Her friend followed suit. Heath strutted back to the table and victoriously shook hands with all the boys.

Heath, in this instance, became successfully masculine both through renouncing the fag—he emphasized he was kissing "girls only," he imitated a fag by coming on to Graham—and through "getting girls" to kiss him.[4] Graham then congratulated Heath on his ability to overcome the girls' resistance to his overtures. This sort of coercion, even when seemingly harmless, embeds a sense of masculinity predicated upon an overcoming of girls' resistance to boys' desire (Hird and Jackson 2001). Indeed, if one of the important parts of being masculine, as stated by the boys earlier, was not just to desire girls, which Heath indicated through his "girls only" admonition, but also to be desired by girls, Heath demonstrated this in a quite public way, thus ensuring a claim, at least for a moment, on heterosexuality.

While the boys laughed and celebrated Heath's triumph of will, the girls may not have had the same reaction to his forced kisses. In a study of teenagers and sexual harassment, Jean Hand and Laura Sanchez (2000) found, not surprisingly, that in high school girls experienced higher levels of sexual harassment than boys did and were affected more seriously by it. The girls in their study described a hierarchy of sexually harassing behaviors in which some behaviors were described as more problematic than others. The girls overwhelmingly indicated that being kissed against their will was the worst form of sexual harassment, rated more seriously than hearing boys' comments about their bodies or receiving other types of unwanted sexual attention.

Of course, it is unlikely that boys, or girls, would recognize these sorts of daily rituals as sexual harassment; they are more likely seen as normal, if perhaps a bit aggressive, instances of heterosexual flirtation and as part of a normal adolescence (N. Stein 2005).[5] In fact, I never saw a teacher at River recognize these seemingly flirtatious interchanges as harassment. In auto shop, Tammy, the only girl, often faced this sort of harassment, often at the hands of Jay, a stringy-haired white junior with a pimpled face. One afternoon he walked up to Tammy and stood behind her deeply inhaling, his nose not even an inch away from her hair. Clearly uncomfortable with this, she moved to the side. He asked her if she was planning to attend WyoTech (Wyoming Technical College, a mechanic school), and she responded, "Yes." He said, "I'm going too! You and me. We're gonna be in a room together." He closed his eyes and started thrusting his hips back and forth and softly moaning as if to indicate that he was having sex. Tammy said, "Shut up" and walked away. Used to this sort of harassment, she had developed a way of dealing with such behavior. But no matter how many times she dismissed him, Jay continued to pepper her with sexual innuendoes and suggestive practices.

Both Jay's and Heath's behaviors show how heterosexuality is normalized as a sort of "predatory" social relation in which boys try and try and try to "get" a girl until one finally gives in. Boys, like Jay, who can't "get" a girl often respond with anger or frustration because of their presumed right to girls' bodies. Marc reacted this way when a girl didn't acknowledge his advances. As usual, he sat in the rear of the drama classroom with his pal Jason. A tall, attractive blonde girl walked into the room to speak to Mr. McNally, the drama teacher. As she turned to leave the class, Marc, leaning back with his legs up on the chair in front of him and his arm draped casually over the seat next to him, yelled across the room, "See you later, hot mama!" Jason, quickly echoed him, yelling "See you later, sweet thing." She didn't acknowledge them and looked straight ahead at the door as she left. Marc, frustrated at her lack of response, loudly stated, "She didn't hear me. Whore." Instead of acknowledging that not getting her reflected something about his gender status, he deflected the blame onto her. In fact, he transformed her into the female version of the fag: the whore.[6]

Getting, or not getting, girls also reflects and reinforces racialized meanings of sexuality and masculinity. Darnell, the African American and white football player who, in chapter 3, talked about how boys were told from a young age to avoid becoming a fag, made it clear that this sort of rejection was embedded with racialized meanings: pacing up and down the stairs that line the drama classroom, he yelled across the room to me.

"There's just one thing I hate! Just one thing I hate!" Shawna, an energetic, bisexual African American sophomore, and I simultaneously asked, "What's that?" Darnell responded, frustrated, "When mixed girls date white guys! Mixed girls are for me!" Shawna attempted to interrupt his rant, saying, "What if the girl doesn't want to date you? Girls have a say too." Darnell responded, not in as much jest as one might hope, "No they don't. White boys can date white girls. There's plenty of 'em. They can even date black girls. But mixed girls are for me." Darnell's frustration reflects a way in which racialized, gendered, and sexual identities intersect. While he felt that he had a claim on "getting girls," as a "mixed" guy he saw his options as somewhat limited. Girls and girls' bodies were constructed as a limited resource for which he had to compete with other (white) guys.

TOUCHING

Just as same-sex touching puts boys at risk for becoming a fag, cross-sex touching affirms heterosexuality and masculinity. "The use of touch (especially between the sexes)" maintains a "social hierarchy" (Henley 1977, 5). In general, superiors touch subordinates, invade their space, and interrupt them in a way that subordinates do not do to superiors. At River High masculinity was established through gendered rituals of touch involving boys' physical dominance and girls' submission.

Girls and boys regularly touched each other in a way that boys did not touch other boys. While girls touched other girls across social environments, boys usually touched each other in rule-bound environments (such as sports) or as a joke to imitate fags. While boys and girls both participated in cross-sex touching, it had different gender meanings. For girls, touching boys was part of a continuum of cross-sex and same-sex touching. That is, girls touched, hugged, and linked arms with other girls on a regular basis in a way that boys did not. For boys, cross-sex touching often took the form of a ritualistic power play that embedded gender meanings of boys as powerful and girls as submissive, or at least weak in their attempts to resist the touching. Touching, in this sense, becomes a "kinesic gender marker" producing masculinity as dominance and femininity as submission (Henley 1977, 138).

At River High boys and girls constantly touched each other as part of daily interaction, communication, and flirtation. In many instances cross-sex touching was lightly flirtatious and reciprocal. In auto shop Brian, a tall white senior, wrapped his arms around Cara, a skinny, white sophomore, who had wandered in to watch the boys work on a car. She said to him, "Let me feel your muscles."[7] Brian responded proudly, "Check out these guns!" As he flexed his arms Cara wrapped her hand around his biceps, laughing and teasing: "Those aren't muscles! I can still squeeze it!" Brian, indignant, responded, "Let me feel yours." The thin girl made her best attempt at flexing her muscles. Grabbing her arms, Brian laughed at her nonexistent biceps, as did Cara. In this instance the touching was reciprocal and lighthearted, though still infused with normative notions of boys as muscular and girls as weak. Brian and Cara touched each other equally, they didn't struggle for control of the situation, and the interaction was not overtly competitive (though a hint of violence hid under the surface of the interaction, as Brian's strength and Cara's weakness were affirmed).

Like rituals of getting girls, touching rituals ranged from playfully flirtatious to assaultlike interactions. Teachers at River never intervened, at least as far as I saw, when these touching interactions turned slightly violent. In her study of sex education practices in high school, Bonnie Trudell (1993) noted that teachers don't or won't differentiate between sexualized horseplay and assault among students. I also never saw administrators intervene to stop what were seemingly clear violations of girls' bodies. While these sorts of touching interactions often began as flirtatious teasing, they usually evolved into a competition that ended with the boy triumphant and the girl yelling out some sort of metaphorical "uncle."

Darnell and Christina, for instance, engaged in a typical touching ritual during a morning drama class. The students had moved into the auditorium, where they were supposed to be rehearsing their scenes. Christina, a strikingly good-looking white junior with long blonde hair, donned Tim's wrestling letterman's jacket. Darnell asked her if she was a wrestler. In response she pretended to be a wrestler and challenged him to a wrestling match. They circled each other in mock-wrestling positions as Darnell, dressed in baggy jeans and a T-shirt, yelled, "I don't need a singlet to beat you, lady!" She advanced toward Darnell, performing karate kicks with her legs and chops with her arms. Darnell yelled, "That's not wrestling!" and grabbed her torso, flipping her flat on her back. She pulled him down and managed to use her legs to flip him over so that he ended up underneath her on his back while she straddled him, sitting on his waist. Graham yelled out, watching in fascination, "What is going on?!" Many of the students had gathered around to watch and laugh at the faux wrestling match. Finally Darnell won the match by picking Christina up and throwing her over his shoulders. He spun her around as she squealed to be put down.

The general pace and sequence of this interaction were mirrored in many boy-girl touching rituals. Boys and girls antagonized each other in a flirtatious way. The flirtatious physical interaction escalated, becoming increasingly violent, until a girl squealed, cried, or just gave up. This sort of daily drama physically engendered meanings of power in which boys were confirmed as powerful and girls as weak.

While the "wrestling incident" between Darnell and Christina expressed seemingly harmless notions of dominance and submission, other "touching" episodes had a more explicitly violent tone. In this type of touching the boy and the girl "hurt" each other by punching or slapping or pulling each other's hair until in the end the girl lost with a squeal or scream. Shane and Cathy spent a large part of each morning in government class beating up on each other in this sequence of domination. While it was certainly not unidirectional, the interactions always ended with Cathy giving up. One of the many instances in which Cathy ended up submitting to Shane's touch began when Shane "punched" Cathy's chin. Cathy, trying to ignore the punch, batted her eyelashes and in a whiny voice pleaded, "Take me to In and Out for lunch." In response Shane grabbed her neck with one hand and forehead with the other, shoving her head backward and forward. Cathy squealed, "You're messing up my hair!" As he continued to yank her head around, Cathy tried to do her work, her pen jerking across the page. While this sort of interaction regularly disrupted Cathy's work and actually looked exceedingly painful, she never seriously tried to stop it. When I asked Cathy why they interacted like that, she answered, "He has always been like that with me. We used to have a class right on the other side of that wall together, and he always beat me in there, too. I don't know. He just beats on me." Her response echoed Karin Martin's (1996) finding that adolescent girls, especially working-class girls, don't have a strong sense that they control their own bodies. While some girls, such as Shawna, were able to assert subjectivity and deny the primacy of boys' desire—as when she confronted Darnell's "Mixed girls are for me!" comment—not all girls felt entitled to or expressed alternative definitions of gender. It may be that Shawna, with her baggy pants, hip-hop style, and "tough girl" demeanor, found it easier to confront Darnell than did a normatively feminine girl like Cathy, whose status depended on her electability to the homecoming court. Cathy's affectively flat response to my question revealed that she simply didn't have access to or couldn't express her own bodily needs, desires, and rights.

Interactions such as the one between Cathy and Shane rarely drew the notice of teachers (except to the extent that the two were disrupting class time), most likely because these encounters were read as harmless flirting. But in the larger context of the school's gender and sexual order they reflected a more serious pattern in which both heterosexuality and masculinity presumed female passivity and male control. River boys often physically constrained girls in a sexual manner under the guise of flirtation. For instance, in the hallway a boy put his arms around a girl as she was walking to lunch and started "freaking" her, rubbing his pelvis against her behind as she walked. She rolled her eyes, broke away, and continued walking. What really undergirded all of these interactions is what some feminists call a "rape paradigm," in which masculinity is predicated on overcoming women's bodily desire and control. A dramatic example of this "rape paradigm" happened between classes during passing period.[8] Walking between government and drama classes, Keith yelled, "GET RAPED! GET RAPED!" as he rhythmically jabbed a girl in the crotch with his drumstick. She yelled at him to stop and tried to kick him in the crotch with her foot. He dodged and started yelling, "CROTCH! CROTCH!" Indeed, the threat of rape was what seemed to underlie many of these interactions where boys repeatedly showed in cross-gender touching that they were more physically powerful than girls.

In all-male spaces some boys talked angrily and openly about accusations of rape. In auto shop Jay told a story about how a girl had accused him of holding a gun to her head and forcing her to have sex with him. For this offense he was put under house arrest for the better part of a year. He angrily reported the injustice of this accusation but followed this with one of his relatively frequent threats about rape. He talked about a girl he thought was "hella ugly" but had "titties": "She's a bitch. I might take her out to the street races and leave her there so she can get raped." All the other boys in auto shop, as usual, responded in laughter.

This sort of thing happened more frequently in predominately male spaces. In the weight room, an extremely physical space, girls were routinely physically restrained or manipulated. Often boys teamed up to control a girl. One day Monte wrapped his arms around a girl's neck as if to put her in a headlock and held her there while Reggie punched her in the stomach, albeit lightly. She squealed and laughed in response. Another day Malcolm and Cameron held a girl down on the quadriceps press machine while she screamed a high-pitched wail. They let her up, but moments later Malcolm snuck up behind her and poked her in the behind. She screamed and laughed in response. These examples show how the constraint of female bodies gets translated as masculinity and femininity, embedding sexualized meanings in which heterosexual flirting is coded as female helplessness and male bodily dominance.

SEX TALK

As Chad noted in his interview, boys needed to ensure their masculinity by talking about sex in a way that was perceived by other boys as authentic so that they wouldn't look like "clowns." Boys' sex talk involves talking about bodies, dating, and girls in general. Often it takes the form of "mythic-story telling" in which boys tell larger-than-life tales about their sexual adventures, their bodies, and girls' bodies (Kehily and Nayak 1997). At River High, these sorts of "sex talk" competitions often erupted in predominately male environments but also occurred in mixed-gender groups.

Sometimes, in their desperate attempts to show they knew about sex, some boys misspoke, revealing themselves, in Chad's words, as "clowns." Standing outside the weight room one day, Jeff desperately tried to maintain a convincing, sexually knowledgeable stance. Pedro and Jeff were discussing the merits of various hair replacement therapies such as Rogaine. Pedro mused about alternative hair replacement strategies, saying, "You could take hair from your butt!" Laughing, Craig suggested "pube," or pubic, hair. This began a debate about the sexual efficacy of shaving "down there." Jeff, looking wary, said, "I don't like sharp objects down there." Josh, having long since established himself as sexually experienced, looked at Jeff incredulously, crying, "You don't like blow jobs?!" Jeff, realizing he had said something wrong but still looking confused, quickly stammered, "Sure I do!" Josh, looking at Jeff disdainfully said, as if speaking to a child, "Teeth." Jeff, quickly trying to recover from his mistake, alleged with hollow bravado, "Oh, if they don't know what they're doing." Josh, with the assurance of experience, argued, "Even if they do!" In this instance, Josh treated Jeff's comment as an inadvertent revelation of sexual inexperience. Of course, whether it actually revealed anything about his past history with blow jobs was not really the point. The point was that he sounded, for a moment, sexually incompetent. Even his attempts at recovery sounded shallow as Josh discursively trumped Jeff's knowledge of blow jobs.

Asserting sexual dominance was, somewhat paradoxically, fraught with danger. On the one hand, overpowering a girl sexually was masculine (as indicated earlier in the rituals of cross-sex touching). On the other hand (as indicated through interviews with boys about the importance of girlfriends), girls' sexual desire undergirded a boy's masculinity. The following example indicates that many boys must tread lightly when talking about how much persuasion they need to deploy in order to convince a girl to have sex with them. In talking about their plans for Winter Ball, Josh told Reggie, "I'll be fucking pissed if I don't get some." Reggie advised him, "That's why you take a girl who's gonna do something." "I got JD!"[9] Josh countered, "I got a big bag of marijuana. The sooner I get her drunk, the sooner I get laid." Reggie laughed. "You have to get her drunk to get laid?" The other boys turned to laugh at Josh. Sean admonished Josh, "You have to change your confidence level." Reggie triumphantly bragged, "I can get laid any time, anywhere." Thus, while overpowering girls' control over their own bodies certainly confirmed masculinity, it was apparently much more masculine simply to overpower them by sheer virility, so that the girls couldn't help desiring a given boy. The sort of "date rape" talk that Josh exemplified simultaneously confirmed and cast doubt upon a given boy's masculinity. As in other practices of compulsive heterosexuality, boys showed that they could overpower girls' desire, will, and bodily control by convincing them (in this case through the use of drugs) to have sex. But if a part of being successfully masculine was, as Chad indicated, being desired by girls, then in this case Reggie and Josh indicated that they were not fully successful at being masculine, since the girls didn't necessarily desire them.

A popular topic of conversation in these male spaces was how and when a given boy was going to have or had had sex. In weight-lifting class, Pedro especially loved to share his exploits. Josh frequently joined in. Often by the end of class a group of boys had gathered around them either staring in amazement or desperately trying to keep up with the tall tales flowing from Josh and Pedro. One afternoon, egged on by the other boys' excited responses to his story about how badly Brittany "wanted" him, Pedro proceeded to act out his previous night's sexual adventures: "Dude, I had sex with my girlfriend last night. She tied me to the bed! I was like, damn!" Josh chimed in, shaking his head knowingly: "Never let a girl tie you up." Pedro laughed and added proudly: "I did her so hard when I was done she was bleeding. I tore her walls!" He acted out the story as he told it, leaning back up against the wall, legs and arms spread above him, thrusting his hips back and forth as he turned his head side to side. In this sort of fantastical story-telling boys assert their heterosexuality by sharing often incoherent sexual fantasies (Wood 1984). Curry (2004) calls these "women-as-objects-stories" in which female bodies serve as the crux of a heterosexual performance designed to bolster a boy's claim on heterosexuality.

Telling stories about sex confirmed boys' knowledge of sex. Some-times these mythic stories became a contest in which one boy tried to beat out the previous story with an outlandish tale of his own. One day in the weight room, for example, Rich sat down on a weight bench and five boys gathered around him as he told a story, after much urging, about sex with his now ex-girlfriend. He explained that they were having sex and "she said it started to hurt. I said we can stop, and she said no. Then she said it again and she started crying. I told her to get off! Told her to get off! Finally I took her off," making a motion like he was lifting her off him. Then he said there was "blood all over me! Blood all over her! Popped her wall! She had to have stitches." Boys start cracking up and moaning. Not to be outdone, other boys in the circle begin to chime in about their sexual exploits. Even those who didn't have stories about themselves asserted their knowledge of sex through vicarious experi-ences. Troy joined the discussion with a story about his brother, a pro-fessional basketball player for a nearby city. He "brought home a twenty-four-year-old drunk chick! She *farted* the whole time they were doing it in the other room! It was *hella* gross!" All the boys cracked up again. Adam, not to be outdone, claimed, "My friend had sex with a drunk chick. He did her in the butt! She shit all over the place!" The boys all laughed raucously and yelled out things like "Hella gross!" or "That's disgusting!" Finally, Travis seemed to top all of their stories with his, "I had sex with this one girl and then the next week she had sex with her cousin!" The boys fell backwards in laughter, yelling "Eeew! Gross!" Eventually they moved back to lifting weights. These stories expressed boys' heterosexuality by demonstrating that they were fluent in sex talk, knew about sex acts, and desired heterosexual sex. Girls' bodies, in this sense, became the conduit through which boys established themselves as masculine.

None of these stories were about sexual desire or how attractive the girls were; rather, they were quite gross, about farts, feces, and blood. These stories were about what boys could make girls' bodies do. That is, the sexual tall tales these boys told when they were together were not so much about indicating sexual desire as about proving their capacity to exercise control on the world around them, primarily through women's bodies by making them bleed, pass gas, or defecate. These stories also highlighted femininity (much like the fag) as an abject identity. Girls had out-of-control bodies, whereas boys exhibited mastery not only over their own bodies but over girls' bodies as well.

These sorts of girl-getting rituals and storytelling practices constitute "compulsive heterosexuality." While on the surface they appear to be boys-will-be-boys locker-room talk in which boys objectify girls through bragging about sexual exploits or procuring a kiss, a closer look indicates that they are also about demonstrating the ability to impose a sexualized dominance.

GIRLS RESPOND

Girls frequently colluded in boys' discourses and practices of compulsory heterosexuality. When interacting with boys, many girls emphasized their own sexual availability or physical weakness to gain and maintain boys' attention. Because a girl's status in high school is frequently tied to the status of the boys she dates, this male erotic attention is critical. Of course, gender practices like this are not limited to teenagers. Grown

women "bargain with patriarchy" by submitting to sexist social institutions and practices to gain other forms of social power (Kandiyoti 1988).

The day before winter break, I handed out lollipops shaped like
Christmas trees and candy canes to thank students for their help with my
research. In government class Cathy took a Christmas tree lollipop,
tipped her head back, and stuck the long candy down her throat, moaning as if in ecstasy. Jeremy and Shane laughed as Cathy presumably
showed off her roomy mouth or throat and her lack of a gag reflex, both
highly prized traits by boys when receiving "blow jobs." Cathy responded
with a smirk, "I don't think I'm *that* good." The group laughed at her
conclusion. It seems that the social power girls gained from going along
with this behavior was more than they gained by refusing. A way to gain
male attention and thus in-school status was to engage in these boys' discourses and practices about sexuality.

This approach, illustrating sexual prowess, was danger laden for girls
at River and is dangerous for teenage girls in general as they tread the
shifting and blurry boundary between sexy and slutty (Tanenbaum
1999). To negotiate this boundary, girls invoked a variety of gender
strategies. Some, like Cathy, promoted their own sexual prowess or acted
as if the boys' comments were compliments; others suffered quietly; and
some actually responded angrily, contradicting boys' claims on girls' sexuality. Teresa, like most girls, quietly put up with boys' daily practices of
compulsive heterosexuality. She was one of the few girls who had en-
rolled in the weight-lifting class. While she told me that she signed up
for weight lifting because "I like to lift weights," she continued by saying
she didn't like exercising in a class with all boys. "It's really annoying because they just stare at you while you lift. They just stare at you." Like
many girls, she quietly put up with this treatment. I didn't see her con-
fronting any of the boys who stared at her.

Other girls developed a more defensive response, though not one
couched in feminism or in opposition to sexism. In auto shop Jay expressed frustration about his upcoming eighteenth birthday, saying that

soon he couldn't "have sex with girls younger than eighteen. Statutory rape." He continued angrily (presumably referring to his rape charge), "Younger girls, they lie, stupid little bitches." He laughed, "God, I hate girls." He saw Jenny, the female student aide in the class, look at him as he said this. So he looked directly at her and said loudly, "They're only good for making sandwiches and cleaning house. They don't even do that up to speed!" She just looked at him and shook her head. Brook, another auto shop student, said to me, "Write that down!" Jay continued to harass Jenny by throwing licorice at her and yelling, "I agree, her sister is a lot hotter!" Jenny looked at him and shook her head again. Jay commanded, sitting back and folding his arms, "Make me a sandwich!" At first she ignored him with a "whatever." Then Jenny carried back the licorice he threw at her and dumped it on him. Jay responded dismissively, shaking his head and muttering, "Fucking crybaby." In this instance Jenny both acquiesced to and resisted Jay's sexist treatment. She sort of ignored him while he made blatantly sexist remarks and tried to get even with him by dumping licorice on him. Like the girl who tried to fight back as she was being jabbed in the crotch with a drumstick, Jenny developed an off-the-cuff response to let the boys know she didn't appreciate their sexism.

Other girls, like Cathy, seemed flattered by boys' behavior, responding with giggles and smiles. In the drama class Emir, who had imitated a fag by "lusting" after the boys on the basketball court, "flirted" regularly with two girls, Simone and Valerie, throughout the class period. He made kissing motions with his lips, ran his tongue slowly over his teeth, and lustfully whispered or mouthed comments such as "Come on, baby. Oooh baby. Yeah, I love you." The girls responded with laughs and giggles, occasionally rolling their eyes in mock frustration. Other girls frequently adopted the smile and giggle strategy. While I interviewed Darnell, he yelled at a passing girl that he liked her "astronaut skirt." She laughed and waved. I asked him what "astronaut skirt" meant, and he explained, "Oh, it's just a little joke. That's an astronaut skirt 'cause your butt is outta this world." As Nancy Henley (1977) points out, this giggle and smile response signifies submission and appeasement, usually directed from a lower- to a higher-status person.[10]

Though most girls submitted to this sort of behavior, not all of them did. As recounted earlier, Shawna told Darnell, when he was declaring, "Mixed girls are for me!" that girls had a say in the matter too. Darnell didn't listen to her, but she didn't accept this definition of the situation. The most apparent resisters were the girls in the Gay/Straight Alliance, whom I discuss at length in the next chapter. But even girls without an espoused political orientation sometimes rejected boys' control of girls' bodies. In the hallway, for instance, Jessica stood behind Reggie as he backed up and rubbed his behind into her crotch. In response, she smacked him hard and he stopped his grinding. Similarly, in the weight room, Teresa sometimes resisted in her own way. Reggie once said to her, "When we gonna go and have sex? When we gonna hit that?" Teresa responded with scorn, "Never!" and walked away. This, unfortunately, happened more rarely than one would hope.

I'M DIFFERENT FROM OTHER GUYS

Thus far this chapter has focused on boys who treated girls as resources to be mobilized for their own masculinity projects, but not all boys engaged in practices of compulsive heterosexuality at all times. Most boys engaged in these sorts of practices only when in groups, and some boys avoided them in general.

When not in groups—when in one-on-one interactions with boys or girls—boys were much less likely to engage in gendered and sexed dominance practices. In this sense boys became masculine in groups (Connell 1996; Woody 2002). With the exception of Chad, none of the boys spoke with me the way they spoke with other boys about girls, girls' bodies, and their own sexual adventures. When with other boys, they postured and bragged. In one-on-one situations with me (and possibly with each other) they often spoke touchingly about their feelings about and insecurities with girls. While the boys I interviewed, for the most part, asserted the centrality of sexual competence to a masculine self, several of them rejected this definition or at least talked differently about girls and sexuality in their interviews.

When alone some boys were more likely to talk about romance and emotions, as opposed to girls' bodies and sexual availability. Darnell, for instance, the boy who had announced, "Mixed girls are for me!" and who had "wrestled" Christina, talked to me in private and with great emotion about a girl with whom he had recently broken up:

> I never wanted a girlfriend, but I got a girlfriend and I never wanted to lose her. Now I don't go out with that girl any more, but I still see her. We actually live in the same apartment complex. She goes to Chicago High School. She's not supposed to go to Chicago and I'm not supposed to go to River, so we kind of stay apart. It's a little hard. It's kind of easy if you were that kind of guy you could just have a girl-friend over there and a girlfriend over here.

While in groups with other boys Darnell behaved much like "the kind of guy who could just have a girlfriend over there and a girlfriend over here," claiming things like "Mixed girls are for me!" But in the interview with me he spoke tenderly about his former girlfriend. When I asked him why he thought he was different, he said, "I had a whole bunch of girls when I was little. I know how certain things can hurt their feelings. I don't like hurting people's feelings." Darnell's discussion of girls and his ability to hurt their feelings provided a very different picture of his ap-proach to women than did his proclamations about which women be-longed to him.

In interviews boys often posited themselves as "different from other guys," while in public they acted just like the guys they derided. Heath, for instance, told me he was "probably less" like an average guy because "I don't try and get with every girl I see." Like others, Heath became a "guy" in public, not in private interactions. Heath was the boy who had dressed like an elf for Halloween and accosted the passing girls in order to procure a kiss. Outside this sort of group setting, Heath dismissed lecherous behavior as something "other guys" did, but when in public he acted just like these "other guys." As Jace told me, when talking about a generic teenage boy, "By himself, he'd probably be cool. He wouldn't do stupid stuff. But in a group he'd do stupid stuff." When I asked him for an example of stupid stuff, he said, "Well, guys check out girls anyway, yell at 'em, 'Oh, yeah, you look good today, what's up?' " Indeed, looking at the differences between both Darnell's and Heath's behavior in groups and individually indicates that Jace highlights an important component of adolescent masculinity—that it happens in groups.

That said, boys not widely considered masculine did, on occasion, speak about girls and their relationships with girls in kind and nonobjectifying ways, even in groups of boys. In the following example a group of boys shared some tender observations about their relationships in a highly masculinized space, auto shop. Ryan looked at a note written to him by his girlfriend before he handed it to me. His girlfriend, who was moving away, wrote that she cared about and would "never forget" him, even though she thought he would forget her. She wrote, among other things, "I feel safe in your arms." I asked Ryan if he wrote notes back. He and his friend Chet both said that they wrote notes to their girlfriends. Both of them also told me they kept their girlfriends' notes in special boxes. They did, however, debate what sort of notes they kept. Chet said he kept all the notes: "It doesn't even matter if it's important." Ryan said he only kept the note if it was important. Another friend, John, chimed in, announcing he kept them because "it's hella long, they spent all that time writing it." While this might initially sound silly, John's comment actually signaled a sweet acknowledgment of a girl's perspective and experience. K. J., the popular dancer we met at the end of the last chapter, spoke up at this point and rerouted the discussion back to the familiar territory of compulsive heterosexuality. He received multiple notes each day from his legions of female fans. His comments about these notes sounded quite different from the sweet comments of Chet and Ryan. K. J. laughed about a note he had received that read, "Every time you dance I have an orgasm." As a sexual actor, K. J. was so virile he could cause a girl to have an orgasm without even touching her. Ryan, Chet, and John laughed, and the conversation soon dissipated. K. J., a high-status, masculine boy, redirected a conversation about girls' perspectives and boys' emotions back to the familiar terrain of boys as sexual actors.

Though discussions among boys like the one between Ryan and Chet were rare, on another occasion I heard a boy, in a group of other boys, refuse to engage in practices of compulsive heterosexuality by claiming that he couldn't talk about his girlfriend like that. Pedro, as usual, was talking to the other boys in the weight room about a variety of sexual practices. He lectured, "You are getting your girl from behind. You spit on her ass cheeks . . . " As he continued he was drowned out by the other boys yelling, "You watched that on a porno!" Undaunted, Pedro said, "Next time you get buttered, hit her on the back of her head after you cum and it will come out her nose!" The other boys howled in laughter as they pictured this highly unlikely sexual scenario. As Pedro goaded the other boys into promising that they would try this particular sexual practice the next time they had the opportunity, a good-looking African American boy spoke up, saying quietly that he wouldn't: "I got a girlfriend, man." As the other boys scoffed he said, "I wouldn't do that to her." The only safe terrain from which to challenge these sexually oriented definitions of masculinity was a relationship. A boy probably could not have argued that talking this way about girls was derogatory on principle without claiming he was speaking about a girlfriend.

Other boys who refrained from participating in these sorts of conversations frequently identified as Christian. Though they professed the same religion, they did not constitute a distinct peer group in the school but were scattered throughout the social scene at River High. Sean, a recent convert to evangelical Christianity, talked through much of his interview about struggling to maintain secular friendships while simultaneously practicing Christianity because of his different views on both sexuality and drug use:

I know if I wasn't with God, I'd be doing everything that they are doing. I don't feel like saying that, but it's the truth. I am like them. But I choose not to do as they do.

Before he converted, Sean, a muscular, handsome white senior who identified with hip-hop culture, had been sexually active with several girls. He found it challenging to refrain from having sex after he converted, saying, "That was a hard one. That was really tough." He looked down on boys who tried to "get girls":

> There will be some guys that they'll go up to a girl, you know? "Hey, girl, come here." And they will keep on bugging them. They'll try to grab and touch them and stuff like this. They're just letting all their, they're acting on emotions pretty much.

Sean saw these boys as out of control. He used a feminized insult, implying that the boys engaged in practices of "getting girls" because they were ruled by their emotions and thus not able to refrain from sexist practices.

Connor, who also identified as a Christian, similarly distanced himself from other boys and their views of sexuality. "I don't care if I have sex or not because I want to save myself until I'm married, because that's something special. I'm really less than most average guys, that's what I think." Connor saw himself as less interested in sex than other teenage boys because he saw it as inappropriate behavior outside a marriage. Ben also refused to engage in sexualizing discourses of girls. He explained:

> I remember the first day we were disassembling a lawn mower and she [Teresa, the only girl in auto shop] was like, right over by me. And there's these two other guys by me. She walks away and then he's like, "Hey dude, can you beat those?" And I'm like . . . "I'm just not into that kind of stuff." He goes, "Oh, okay, good stuff."

Like the boy who refused to engage in compulsive heterosexuality by claiming a girlfriend, some boys claimed a religious affiliation.

Christian boys, like Sean, frequently cast themselves as more mature than other boys because of their sexual restraint, drawing on masculinizing discourses of self-control and maturity. Like practices of compulsive heterosexuality, these sorts of gender practices indicated control and mastery, not over others (girls), but over themselves. Talking with Darren and Brook, who both identified as Christian, during auto shop, I asked them if they ever felt left out of conversations with other guys. Brook responded, "Yeah, sometimes. But I'm not, like, ashamed of what I think, you know?" I asked in response, "Do you ever feel less masculine because of it?" Brook said, "No. If anything, more. Because you can resist. You don't have to give in to it." Darren chimed in, "That was profound, dude!" I then asked, "Do you think other guys ever think, 'Oh, those guys are such pussies. They just can't get laid and it's an excuse'?" Brook replied, "Probably, yeah. There are going to be those stereotypical teenage guys again that think that." Unlike other boys, who, for the most part, talked about sex as if it were a recreational activity, both Brook and Darren wanted sex to be "special." Brook said that while "sex is all over the place, I haven't had sex." Like other boys, he hurried to assure me that "I'm a teenage guy, don't think I don't think about it." But unlike other boys, he exercised will and mastery, not over girls' bodies, but over his own by waiting to have sex. Like these boys, Cid explicitly invoked a discourse of control as he spoke about how "most guys are gawking at the girls. I notice that and I just don't want to be like that. I don't know if I'm controlling myself or if it just happens. Either way I don't want to be like that . . . It makes me feel better about myself, like I don't have to be like them."

Religion played a key role in how or if boys deployed practices of compulsive heterosexuality to shore up a masculine appearance and sense of self. In fact the table at which the Latter Day Saints students convened during lunch was (apart from Gay/Straight Alliance meetings and the drama classroom) the least homophobic and sexist location on campus! At first this seems to be a strange finding because many Christian sects or denominations are regarded as conservative and sexist. These boys weren't necessarily any less invested in a masculine identity predicated on gender inequality. However, Christian boys at River High had institutional claims on masculinity such that they didn't need to engage in the sort of intense interactional work that Kimmel (1987) claims is characteristic of contemporary "compulsive masculinity." As a result, unlike nonreligious boys, they did not need to engage in the continual interactional repudiation of equality with girls. Their respective religions buttressed male power through their teachings such that the interactional accomplishment of masculinity was less central to their identity projects. Thus the Christian boys at River may have been less interactionally sexist, but their investment in gender difference and gender inequality was little different from that of the other boys at River. In a society in which the gendered order has undergone a rapid change due to challenges to male power, and men and women are relatively equal under the law, one of the ways to maintain power is through interactional styles. But because the Christian institutions of which these boys were a part have remained relatively stable regarding issues of gender difference and equality, these boys had less need for interactional practices of gendered power.

FEMALES ARE THE PUPPETS

At a country square dance a few years ago I saw an offensive game between two men on opposite sides of a square, to see who could swing the women hardest and highest off the ground. What started out pleasantly enough soon degenerated into a brutal competition that left the women of the square staggering dizzily from place to place, completely unable to keep up with what was going on in the dance, and certainly getting no pleasure from it. The message that comes through to women in such physical displays is: you are so physically inferior that you can be played with like a toy. Males are the movers and the powerful in life, females the puppets.

It is heartbreaking, thirty years after Nancy Henley (1977, 150) wrote this passage, to document the continuing centrality of what she called "female puppetry" to adolescent masculinity. Like these square dancing men, boys at River High repeatedly enforced definitions of masculinity that included male control of female bodies through symbolic or physical violence.

As a feminist researcher I was saddened and quite frankly surprised to discover the extent to which this type of sexual harassment constituted an average school day for youth at River High. Though much of the media and many cultural critics repeatedly claim that we have entered a postfeminist age, these scenes at River High indicate that this age has not yet arrived. In fact gender practices at the school—boys' control of girls' bodies, almost constant sexual harassment, and continual derogatory remarks about girls—show a desperate need for some sort of sexual harassment education and policy enforcement in schools.

Just as in the square dance that Henley described, girls' bodies at River High provided boys the opportunity to demonstrate mastery and dominance. These practices of compulsive heterosexuality indicate that control over women's bodies and their sexuality is, sadly, still central to definitions of masculinity, or at least adolescent masculinity. By dominating girls' bodies boys defended against the fag position, increased their social status, and forged bonds of solidarity with other boys. However, none of this is to say that these boys were unrepentant sexists. Rather, for the most part, these behaviors were social behaviors. Individually boys were much more likely to talk empathetically and respectfully of girls. Even when they behaved this way in groups, boys probably saw their behavior as joking and in fun (Owens, Shute, and Slee 2005). Maintaining masculinity, though, demands the interactional repudiation of this sort of empathy in order to stave off the abject fag position. It is precisely the joking and sexual quality of these interactions that makes them so hard to see as rituals of dominance. These interactional rituals maintain the "cruel power of men over women by turning it into just sex" (Jeffreys 1998, 75). The data presented in this chapter make gender equality seem a long way off. The next chapter shows how several groups of girls, much like the boys in the drama performances, provide alternative models of gender practices in adolescence, emphasizing play, irony, and equality rather than dominance and submission.

CHAPTER FIVE

Look at My Masculinity!

Girls Who Act Like Boys

"Girls can be masculine too, you know," Genevieve pointed out to me when I told her I was writing a book on teenage boys and masculinity. Indeed, Genevieve had a point: girls *can* be masculine. At River High several girls identified themselves and were named by other students (both girls and boys) as masculine or as "girls who act like guys." They dressed, talked, and carried themselves in many ways "like guys." None of their peers identified them as actual boys. In other words, these girls weren't trying to "pass" as male, nor did students refer to them as "tomboys," the common way we think of boylike girls. None of the girls thought of themselves as boys trapped in girls' bodies or identified as transgendered.[1] Several of them, although not all, identified themselves as lesbian.

Most, though not all, of the girls were members of two social groups. I call these two groups the Basketball Girls and the Gay/Straight Alliance (GSA) Girls.[2] The Basketball Girls, athletic, loud, popular, and well liked, were commonly identified by other students as "like boys." The GSA Girls, as their name indicates, were all members of the school's GSA, a club formed to support gay students on campus. They were socially marginalized and less well known and were more likely to describe themselves than to be described by others as masculine. In addition to these two groups of girls, one other girl at River was commonly identified by students as masculine—Jessie Chau. She was not a member of either group and was a senior when the GSA Girls and the Basketball Girls were mostly first-years and sophomores. Like the Basketball Girls she dressed like a boy, was an athlete, and was incredibly popular—serving as both class president and homecoming queen.

By looking at these girls this chapter examines what it means to define masculinity as a set of practices associated with women as well as men. By moving in and out of masculine identifications these girls engaged in what Schippers (2002) calls "gender maneuvering." *Gender maneuvering* refers to the way groups act to manipulate the relations between masculinity and femininity as others commonly understand them. By engaging in public practices that students associated with masculinity (certain clothing styles, certain sexual practices, and interactional dominance), these girls called into question the easy association of masculinity with male bodies. Their gender maneuvering challenges both commonsense and academic understandings of masculinity as the sole domain of men.

These girls engaged in non-normative gender practices in a variety of ways. In their daily interactional practices they engaged in gender resistance, acting in ways most people don't associate with teenage girls. However engaging in non-normative gender practices doesn't always and consistently challenge the gender order. Doing gender in this way opens up issues of gender resistance and reconstruction, illustrating that gender resistance can, but doesn't always, challenge sexism (Gagne and Tewksbury 1998). Like boys who "inhabit and construct non-hegemonic masculinities," thereby both subverting and reinforcing normative gender relations (Renold 2004, 247), these masculine girls both challenged and reinscribed gender norms. This chapter concludes with thoughts about how to discuss female masculinity and implications for how scholars study both male and female masculinity.[3] While all the girls' practices of gender maneuvering had the potential for challenging the interactional gender order, the GSA Girls' gender practices, with their clear political project, contained the most potential.

TOMBOY PASTS

Acting like a boy was not unique to the Basketball Girls, Jessie, and the GSA Girls, nor is it something that occurs only at River High. Many girls and women claim that they were tomboys as children. In *Gender Play*, Barrie Thorne (1993) talks about female students in her college classes who proudly shared stories of childhoods in which they considered themselves tomboys. Similarly, when he asked his undergraduates, "Who was a tomboy as a child?" Michael Messner (2004b) noted that women raised their hands more often than men did when he asked, "Who was a sissy?" In fact, Lyn Mikel Brown (2003) argues that the story of the tomboy girl triumphant over the sissy feminine girl is a common one. Instead of redefining girlhood as tough and powerful, these tomboy stories belittle normative femininity and celebrate masculinity. The girls at River High, both those who were normatively gendered and those who identified as masculine, spoke with pride about tomboy childhoods. Identifying as a tomboy aligns a girl with a romanticized history of masculine identification before she encountered a more restricting femininity.

Several girls who, at the time I spoke with them, identified as normatively feminine shared stories about how they had acted more masculine when they were younger. They illustrate the trajectories of gender identity, in which gender non-normativity may be considered cute in childhood but problematic in adolescence or adulthood. Jenna and Sarah, energetic, thin, attractive white cheerleaders who wore their straight blonde hair up in high bouncy ponytails and frequently pulled out compacts to apply or freshen up already perfectly crafted makeup, rehearsed their lines for an upcoming play as they sat outside drama class. Their talk turned to River High's football team. Sarah announced, "I wanted to play football when I was little! I love football! And my dad totally wanted me to play. But my mom didn't, and I think that's why I didn't get to play. So I became a cheerleader." It seemed as if, in her mind, being a cheerleader was as close to becoming an actual football player as she could get.

While certainly cheerleaders and football players inhabit the same playing field, the gendered meanings of the two roles are worlds apart, with
cheerleaders working as football players' perky heterosexual helpmates
(Adams and Bettis 2003). Like Sarah, other girls often told stories about
mothers encouraging them to give up "acting like a boy" as they grew
older. During Hoop Skills (the basketball class), Latasha, a petite African
American sophomore, said with pride and a bit of regret, "I used to dress
like a boy. But I fixed up this year. My ma didn't like it." Her appearance
underscored her claim. She now sported large gold hoops, gold jewelry,
tight pants, and a tight shirt, with makeup and a gold heart painted on
her cheek.

Boys also commented on girls' increasing feminization as they grew
older. As Allen and I talked about "girls who act like guys," he said, "You
can't see too many of them at the high school level, it seems to me, as I
did when I was younger in the middle school." When I asked him "Why
do you think that is?" he responded, "At the age of high school I guess
people want to be the same. When you're younger . . . you are a kid. You
are wide open. You're not really sure. You just do what you want." Allen
attributed girls' changing gendered practices to social pressure, which, in
the case of the girls who identified as tomboys when they were younger,
seemed to be true. Mothers, and most likely other adults, began to discipline girls to assume more typically feminine dispositions. The change
from tomboyism to femininity discussed by Latasha, Sarah, and Allen reflected the representational transformation in the yearbook in which
both girls and boys moved from a variety of clothing options to strictly
gendered uniforms in their senior photos. The public face of the tomboy
belongs to childhood. This sort of female masculinity in childhood is not
only accepted but celebrated (Halberstam 1998). However, this same
masculinity in adulthood threatens to destabilize the gender order.

Interestingly, I never heard these sorts of childhood stories from boys.
None of them told me they were or knew of boys who used to act more
feminine when they were younger. Nor did any of them express sadness
about experiences they had missed out on, such as playing with Barbies

or dressing up in skirts and heels. The fact that I didn't hear these stories doesn't mean they don't exist. When teaching college classes about masculinity, I've heard stories from my male students about being ruthlessly teased and eventually giving up playing with dolls and Barbies because of this gendered torment. Instead of pride, their stories are tinged with shame. We don't have a cultural narrative, such as that of the tomboy, with which to frame and understand these experiences, so they may be more likely to be silenced.

In high school, female masculinity, once understood as a tomboy identity, translates into a sexual identity. Much as they did with boys, youth at River High associated girls' gender non-normativity with same-sex desire. When I explained to them that I was "writing a chapter on girls who do guy things," Sarah (the aforementioned cheerleader) asked, "Oh, you mean lesbians?" However, the loathing many boys expressed for male same-sex desire didn't appear when boys (or girls) talked about either tomboys or lesbians. James said, "I haven't really heard anybody tease them [lesbians]." In explaining the differential treatment of gay boys and lesbians, students repeatedly asserted that because boys thought that same-sex activity between women was "hot," lesbians were desired, not shunned. When I asked James about this, he told me, "Guys like it for girls. Guys will see two lesbians and they'll be like 'Yeah!' Then when guys see two guys they're like—'Uughh!' " Marco also drew on a discourse of eroticization: "Girls are pretty. They have soft skin, you know? Guys don't. They're hairy. They stink. I can see where a girl would be a lesbian." Ray told me that most guys fantasized about lesbian relationships: "[To] see two hot chicks banging bodies in a bed, that's like every guy's fantasy right there. It's the truth. I've heard it so many times: 'Give me two chicks banging bodies.' " So-called "lesbian" sex is a trope frequently deployed in heterosexual pornography that, far from legitimizing same-sex relationships, titillates and arouses male readers (Jenefsky and Miller 1998). Eroticizing women's same-sex relationships renders them harmless and nonthreatening to the gender order (Rich 1986).

In general, girls who transgress gendered and sexualized expectations don't need to do the same sort of interactional work boys do when they are permanently or temporarily labeled as fags. Unlike gender and sexual non-normativity for boys, which decrease a boy's social status, gender and sexual non-normativity for girls can actually increase their social status. In certain circumstances, such as those in which girls' non-normative gender practices mirror the boys' masculinity processes that I've discussed thus far, such non-normativity can result in popularity. However, as the GSA Girls' gender practices indicate, challenging gender norms, especially when the challenge is framed as a political one in direct opposition to sexism and homophobia, doesn't necessarily result in increased social status for girls.

REBECA AND THE BASKETBALL GIRLS

Not surprisingly, more often than not the Basketball Girls could be found on the basketball court. While in total there were about ten to fifteen of them, Rebeca, Michelle, Tanya, and Tanya's little sister, Sheila, were the girls students talked about when I asked them if they know any "girls who act like guys." They were a racially diverse group (as was the larger crowd)—Rebeca was Latina, Tanya and Sheila were white, Michelle was Filipina. They were all sophomores during the first year of my research, with the exception of Sheila, who was a freshman. The Basketball Girls acted like boys in a variety of ways. Their athleticism and involvement with a male sport instantly aligned them with masculinity (Messner 2002; Theberge 2000). They spat, walked in a limping "gangsta" style, wore boys' clothing, ditched class, and listened to loud hip-hop music, dancing and purposefully singing only the "naughty" lyrics. They performed special handshakes and made fun of me when I didn't execute them correctly. Their energy was never-ending. At the homecoming football game, which they all attended, I grew dizzy watching them run up and down the bleachers, screaming, laughing, and pulling each others' long ponytails. They continually shoved each other and wrestled on the top bleachers, every once in a while falling into me, at which point they'd laughingly reprimand each other and profusely apologize to me because I was, in their words, a "grown-up."

Before this group physically appeared, one could almost always hear them coming because of their hollers, screams, and laughter. Michelle described their "loudness" to me at length:

> They're fun to be around. They loud. They not quiet people . . . When I'm by myself I don't really be yelling and stuff, but when I'm with my friends, yeah, I be like that . . . When I'm around my friends I can't be quiet. We [are] just always loud. That's how it is. When we go around school, everybody already knows. We're always together, and we always act loud. Everybody's like, "If you guys were ever in class together I feel sorry for that teacher." That's how we was in sixth period. We were hecka loud in that class.

Other students also described the Basketball Girls as loud. Jason observed, "They are sometimes a little rowdy and loud. Like after school they hang out sometimes and they're running around yelling and stuff, but you just overlook it. I think they're cool."

The Basketball Girls were instantly recognizable because their attire set them apart from other female students. They wore long hair, typically slicked back into tightly held ponytails that hung long down their backs. They dressed in baggy hip-hop clothes generally indistinguishable from boys' hip-hop clothing: oversize shirts, baggy pants precariously balanced low on their hips and held up with a belt, immaculately clean athletic shoes unlaced with socks rolled up under the tongues so that they stuck out, and large jewelry. One day Michelle came to school dressed entirely in white—white cargo pants, a white baggy T-shirt, and a white sweatshirt with one arm in the sleeve and the other sleeve hiked up over her shoulder (a typically "boy" way to wear it), and white tennis shoes. While hip-hop culture is often derided for its rampant misogyny, girls and women find ways to appropriate the culture and style in order to express independence and agency (Emerson 2002). This is what the Basketball Girls did in their interactional style, clothing choices, and musical tastes.

None of the Basketball Girls said they self-consciously dressed like boys; instead they said they dressed in baggy clothes for comfort. Michelle said she liked to dress in baggy clothes "'cause it's comfortable. I don't like wearing tight stuff." She told me that other girls dressed in fitted clothing "'cause they want to look cute for people. I really don't care what people think about me, or whatever." She did say other people commented on her unusual clothing choices: "Yeah, they'll always be like, why I dress like this? I'm comfortable. That's what I like."

Rebeca told me that she had dressed this way "my whole life practically." When I asked her why she didn't dress like her girlfriend, Annie, a perky white cheerleader who wore typically feminine, low-slung, tight pants and fitted shirts, Rebeca told me, "It doesn't go right with me. I don't feel the vibe there. I don't like it." She said that her friends "dress fine. I mean, I don't care how they dress. I mean, I like the way they dress and everything. I just like the way I dress." I asked her if anyone ever commented on the fact that she didn't wear tight clothing. Rebeca told me, "I get that a lot." Her friends (not all members of the Basketball Girls) often teased Rebeca about her masculine self-presentation. On Halloween Rebeca was hanging out at basketball practice with Latasha and Shelly talking about whether they planned to go trick-or-treating that evening. Latasha teased Rebeca, "Are you going as a girl?" They all laughed. Shelley jumped in, saying, "Yeah, I wanna see you in a dress!" Latasha modified this by saying, "No, just tight pants and a tight shirt!" All three continued to laugh at the idea of Rebeca in "female drag."

The Basketball Girls sometimes joked about dressing like other girls at River. One morning Tanya, Rebeca, and Sheila skipped class to sit on top of tables in the school's central quad and listen to rap music. They discussed what they were planning on wearing to the "Back to School Dance" the upcoming Friday. Rebeca asked Tanya, "You goin' to the dance?" Tanya answered, "Yeah, I'm gonna wear a skirt." Rebeca's mouth dropped open: "For real?" Sheila, Tanya's little sister chimed in, "Yeah, I'm wearin' a dress, some makeup, and my hair all down." Rebeca, flabbergasted at this point, asked, "FOR REAL?" Both Tanya and Sheila laughed loudly, "NAH!" All three of them cracked up in laughter. Such laughter was both a celebration of their gender transgressions and possibly a way to manage anxiety about it.

The Basketball Girls constantly disrupted whatever environment they were in with their never-ending (but very entertaining) energy. None of them had cars or licenses, so they ate lunch in the cafeteria. More than once they got into a food fight in the cafeteria at lunchtime. During one particularly entertaining round, they hollered at one another as their food fight turned into an impromptu soccer game. They kicked empty water bottles back and forth across the cafeteria, yelling "Goal!" every time they shot a bottle between table legs. Another time they incited a food fight by continually throwing candy eggs at the heads of a group of girls in the cafeteria, laughing raucously each time an egg pelted its target. They continued this behavior down the hallway, laughing hysterically as they hit these girls with the eggs.

The Basketball Girls' high-energy antics and proclivity to fights often brought them into conflict with the school's disciplinary rules. Rebeca, for instance, said of her disruptiveness in the basketball class, "I don't like the varsity coach 'cause she's my teacher. She hates me, I hate her. She just mugs me. I mug her back." I asked Rebeca, "What's mugging?" She answered,

> Like givin' me a dirty-ass look. I'm just like, whatever. I be hella loud in that class . . . I'm seriously jumping up on the bleachers. Throwing balls all over the place, just shooting wherever I want to. Not even listening to the teacher. And she just, like, sits there, like [soft voice], "I hate you. Hate you." No, she doesn't say that, but I know she's sayin' it. She doesn't like me.

All during Hoop Skills class, not one of the Basketball Girls stopped moving. While some of the other students tired out and wilted in the corner, these girls constantly made drum noises by pounding the bleachers rhythmically, ran up and down the court, jumped on each other, and shot baskets. In fact, one day, Tanya was so disruptive the coach asked her to leave class. Upon exiting the gym, she started to jump up and down outside, making faces in the window at the rest of the class as they laughed at her clowning.

One day at lunch I sat with the Basketball Girls as we watched Tanya's father escort her off the school campus. Casey, a middle-aged blonde security guard, walked up to the Basketball Girls' lunch table, shaking her head and saying, "She's back for a day and then she's suspended again." Tanya had shown up late for a class in which the teacher had locked the door to prevent disruptions. Frustrated at being locked out, Tanya started to kick the door loudly and repeatedly. The teacher called security and she was suspended. The rest of the girls were no strangers to fights. At football games their shoving matches were frequently interrupted with pronouncements of which girls they planned to fight, followed by furtive and intense discussions involving mediators between them and groups of girls from a rival school.

Their aggressiveness frequently inspired fear in other students. Ricky said of them, "They're tough! Oh, they're tough! Every time I see them they're like [deep voice], 'Yo man, whatsup!' I'm like [makes a scared face]. I'm used to 'Oh, hi!' [high-pitched female voice]." I asked Ricky if other students gave the girls a hard time. He told me, "I can't imagine that they do, because they're so tough. They have the ambition and the attitude to kick some ass. They [other students] know that if they say anything they're gonna get their ass kicked. So they don't say anything." He was right, I never saw other students fight back against the Basketball Girls, nor did I hear disparaging comments made about them.

None of them had boyfriends. With the exception of Rebeca, who identified as a lesbian, it was unclear whether the others identified as straight or gay. However, they make it clear that boys were not high on their priority list. Michelle said, as we talked on a metal bench outside the locker rooms one afternoon, "I don't really have no time for boyfriends. When I did have one it wasn't fun. I like hanging out with my friends all the time, doing stuff with them. When you're with a boy you don't really have time for them. I don't have time to be with a boy." Regardless, the prevailing view among the student body was that the Basketball Girls were gay. Calvin described them as a "hecka loud" group of girls who "all look like boys, all dress like boys," and are "all gay."

Little five-foot-high Rebeca was, in one student's words, "the leader of the pack." Jose described her by saying, "She kind of looks like a guy but it's a girl." She was well known, well liked, and almost always within earshot. She was a darling girl with a vivacious smile and tangible energy, and she made friends easily. At a football game when I said I was writing "a book on boys," one of her (non–Basketball Girl) friends squealed that "you should interview her! She dresses like a boy and she's a lesbian! She turns straight girls gay!" Indeed, both straight boys and straight girls at River High commented on her attractiveness. Her current girlfriend, Annie, had been straight until she met Rebeca, thus adding to the impression that Rebeca possessed mystical attraction.

Rebeca's lesbianism and masculine sense of self often became a joke with her friends who were outside the Basketball Girls. As I interviewed Rebeca on the lunch tables in front of the school, Lisa, one of Rebeca's non–Basketball Girl friends, approached, asking, "What are you guys recording?" She wanted to know if I was writing about Rebeca, and I said, "Sort of." Laughing, she asked what my research was about—"lesbians?" Rebeca and her friends, including me, all laughed at this. Rebeca, retorted, "You're gay, Lisa!" Ana yelled back, "Lisa's not gay, Lisa's straight!" Rebeca teased, "You sure about that?" Ana yelled, "I'M POSITIVE!" They both laughed as Rebeca concluded, "I love doing that to her!" and they laughed some more. This good-natured teasing permeated discussions of Rebeca's sexuality and her gender practices. Her friends teased her, not when she acted like a boy, but when she acted like a girl. For instance, when Rebeca spoke about her recent heartbreak, Ana teased her. "She cried, she was so emotional," Ana mocked, making crying sounds, while Rebeca faked indignation.

Rebeca prided herself on being an "out" lesbian. She told me that she came out at a very young age:

I came out in seventh grade. I dated a lot of boys so I tried to hide it. I told everyone in ninth grade because I started dating this senior girl. I hate guys. Guys are gross to me. Eww. I mean when I was in middle school I went out with a lot of guys. I kissed 'em and everything. I didn't feel anything. I was just like, ugh, this is so gross.

Even though she was quite comfortably and publicly "out," Rebeca didn't align herself with the visible group of gay kids at the school, the kids who were active in the GSA. She told me, "I went to it a couple times, but it didn't do anything [for me]. So I really didn't care." Rebeca's experience with the GSA sums up the relations between the Basketball Girls and the GSA Girls. Neither was fully comfortable in the other's social territory. Part of Rebeca's discomfort probably stemmed from the fact that the Basketball Girls resisted politics in general. In high school, it is profoundly uncool to care deeply about most things (save for sports and dating). For instance, the Basketball Girls made light of National Coming Out Day, which fell on the same day as the homecoming football game. As they ran up and down on the bleachers, Annie, Rebeca's cheerleader girlfriend, ran up to Rebeca and yelled, teasing her, "It's National Coming Out Day!" All the girls laughed, including Rebeca, and went on with their roughhousing. This was the only time I heard the girls refer to larger political or social aspects of sexuality.

Rebeca credited her lesbianism with making her more popular. When I asked her if people treated her differently because she dated girls, she said, "I get a lot of nice comments. Like, 'You're a pimp, you have all the girls!' I get a lot of that." I responded, surprised, "So everyone's totally cool with it?" "Yeah, they're like, 'Hey hook me up with some of your girls!'" Rebeca immediately posited boys as her audience, as those who would approve or disapprove of her sexuality. It seems that, as with boys' potential same-sex desire, boys were the ultimate arbiters of what was acceptable and not acceptable at River High. Michelle also told me Rebeca didn't experience homophobia from her classmates. Rather, she told me that both boys and girls were attracted to Rebeca.

They know she's gay, so they don't really have anything to say. Everybody knows her as *the pimp*, cause everybody be jackin' her real hard, they really do. Not boys. Girls. Well, boys be jackin' her too. When she dresses like a girl, she's *hecka* pretty. When she dresses like a boy all the girls will be jackin' her. But she don't like the boys, so . . .

Michelle used the word *jackin'* to indicate a level of attraction. She explained that depending on Rebeca's gendered presentation of self, either boys or girls were drawn to her. Like Chad, Rebeca had the ability to inspire intense desire in others. And, as with Chad, this sexual desire increased her social status, conferring upon her the high-status identity of "pimp."

At River High when a boy dated a lot or had sex with a lot of girls, he was admiringly called a "pimp." It was a term of honor and respect. At River High, if a girl dated a lot of boys, then she was called a "slut" or a "ho," never a "pimp." Rebeca often recast herself as a "pimp" rather than a "ho." I teased Rebeca at one point by asking her if her nickname was "pimp." She replied defensively and with a smile, "I am pimp!" What follows is an interesting interchange between Rebeca and Ana (one of her non–Basketball Girl friends) on the definitions of *pimp* versus *ho*:

ANA: You aren't a pimp. Who are you pimpin'?

REBECA: I'm not a pimp? I'm pimpin' every single girl here. Including you!

ANA: Oh yeah, right! Including me! Uh uh! Uh uh! No! You ain't pimpin' no one! You think you're pimp. You're a pimp last year. 'Cause you played hecka girls last year. Over the summer. You know how many girls you played over the summer?

REBECA: Now, that was kind of funny.

ANA: That was kind of mean! You're an H-O!

REBECA: No, I can't be a ho. Go look up definition of *ho* in the dictionary.

ANA: It's gonna tell me it's a gardening tool! (laughs)

C. J.: Wait, why can't you be a ho?

REBECA: 'Cause I *can't* be!

ANA: You're not a pimp 'cause you're not.

REBECA: Okay, Ana.

        (Ana walks away)

REBECA: I hate her! (smiling and shaking her head)

Rebeca here engaged in a discursive contest over what it meant to be a pimp. She refused a feminized interpretation of her actions in which she had to be a girl; instead she claimed a masculine position as a pimp in sexualized interactions with other girls. She wasn't chasing them. They were chasing her, because she had the virility to incite that sort of desire. Ana, good-naturedly, tried to keep Rebeca in a feminine, penetrated position.

Other Basketball Girls also repositioned themselves as masculine by invoking a "pimp" identity. Michelle, for example, told me about her plans to attend Winter Ball the previous year: "I was going to be like a pimp, and I had like four girls goin' with me." She said she had "rented a zoot suit and it was really cool." Michelle, however, ended up not attending Winter Ball, seemingly because of lack of funds.

In addition to reframing her sexual and romantic practices as "pimp," Rebeca consistently made discursive moves reframing her body as a male one. She posited herself as the center of female desire, saying, "I can't help it if I have girls on my jock!" *Jock* is a slang term for "penis." In a separate incident at lunch Rebeca and her girlfriend, Annie, were playfully shoving each other. Annie put her hands on Rebeca's chest and shoved her back, laughing. Rebeca yelled, "Stop punching my muscle!" and grabbed at her own chest defensively. All the girls laughed. Once again playing the straight person to Rebeca's gender-bending humor, Ana asked, shaking her head, "Why does she call her boobs her muscle?" Rebeca responded, pointing to Annie, "You have boobs. *I* have muscle." In both these instances Rebeca not only aligned herself with masculinity but refashioned her body as a male one, rejecting breasts and replacing them with muscle, rejecting a vagina and replacing it with a "jock." She flirted, in these instances, with embodying maleness by claiming male body parts. In a way she drew on popular understandings of masculinity in which masculinity has to line up with a male body. In the end, though, she never expressed desire to actually be a boy.

Rebeca also participated in a masculinizing process when she engaged in sex talk and rituals of "getting girls." Rebeca's interactions with girls outside her social circle often looked similar to the way masculine boys behaved around girls they found attractive. One day Rebeca stood outside the girls' locker room talking to a couple of boys. A thin, attractive girl walked past wearing snug, low-waisted jeans, a white tank top, and a lacy brown shawl tied tightly around her waist. Rebeca yelled to her, "LET ME SEE YOUR SHAWL!" Rebeca then turned to the boys and said, "I saw a girl wearing one of those the other day, and I thought it was for, like, . . . " She completed the sentence by reaching out as if to grab each side of the sash and pull it toward her, laughing and thrusting her hips as if imitating sex. Both of the boys laughed, as one of them said, "I *bet* you did!" As the girl walked past hesitatingly, Rebeca continued talking, "You look *good* in that shawl." Lyn Mikel Brown (1998) calls this sort of language "ventriloquation" to refer to the ways in which girls adopt boys' points of view. In this instance, Rebeca engaged in masculinizing practices that objectified other girls and thereby enhanced her own social standing with boys. She engaged in ventriloquation in order to appropriate the social power that accompanied masculine identities.

Though she daily enacted these sorts of masculinity processes, Rebeca occasionally participated in feminizing processes. She surprised me by telling me, at length, about her experience wearing both a formal dress and makeup to the Winter Ball:

> I had makeup on and everything. I went with two people. I went with a guy and a girl. I walked in with them. They were like, "Who's that? Is she new?" I heard whispers and everything. Somebody went up to me and was like, "Are you new?" I was like, "No, I'm Rebeca." She was like, "ARE YOU SERIOUS? GUYS, GUYS, COME HERE—IT'S REBECA!" Everybody, like, came around me, they were like, "Oh my God! You are so beautiful!" I was like, "Thanks" [she was shrugging

her shoulders and looking embarrassed here]. Everybody took pictures of me. I had, like, the camera on me the whole night.

When I asked Rebeca how this attention for a feminized appearance made her feel, she replied, "I was like, damn! Oh my God, I'm famous! [laughs]. I was like, wow. 'Cause everybody's like, 'Are you gonna wear a dress?' I'm like, 'No, I'm gonna wear a tux.' They're like, 'Are you serious?' I'm like, 'Yup.' And I surprised 'em by coming." However, when I interviewed Rebeca after Winter Ball she told me she had wanted to wear a tux and not a dress to the formal dance. When I asked her, "So why'd you decide to wear a dress instead of a tux?" Rebeca displaced the responsibility onto her mother, saying, "My mom wouldn't have let me step out of the house wearin' a tux." Like other girls I spoke with at River High, Rebeca blamed her mother for restricting her desired masculine gender expression. There was something unconvincing about her explanation, given her daily "boy" attire. While her mother may have been part of the reason she conceded to wear a dress, school ritual brought to bear its own set of power relations on Rebeca's decision to enact normative femininity.

Rebeca blamed the makeup on her sister: "My sister talked me into it. She was like 'You'll be hella pretty.' I'm like 'Okay. I guess.' " Rebecca laughed, saying, "It was gross! It was hecka nasty. I did not like it. It felt like blah! I did not like it! I was like sweating and I go like this [rubbing her eye] and I see my finger is black! I was like, 'Oh my God, this is not working.' Makeup's hecka nasty. I *hate* makeup." However, when I asked Rebeca what she was going to wear to the next Winter Ball, she said she was going to wear a dress and makeup again even though "it's gonna be a pain." Indeed, at the Winter Ball itself Rebeca complained to me about how she couldn't wait to get out of her dress and into a pair of pants. I asked her why she didn't bring any with her, and she said that because none of her friends wanted to, she didn't.

Rebeca's ability to remain in gender flux certainly added to her popularity. Her capacity for revealing either her presumed core femininity, thus exposing her masculinity as drag, or revealing her femininity as drag and her masculinity as real was equally intriguing. It was as if she were endowed with some sort of power that the rest of the students didn't have. Thus she became an object of intense fascination as a liminal figure who demonstrated an ability to move between the worlds of masculinity and femininity. As such, she seemed to have some sort of power, not available to most teenagers, to inhabit multiple identities. In her study of proms at a variety of high schools, Amy Best (2004) notes a similar phenomenon in which girls "demonstrate their skills at assembling a range of signs and symbols upon their bodies in a way that transformed who they were in school" (199). Occasionally girls who refused dresses and frilly clothes in their daily lives donned these feminine symbols at proms, much as Rebeca did. As Best notes, "Part of the pleasure of prom is to be someone different from who you are at school" (199). For Rebeca, playing with gender in this way was both pleasurable, in that she received even more attention from her peers, and uncomfortable, in that the clothes and makeup were restricting and awkward.

To my surprise, Rebeca experienced the school administration as supportive of her sexuality and her relationships. She told me that even during her public and dramatic breakup with her previous girlfriend, Jana, the school administrators had helped them out. Rebeca told me that she and Jana "went out for ever. We were engaged. That's how strong our relationship was. We were engaged." Rebeca continued to tell me of her heartbreak when she found out that Jana was cheating on her with a guy. She said that her heartbreak was so severe that

> we argued in the hallway and we almost got in a fistfight. Then the principals broke us up because everybody at this school, all the teachers, everybody knew we were together, knew we were a couple, a couple like married. Everybody at this school was like, "Congratulations!" The principals brought us in the office and we sat down and they started talking to us. They were like our counselors. He [Mr. Hobert, the principal] sat me down and [I was] just crying. I told my principal, "She's really messed up for what she did!" My principal was like, "What do you want to do?" He asked Jana, "Do you want to be with her?" She was like, "No. No. No. I don't love her no more." I was like, "Are you serious?!" She was like, "I don't wanna be with her. I don't wanna be with her." I was like,

"No! This cannot happen! You have to be with me! I gave you everything! We're married!" I ran out of that office so fast and I started crying.

Even in this midst of her heartbreak, Rebeca didn't find the school homophobic; rather, her lesbianism translated into popularity and extra
support and counseling from the administration (in a school so large that
most students never speak to the principal or other administrators). In
some sense the administrators, much like the other students at River
High, were charmed by Rebeca. Her non-normative gender practices
were couched in a way that was simultaneously charming and disruptive.
But without a political critique of gender norms or heterosexuality at
River High, these gender transgressions were, in the end, nonthreatening to the existing gender and sexual order.

In a sense, however, speaking of the Basketball Girls as masculine or
feminine doesn't get at all the aspects of their gendered portrayal. The
way they "did gender" also involved racialized meanings. Much like
African American boys who identify with hip-hop culture, the Basketball
Girls struck a "cool pose" (Majors 2001). Their interactional style,
choice of sports, and favorite music and clothing all drew upon those
present in hip-hop culture. Like boys identified with hip-hop, they were
vaulted to popularity. However, they did not embody the threat of
African American maleness. While African American boys in school were
seen as threatening to the social order, the Basketball Girls were more
likely to be seen as rascals, even though they self-consciously identified
as not-white. Michelle explained this to me by saying that "sometimes
white girls act quieter . . . Most white girls are quiet . . . I don't know why
that is." She qualified this statement with "But some of the white girls I
hang around with, they act loud too, so I don't know." So while she and
the rest of the Basketball Girls identified as a variety of races and ethnic-
ities, they did consciously see themselves as different from most white
girls.

The Basketball Girls were a high-energy, popular, and engaging
group of girls. On the one hand these girls rejected prescriptions of

normative femininity, resisting, for instance, heterosexuality, makeup, and dresses. They didn't engage in appropriately feminine sports such as cheerleading, dance, or even soccer. Instead they not only played but were passionate about basketball, a sport associated with men and masculinity (Shakib 2003). In this way it seems that the Basketball Girls were reconstructing what it meant to be a girl. They also engaged in practices that looked a lot like "compulsive heterosexuality." Like sexist and athletic boys, they were at the top of the school social hierarchy, instilling both fear and respect in other students (Connell 1996; Eckert 1989; Eder, Evans, and Parker 1995; D. Epstein 1997; Kehily and Nayak 1997; Martino 1999; Parker 1996). In this sense, their "gender maneuvering" both challenged the gender order and reinscribed it. They challenged the gender order by acting and dressing like boys. They reinscribed the gender order by engaging in many of the dominance practices that constitute adolescent masculinity, such as taking up space, teasing girls, and positioning themselves as sexually powerful.

THE HOMECOMING QUEEN: JESSIE CHAU

Clad in wind pants, a T-shirt, and a baseball cap, Jessie Chau sat in Mrs. Mac's advanced placement government class like a boy—positioned sideways, her legs spread wide and her arms splayed across both her desk and the desk behind her. Jessie, a confident, attractive, Chinese American athlete and out lesbian, was River High's homecoming queen and president of the senior class. She was a senior when the Basketball Girls were sophomores, so she might be regarded as a sort of trailblazer for this type of gender maneuvering at River High. She didn't have a group with which to engage in non-normative gender practices but rather did so on her own—innovating and compromising gender practices at different points in her high school career. Like the Basketball Girls she was popular and well liked. Girls wanted to be her friend, boys wanted to date her. Like the Basketball Girls she dressed in "boy clothes," played sports, and, like Rebeca, identified as a lesbian. Jessie, however, lived these gender and sexual transgressions on her own, without the benefit of a like peer group to support her. Several years older than the Basketball Girls, she had forged this alternative set of gender practices solo.

Boys expressed a combination of confusion and admiration for Jessie. Richard, a conservative white senior, told me,

> She dresses like a man. . . . It's kind of weird. She has always been popular since she was in middle school. It's inevitable for her to be number one. . . . Jessie is a great girl. She's really nice. She's really cool. I just think it's kind of weird that she dresses like a man. She's a softball player and she's hella good. She's a tomboy.

This was one of the few times I heard the word *tomboy* used to describe a girl who acted like a boy at River. Jace explained her popularity by saying, "Most people at River, I mean, guys are going to be like, 'Hey that's cool!' and she's friends with tons of girls." Like the Basketball Girls Jessie benefited from sexist male fantasies about lesbian sexuality, as Jace indicated with his "Hey, that's cool!" comment. Similarly, because same-sex desire did not threaten girls' gender identity in the way it did boys', Jessie's sexuality and gender transgressions had little effect on her friendships. For instance, when Cathy talked to me about Jessie's sexuality, she said,

> She had a boyfriend her junior year and they broke up. Then people could kind of tell. Because she was real jocky and stuff. People were just like, "I wonder if she is?" She was always with this girl, Sandra. She told me one day, "Cathy, I want to tell you something and I don't want you to think differently of me." I was like, "I'm cool with it, I don't care." Some people are a little homophobic. She would sit behind me and play with my hair . . . I don't think it was weird at all that she won. She was the nicest one out there. Being gay had nothing to do with it.

Cathy talked fondly of Jessie and of being touched by Jessie. This fondness couldn't be more different from the at best guarded way straight boys talked about gay boys. While, as Cathy highlighted, Jessie's sexuality certainly made for juicy gossip, such tales did not seem to affect her popularity or likability. If anything, her non-normative gender practices and sexual identity bolstered her popularity among many students.

Jessie self-consciously dressed differently from other girls at River High. Her clothing reflected contemporary "lesbian" styles, mixing both feminine and masculine signs such as baggy pants and fitted shirts (Esterberg 1996). This aesthetic marked her as different from most girls at River High though not necessarily as masculine. She did not share this style with a peer group as the Basketball Girls did. She told me that her friends actively encouraged her to dress more like other girls.

> It's kinda like my friends try to push it on me, 'How come you don't dress more like a lady?' and all that stuff. I don't know if you've seen me on a regular day, but I don't wear tight jeans. I don't have one pair of tight jeans in my closet. I don't have one skirt in my closet. I have dresses in my closet, but they go in a separate closet [laughs]. I don't wear the baby tees and stuff like that. On a good day I'll throw on a shirt and a pair of pants and just go.

In response to her friends' urgings, Jessie had developed a critique of typical girls' attire. She argued that other girls at River dressed in ways that emphasized their heterosexual availability.

> There's girls at the school who wear shirts that are too provocative. It screams attention. It's just like, what are you trying to get at, you know? I don't want to sit there and try to talk to somebody when their boobs are hanging out at me and I'm just, okay [both of us laugh]. I mean, it's hard not to look when someone's wearing something like that! I mean it's hard to concentrate.

Jessie was most likely both distracted by and critical of such apparel choices. Given that she both was attracted to other girls and was a girl herself, she had a unique criticism of typical girls' clothing. She did not want to be looked at in the same way as these girls, so she specifically bought boys' clothing: "It's just like I don't try to impress anybody. I dress in like a turtleneck and a pair of khakis. And it doesn't look bad. But it doesn't look like I'm dressing like a girl. I don't, most of the clothes I buy aren't girls' clothes. They're boys' clothes. I mean, I'm not ashamed of it." In part Jessie claimed that dressing this way was a function of her priorities. She wanted to be comfortable and spend a small amount of time on her appearance. Neither of these things were typical priorities for girls at River. She didn't understand why girls would dress in clothing that seemed so at odds with the functions of daily life:

> Girls will dress in skirts and stuff for school and it's like, how can you sit in a desk for, like, seven hours and wear a skirt! Gimme a break! You can't! You can't! You just can't do it! It's like, why you gonna get up an hour earlier when you can sleep in an hour later, you know? [laughs] I mean, my hair used to be down to my butt. I cut it to here because my day would go so much quicker if I just didn't have to deal with it.

Unlike other girls, she felt she didn't need to impress or draw attention with her body. Instead, it seemed that she saw her body as functional, active, and agentic, judging by her love of dancing and her passion for sports. Though she lacked a coherent political critique and instead held individual girls responsible for their clothing choices, her own choices left her empowered and confident in the face of a sexist and homophobic social world.

Like the Basketball Girls, Jessie was no stranger to fights. She and her friend Nel spoke fondly of the previous year's CAPA, during which there had been several fights. Jessie seemed to think they were great fun, talking about how she was cheering for Nel during one of the fights. Nel bragged about starting a fight, saying "it was cool" because she knew that "Jessie had my back." Jessie's on again/off again rival was Rebeca. For a while those two couldn't stand each other, in no small part because they were "talkin' to," or flirting with, the same girl, Jana, Rebeca's ex-girlfriend. Jessie explained, "Jana tried to get at me and Rebeca got pissed off." All three of them attended a dance early in the school year, soon after Jana tried to "get at" Jessie. Jessie told me, "I was just walking out and Rebeca said I was an ugly bitch or something. My friend hears her and slaps her. I just like, 'Oh my God.' " The fight didn't escalate because, as Jessie explained, "You know, I could have beat her ass a long time ago. But I didn't, out of respect for [their] relationship. You're my friend and I don't want to start anything. I try my hardest to be nice to her." Jessie laughed at Rebeca's attempt to apologize later: "She knows I'd beat the shit out of her if anything happens. Honestly, she's up to my hip. She's really short and she looks like this little boy." Like the Basketball Girls Jessie saw herself as tough and ready to fight. She and Rebeca never did come to blows, but both spoke often about the possibility of a fight between the two of them.

One of the reasons Jessie didn't like Rebeca was that she saw Rebeca as "flaunting" her sexuality: "They flaunt it all the time at school. I don't need to flaunt my stuff to prove a point. I don't understand what their point is. They're in a relationship and they're together. I just think that they try to show it off too much." The vehemence with which she said this revealed some of Jessie's coping strategies around being gay in high school. While she dressed and acted in many ways like a boy, she balanced this with a sort of "don't ask, don't tell" approach to her sexuality. In large part, this approach reflected her own ambivalence about her non-normative gender practices and her lesbian identity. This said, she did acknowledge the "double standard" applied to heterosexual and gay relationships:

> There's straight couples all over the place and they can just go anywhere and be together and it's okay. Then you have the gay couples that get together and people just gawk and stare at you like you are some alien. I think it's okay that they are open about their relationship. But sometimes I just think they are trying to prove a point.

Jessie was nervous enough about other students' stares that she attended the Homecoming Rally with her male friend Gary as her escort. She also attended dances with male friends, with the exception of her senior prom, when she finally took her girlfriend, Sasha. That said, Jessie also highlighted that she desired women in subtle, and possibly male-identified, ways. She was, for instance, a fan of the Playboy Bunny insignia. She designed an art project in which she crafted a "bunny" out of chipped glass, saying, "I just like it! I've got one on my backpack. I've got one on my car. I just like it. It's cool." Like Rebeca, she engaged in "ventriloquation" by adopting and displaying a symbol associated with pornographic representations of women.

During homecoming, which is, like many school rituals, a time of intensified gender and sexual norms, Jessie's non-normative gender and sexual identity caused quite a stir among the student body. When chosen as homecoming queen, Jessie told me that her clothing choices were a subject of gossip. Students saw her non-gender-normative clothing choices as contradicting the traditional requirements of homecoming queen.

> The funny thing is that I get so much trash talked about me as far as homecoming goes: "Oh, like, she's gotta wear a dress." All girls that made it put on their little tight clothes. "I'm trying to get votes," you know? Me, I come in my pajamas, I don't care! I think the reason why I got votes is because I didn't fake it. I think that I was original and I was nice to people and I was myself. I'm a big, like, comedian person. I like to make people laugh. I like to talk and hang out and have a good time.

During the several weeks leading up to the Homecoming Rally and vote, Jessie almost got in several fights, for, while she was popular, there were students at River who opposed her election because she was gay:

> They say they don't think I'd be a good enough person to represent their school. I almost dropped out of homecoming just because I didn't want all the trash talked about me. I'm not one to not stick up for myself. I almost got in two fights before homecoming day. I would have gotten everything taken away from me, though. Because I'm senior class president. So I would have been impeached and then homecoming and then my scholarship. I mean it's just too much to lose. If I didn't have anything to lose, then damn, I would have done it.

Clearly, Jesse did not drop out of the homecoming race. Winning homecoming queen floored her. She said that she actually cried when she won: "I was just like, I even cried! I was totally surprised. I never cry. I take after my dad. My dad's just like a really hard, stern-faced man. I just broke down in tears, and I was like, 'Oh God! Oh God!' " She fluttered her hand at her face as she imitated herself, laughing. She said that many of the other students were equally surprised, saying, it "shocked everybody" because "throughout my whole life I've always hung out with boys." Some people were rude: "They were like, man, it's just like a dude."

While Jessie prided herself on her refusal to exploit her body to gain votes, she did cave to what she felt as strong pressure to conform to normative gender self-presentation during the formal homecoming rituals, in which she wore a dress. When I asked her why, she said, "Um, I dunno. I'm a person about pantsuits. I just sit back and relax [putting her arm over the chair at this point and spreading her legs out in front of her]. Do my own thing. They were just like, 'No, Jessie, you have to wear a dress.' " I asked her who "they" were, those people telling her she had to wear a dress. In her answer, Jessie aptly highlighted how social structures have a life of their own: "It's just, it's just policy. It's like nobody ever . . . I was like, uhh [groan], might as well keep tradition and wear a damn dress." There was not, as far as I could find, an official policy requiring that homecoming queens wear a dress. That Jessie felt there was a policy highlights the power of the interactional order and the pressure to "do gender" embedded in school rituals. She described herself as being very uncomfortable during homecoming: "The dress I wore during the day I wore during the night, and it was outside. It was freezing outside." Her dress was a tight, sparkly, floor-length gold dress with spaghetti straps. Indeed, she looked uncomfortable as the form-fitting dress and the high heels confined her usual long confident stride to short, frequent steps. Even the ladies who worked in the school office, who sat behind me at the Homecoming Rally, talked about how much Jessie didn't like her homecoming dress, saying, "You know she hates that dress. She just does not like that dress."

Jessie fittingly described how constraining the dress was when she talked about sitting on the homecoming float: "Yeah, I'm sitting there and I'm getting on the float, and they're like, 'Jessie, don't spread your legs so wide!' It's hard. I'm trying to sit with my legs all crossed. I'm just like, 'Oh God, I swear I got a cramp.'" She was so uncomfortable in her dress that she changed her clothes at the homecoming dance afterwards: "I took pictures of me and one of my other friends, we, like, changed clothes. I was wearing pink pajama pants and a white shirt."[4] Jessie's experience of her formal attire reflects what feminists have long highlighted about the confining and nonutilitarian nature of much of women's clothing.

Jessie both resisted normative definitions of femininity and engaged in them in her varying bodily comportments, clothing choices, and romantic relationships. Like the Basketball Girls she was an athlete, though she drew on the "cool pose" to a more limited extent than they did, and she remained somewhat of a liminal figure, moving in and out of masculine and feminine bodily comportments. Also like Rebeca, she was engaging, beautiful, and charming, all traits that allowed her some leeway in a non-normative gendered presentation of self. She engaged, though to a lesser extent than the Basketball Girls, in sexist practices. She also, I think, exhibited quite a bit of bravery as she bucked many school norms of gender and sexuality to serve as an out gay homecoming queen.

THE GAY/STRAIGHT ALLIANCE GIRLS

Where the Basketball Girls and Jessie espoused a sort of hip-hop ethos, the girls in GSA displayed a more "goth," alternative, or "punk" ethos. The GSA Girls, Genevieve, Lacy, Riley, and T-Rex, often dressed in black clothing with rainbow accents, Doc Martin shoes, or army fatigues. Three of them sported multicolored hair that often changed hue. Riley, a self-described "riot grrl," favored bright pink or blonde short hair accented with barrettes, whereas Genevieve and Lacy tended toward deeper browns, burgundies, and reds for their long dark hair. Tall and imposing, T-Rex wore baggy "skater" clothes, had long blonde hair, and often wore contacts with stars on them. T-Rex was the guardian of the group, describing herself as "their bodyguard." Lacy dressed more traditionally feminine, often wearing long flowing dresses and occasionally wearing baggy cut-off jean shorts and old T-shirts. Genevieve wore button-down shirts and a daily changing variety of ties. Like the Basketball Girls, the GSA Girls were almost always together in and out of school. They were an emotionally intense group of girls, deeply committed to social justice and equality.

They were all active members of the school's GSA. GSAs are school clubs that are increasingly popping up throughout the country. They function as "safe zones" for students where they can be free from gender- and sexuality-based teasing and taunts. The meetings consisted of planning political and social activities such as the Day of Silence, movie nights, get-togethers with other GSAs, and the Gay Prom. As many as seventeen kids came to the biweekly GSA meetings, and about five to ten attended regularly. The GSA Girls and Ricky formed the core of the GSA. Students who attended the GSA were a racially diverse group. While many of the members of the GSA did not identify as gay, lesbian, bisexual, or transgendered, T-Rex was the only straight-identified girl in the GSA Girls group.

GSA Girls purposefully challenged the sexualized and gendered authority of the school. In one meeting Lacy, the GSA president, helped a boy who said that his friend was harassed by a homophobic teacher. Lacy told him and the rest of the participants in the meeting about California's AB 537, an assembly bill that protects gay students from homophobic harassment in school. Lacy encouraged the boy to speak to school administrators, invoking that law for protection. The GSA Girls constantly challenged norms, especially those having to do with gender and sexuality. They often said things like "Why be normal?" and "Normal is bad."

The students and administration at River High were antagonistic to the existence of the GSA. The girls were keenly aware of this antagonism, experiencing both violence and lack of acknowledgment from school authorities and other students. The previous year one of the GSA

Girls had had her locker broken into. Other students tore down posters advertising GSA meetings. The GSA Girls perceived that the administration made it difficult for them to advertise their group. Lacy often worried in second period, as announcements were read over the intercom, that the GSA announcement would not be read, an omission that had in fact happened many times. Once, while enduring the daily ritual of waiting to hear the GSA meeting announcement, she explained that GSA members did not even know about the special lunch organized to highlight student groups until shortly before lunchtime on the day of the event.

GSA meetings provided time for students to discuss inequality and social change. One day Lacy ran an exercise about socialization in which she asked the assembled group of fifteen to brainstorm how they were taught, as children, right versus wrong behaviors. She wrote their answers on the whiteboard at the front of the classroom. On the "right" side students suggested marrying a rich Catholic man, going to school, making money, going to church, morality, respecting adults, no smoking, no lying, no stealing. On the "wrong" side were listed eating yellow snow, Internet porn, playing doctor, dirty walls, cussing, drugs, premarital sex. This spawned a discussion of right and wrong in general. Ricky shouted out that he learned that "eye shadow going on before eyebrows was wrong!" The group laughed as Ricky explained, "That's what happens when you grow up in show business!" Ally contributed: "I learned that girls were supposed to have long hair and wear skirts, and pants go on the boys." Again Ricky chimed in, "I totally break that rule!" flipping his shoulder-length hair dramatically. Lacy then asked them what they still thought was wrong from that list. The students said that playing doctor was not wrong, premarital sex was not wrong, and that eating snow was not wrong. They then turned back to the "good" side and said that going to church wasn't necessarily good. And when Lacy pointed to "being normal," the whole group shouted out "No! No! No! No!" Lacy used this as an opportunity to discuss where homophobia comes from. Some students suggested that people were raised that way. Others suggested the government was responsible. GSA meetings served as a place to both challenge norms and explore possibilities for social change. It also gave these youth a place to be with other kids like themselves and to plan a social life outside school.

For Genevieve, Lacy's girlfriend, the GSA was a safe space at school where she could be with people like her. When I asked her, "What does it feel like for you to be in a GSA meeting?" she answered:

> It's really weird, being with people that are like me and then being around people that aren't like me. A lot of times I forget that everybody, that there's a lot of people that aren't gay. I go to GSA and it's normal to me. Then it's like, wow, there's a guy and a girl. That's weird. I see it every day, I don't care, I'm like, whatever, but if I think about it it's different and I feel different, that's the only time I think about it.

But the students often felt that this space was under threat due to both administrative negligence and peer harassment. For instance, students expressed fears of being disrupted or attacked by other students. Genevieve said that she believed that a homophobic student would probably disrupt one of their meetings. During a GSA meeting, Natalia, a white bisexual girl with multicolored hair and baggy pants, shared a nightmare that she had had the previous week. She told the GSA she had dreamt that a bunch of "jocks" had come into a meeting and started "shooting up the place." The other students laughed, but some also commented that they wouldn't be surprised if that happened. The GSA meetings were a safe place and a space that was constantly under threat.

Even in the context of these homophobic experiences, Genevieve described her school experiences before coming to River High as even more homophobic. She had lived with her mother in Minnesota and her father in Arkansas before moving in with her grandmother in California. "In Arkansas, whenever people would find out that I was gay, I couldn't walk down the hall without someone being like, 'faggot,' 'fuckin' dyke,' or whatever." She tried to start a club at her previous high school because "they didn't have any sort of support group or club, but they said no." Before living in Arkansas she had attended school in Minnesota, where students were less vitriolic but generally unsupportive because the town was "hard-core Christian." While she repeatedly noted the homophobia at River High, she said that the presence of the GSA made a big difference. She described being surprised when she came to River High and found out that "wow, there's a GSA. What's a GSA?" She hastened to tell me that the students at River High "don't like the GSA."

Though other students at River High didn't readily describe the GSA Girls as "girls who act like boys," the GSA Girls themselves often described their own gender practices as masculine. Genevieve dressed masculine, although in a different way than the Basketball Girls. Much to the consternation of her conservative, religious grandmother, her fashion trademark was her ever-present tie.

> I don't wear ties around my grandma. She asked me what I wanted for my birthday. I said, "I want a tie." She's like, "You already look like a boy enough." I said, "Grandma, I do not look like a boy. I have breasts and I don't hide them, and I don't wear big baggy boy clothes." But she's like, "You have those boy shirts."

Genevieve's clothes were form fitting, but they were also masculine. She routinely wore button-down shirts with pants and ties. She identified these ties as masculine. In the hallway one day she ran up to me and grabbed her tie, excitedly bouncing up and down as she exclaimed, "Look at my masculinity!" then added a little strut as if for emphasis. She did have large breasts, which seemed a bit at odds with the boy's clothes she wore. She said that she wore the ties because she thought "they're very cute. I feel masculine. I feel bigger and better." Genevieve combined masculine and feminine gender markers in her appearance, wearing typically masculine attire—jeans, button-down shirts, and ties—while making sure they accentuated her curves.

Genevieve also refused to wear makeup, a key signifier of femininity, and put down girls who did wear it:

> I hate it when girls can't leave their house without putting makeup on. I hate that! I went out of my house without makeup on. Just like I feel

like wearing a tie. But some girls are like, "I can't leave the house without makeup." Three hours later they're finally coming out.

Genevieve claimed she was not going to wear makeup because "I'm not going to hide who I really am." Makeup, for Genevieve, not only was too feminine but also was a lie about her true self.

Genevieve discursively worked to recast herself as masculine by attributing a phallus to herself (much like Rebeca's claiming a "jock"). She described the boys at River High by saying, "They can suck my cock. They're rude. I'm serious. I just don't like them." By claiming a phallus Genevieve symbolically regendered her body. Importantly, Genevieve claimed a penetrative phallus, much like the boys in chapter 4. Like them she exercised dominance through a sexualized discourse in which she framed herself as a powerful penetrator and the boys as feminized receivers. She turned their language upon themselves by reappropriating it defiantly.

Genevieve, Lacy, and Riley self-consciously played with gender at ritualized school events such as the prom and Winter Ball. For the GSA Girls, these events were not a time for the enactment of normative gender codes but rather a time to challenge gendered norms. Instead of joking about and superficially dismissing feminine dress, the GSA Girls talked about the gendered meanings of clothing. As a result, they invented gender-blending outfits featuring masculine and feminine markers.

When the girls talked about going to Winter Ball, Genevieve and Lacy playfully argued over who was going to wear the dress. Genevieve told me that she wanted to wear a suit to Winter Ball but complained that her grandma would prevent her: "I'd have to sneak because my grandma would be like, 'Nope.' " Lacy told me, at one point in their negotiations, that she was upset because Genevieve wouldn't wear a dress. Lacy said, "I made her try on this black velvet dress and she looked sooo hot! It came down to here and up to here! [motioning down to her chest and up to her thigh]. She finally said she'd wear it if I found her shoes. So now she can just say 'no' to any pair of shoes!" Lacy concluded by sighing in mock frustration, rolling her eyes, and smiling. Both of them smiled at the end of this discussion.

At the dance, Genevieve was in fact quite proud as she ran up to me in this same long black dress, saying "I'm wearing a dress!" When I asked her why she had decided to wear a dress, she pointed at Lacy and said, "'Cause she wanted me to look sexy." She quickly added with pride, as she pointed to the jewelry on her neck, "But I'm still wearing a tie!" Around her neck was a black velvet choker with a prominent cubic zirconia tie in the middle.

Genevieve and Lacy both claimed masculine and feminine attributes in their clothing styles, interactional styles, and interests. While, with her long flowing skirts, Lacy appeared normatively feminine, at times at least she proudly talked about ways she saw herself as masculine. One day, when we were sitting in the drama class room, Lacy told me, "My car is my manhood. Ask anyone. Guys talk about dick size. I'll talk about my car." She told me that Genevieve teased her about her car obsession: "You're such a butch guy. It's just a car." Like the Basketball Girls, the GSA Girls lightheartedly teased each other about gender maneuvering.

The GSA Girls talked with ease about relationships among a butch-femme aesthetic, romantic relationships, and gendered oppression. Romantic relationships were a frequent topic of conversation during GSA meetings. Talking about their relationships in this club provided both a forum for personal advice and a place to talk about these relationships in terms of larger meanings about masculinity and femininity. For instance, during one GSA meeting Ally said, "I think no matter who you date there is always one who is more masculine and one who is more feminine." Riley responded,

> I totally don't think that is true! Gender roles suck! When I was dating Jenny sometimes I wanted to wear pants and walk on the outside of the sidewalk. She wouldn't let me. It's weird dating in gender roles if you are not particularly in one. I would wear something and she would be like, "You look too butch. Take that off."

Talking analytically about "gender roles" was something that really only happened among the GSA Girls and during GSA meetings. This sort of political engagement and social criticism probably elaborated the GSA Girls' vocabulary about complex issues of gender, identity, and sexuality.

Not surprisingly, Genevieve found the school not only hostile to her relationship but hostile to any politicization around same-sex relationships. Genevieve, Lacy, and Riley experienced antagonism from both the students and the administration at River High school in terms of their gendered and sexual identifications. Genevieve hated it "when guys are like, 'Oh, I'm okay with two chicks in bed, but I'm not okay with two guys.'" She saw the boys' seeming acceptance of lesbians as an indication of sexism, not antihomophobic attitudes. Genevieve did not see herself as a sexual object for these boys but rather rejected their sexualization of her and her relationship. Conversely, Rebeca's friends talked about guys desiring her as a badge of pride. Unlike Rebeca, Genevieve felt antagonism from the students and the administration at River High school in terms of both her gendered self-presentation and her lesbianism. Genevieve told me, "I've been getting really dirty looks from that guy, some guy in authority at our school. I don't know what he is. I don't care what he is. All I know is that he looks at me and Lacy really rude."

Interactions between the Basketball Girls and the GSA Girls were rare. Though the girls of both groups engaged in gender maneuvering, they were at opposite ends of the social hierarchy and had very different political and interactional styles. Often when I was around they would come together in order to talk to me. I sometimes tensed during these interactions, realizing that their different ideologies about gender and politics might conflict and fearing that I would have to mediate. One afternoon their different approaches did appear during an interaction. As the school bell rang Rebeca yelled "It's C. J.!" as she and her girlfriend, Annie, ran up to me. I congratulated them on their three-month anniversary as Lacy and Genevieve walked up holding hands. An uneasy tension hung in the air, since the two groups usually didn't interact with one another. To ease the tension I spoke first. I asked the group if they were planning to attend Winter Ball. Rebeca responded excitedly, "I am! I'm wearing a dress!" Genevieve piped up, "Me too!" Surprised that after all of her talk about wearing a tux Rebeca planned to wear a dress, I asked her why. "My mom is so gay!" she responded. "She won't let me out of the house in a suit!" Lacy challenged her, "Why are you calling something you don't like gay?" Rebeca stated, "I always do that. I always call people I don't like gay." As if unable to continue with this line of discussion, the girls dropped the subject and began to talk about Rebeca's shoes. Lacy's question to Rebeca demonstrated her politicized understanding of sexuality, challenging Rebeca's use of a homophobic epithet. It was as if Rebeca couldn't make the connection between homophobia at River High (which she didn't experience) and her own derogation of the term *gay*.

The GSA Girls also challenged this casual, daily homophobia at institutional events. In chapter 2 I documented how River High endorsed heterosexuality and gendered difference through school-sponsored rituals. The school's resistance to expressions of non-normative feminine identities was made clear when National Coming Out Day fell on the same day as homecoming, a day when the school celebrates heterosexual pairings through the Homecoming Assembly and football game (resulting in the GSA Girls' joking references to National Homecoming Out Day). Several of the students from GSA had been busy creating special shirts that read "Nobody Knows I'm a Lesbian" or "Nobody Knows I'm Gay" for National Coming Out Day. They wore them proudly to the Homecoming Rally, which, just like the Mr. Cougar Rally, consisted of the six homecoming princesses competing in skits to be voted as that year's homecoming queen. These shirts were planned to contrast sharply with the celebration of heterosexuality that was the Homecoming Rally. As with Mr. Cougar, the weeks leading up to the Homecoming Rally, game, and election were filled with student competitions, spirit days, and votes for homecoming princesses and queens.

The final skit of the Homecoming Rally, entitled "All for You," starred Jessica and Angelica, two Latina seniors. Clad in tight jeans and black tank tops, the two princesses began dancing to a popular dance song by Janet Jackson. Their dance moves consisted of repeatedly gyrating their hips in sexually suggestive dance moves. During the song that followed, seven girls, including Jessica and Angelica, each grabbed a boy as Janet Jackson sang, "How many nights I've laid in bed excited over you / I've closed my eyes and thought of us a hundred different ways / I've gotten there so many times I wonder how 'bout you . . . If I was your girl / Oh the things I'd do to you / I'd make you call out my name . . . " The girls walked up behind the boys and ran their hands down the front of the boys' bodies. Then they turned the boys around and made them kneel in front of them so that the boys were face to face with the girls' crotches. The girls took the boys' heads in two hands and moved them around as the girls wiggled their hips in the boys' faces. The dance ended with the boys getting up and the group posing together with Jessica and Angelica lying down in front with one leg jutting into the air, crotches exposed. This skit followed two other skits featuring homecoming princesses performing similar, only slightly less sexually explicit, dances.

After the Homecoming Rally and its celebration of girls' heterosexual availability, Lacy, Genevieve, and Riley ran up to me wearing all black with rainbow pins and belts. Given the GSA's preparations leading up to National Coming Out Day, I was wondering why they weren't wearing their special gay pride T-shirts. I didn't have time to ask where their shirts were as they tumbled over each other, indignantly explaining to me what had happened. Lacy angrily unbuttoned her sweater revealing her black and white "Nobody Knows I'm a Lesbian" T-shirt, and said, "Mr. Hobart came up to me and said I have to cover this shirt up. I couldn't wear it!" Riley and Lacy, equally resentful, cried, "He made me take mine off too!" Riley unfolded the shirt she had painted in rainbow colors. Neither of them was wearing a gay pride shirt anymore. Lacy, incensed, cried, "And look what they can do up there! All grinding against each other and stuff! And I can't wear this shirt!"

When I asked Genevieve later why the girls couldn't wear the shirts, she explained,

'Cause this school says that if you are wearing a shirt saying that you're a lesbian that says that you are supposedly having sexual acts with the same sex. I find that stupid, because what if someone was walking around saying, "Hey, I'm a heterosexual," does that mean that you're sexually active? I was very very very angry that day. 'Cause that was the Homecoming Assembly day, my God! Did you see what those girls were doing? Not that I was complaining, but I did have a complaint toward the authority of the school. The school will let chicks rub their crotches and shake their asses in front of all these students in the school. Like nastiness, but my girlfriend can't wear a "Nobody Knows I'm a Lesbian" shirt.

While the principal argued that the problem was not homosexuality but sexual activity, the explicitly sexual displays in the homecoming skits seemed to indicate that something more than concern over sexual activity was going on. The girls argued that equality, not sex, was the point of their T-shirt slogans. It seems the school had very little problem with students addressing sex as long as they focused on girls' heterosexual availability. Mr. Hobart had effectively set up a two-tiered system in which explicit expressions of heterosexuality such as sensual dance moves, skits that told stories about heterosexual relationships, and an entire ritual based on male and female pairings were sanctioned, whereas expressions that challenged such an order, such as T-shirts expressing alternative identities, were banned.

By engaging in a variety of gender practices that challenged sexism and homophobia, the GSA Girls actively reconstructed gender. Instead of giving in to a binary gender system and identifying as either male or female, they drew upon a variety of gender markers. They purposefully wore gender-bending clothing. They saw themselves as agents of social change as they challenged school norms about gender and sexuality. Similarly they self-consciously rejected strict gender roles in dating relationships, moving in and out of feminine and masculine identifications. Their anger at inequality and injustice was a powerful tool that they expressed through politicized gender maneuvering.

EMBODYING MASCULINITY

The non-normative gender activities in which these girls engaged may be considered a form of what Geertz calls "deep play" (1973). Their gender practices reveal larger tensions around gendered inequality, sexualized power, and contemporary American notions of youth. This sort of cross-gendered dressing and behavior is a way of challenging currently held notions of masculinity and femininity as well as challenging the idea that youth are passive recipients of socialization rather than active creators of their own social worlds (Thorne 1993). The Basketball Girls, Jessie, and the GSA Girls were recognized by others as masculine because of the way they "did gender" (West and Zimmerman 1991): their clothes, their lingo, the way they held themselves, their romantic relationships. However, none of them fell into the category of "boy." Rather their gender displays drew on tropes and practices of masculinity in such a way that these girls were categorized as masculine by themselves and others. In this way they destabilized, to a certain extent, the sex/gender binary and the easy association of masculinity with boys and femininity with girls. The girls' gender transgressions opened up spaces for social change. As Judith Butler (1993) points out, "doing gender" differently can both reinscribe and challenge the gender order by destabilizing gender norms. This sort of activity challenges the naturalness of the categories of masculinity and femininity by destabilizing the association of these identities with specific bodies.

The Basketball Girls, Jessie, and the GSA Girls all engaged in gender resistance, but they did it in different ways. The Basketball Girls' and Jessie's doing of gender both resisted and reinscribed gender norms; the GSA Girls' doing of gender more consistently challenged an unequal gender order in which femininity, to a large extent, was defined by submission and masculinity by dominance. Their different gendered and sexualized practices show that a politicized understanding of gender is central to challenging the gender order.

Historically, differences in gender practices in American lesbian communities largely fell along class lines: in general, working-class lesbians tended to be more invested in dual gender roles and less invested in linking a (largely middle-class and white) feminist agenda with their sexual identities (Faderman 1991; A. Stein 1997). Although the Basketball Girls and the GSA Girls conformed to this pattern in the two different sets of gender practices that they displayed, they complicated it with respect to their backgrounds. The Basketball Girls tended to have stable working- or middle-class families and lived with married parents where either both worked or one was a stay-at-home mother. Conversely, the GSA Girls were from homes where one parent had died and the other was unemployed (Riley), a parent had committed suicide (T-Rex), both parents were absent due to drug use and neglect (Genevieve), or one parent was alcoholic (Lacy). While their economic class status might not be that different, the girls were divided between "hard living" and "settled living" families (Bettie 2003).[5] "Settled living" families have predictable, orderly lifestyles with some modicum of job security. "Hard living" families are characterized by less stable employment, marital strife, and, often, drug use. Life for them is not as stable or predictable. In fact, the GSA Girls' experiences of injustice in their families might have catalyzed their political activism around social inequality.

While all of these girls were aligned with masculinity, they were aligned differently. The Basketball Girls were seen by others as masculine; in fact, other students usually held them up as an example of girls who "acted like boys." The GSA Girls were only occasionally cited by other students as masculine, though they self-consciously discussed themselves as masculine. For the most part the Basketball Girls and Jessie firmly rejected fully feminine identifications—stopping short of changing their names or self-referential pronouns. The GSA Girls occupied a more self-consciously ambiguous gendered position, alternately purposely rejecting and embracing markers of femininity and masculinity. Several axes of comparison between the two groups—clothing, dominance, rejection of femininity, and sexuality—provide new ways to think about relationships between masculinity, femininity, sexuality, and bodies.

All the girls resisted, to different extents, normatively feminine clothing. Rebeca and Jessie wore masculine clothing on a regular basis, except at highly gendered school rituals. Genevieve, however, wore masculine and feminine clothing daily and at highly gendered school events, such as the prom. Her clothes—button-down shirt, ties, and pants—drew on traditionally masculine styles. However, she wore them tailored in such a way that her form-fitting pants and button-down shirts accented her breasts and hips. As a result her clothing displayed a playful ambiguity of gender rather than a strict adherence to a binary gender system. Genevieve reflected on her clothing choices and took explicit pride in her "masculinity," as she called her tie. Even when she went to highly gendered events such as the prom she took pains to mix gendered attributes, such as wearing her cubic zirconia tie with a slinky velvet dress. Rebeca and Jessie refused explicitly gendered interpretations of their masculine clothes, simply claiming that they wore them because they were comfortable. Others required that they account for their clothing practices (teasing them for their clothing) in ways they wouldn't have if they had actually been boys dressing in the exact same clothes. Though their logic wasn't explicitly feminist, Rebeca's and Jessie's desire to be comfortable was, in itself, a critique of femininity and the confining and oppressive nature of women's clothing.

Both Rebeca and Genevieve routinely denaturalized the sexualized receptivity of a female body by claiming a phallus and positioning themselves as sexualized penetrators rather than receivers of sexual activity. Rebeca repeatedly disavowed a feminine body by saying that she had girls on her "jock" and arguing that she had "muscles" instead of breasts. She also made sure that her girlfriend *did* have "boobs" and not muscles. Genevieve also claimed a phallus, but she did so only to insult boys she saw as homophobic or sexist. She actually sounded like boys in the River High weight room who talked in lewd terms about their sexual adventures with girls. Genevieve used masculine, penetrative insults ironically (if they had come from a boy she probably would have considered them homophobic or sexist) and turned them back upon the boys much as gay activists have reappropriated the word *queer* in their rhetoric.

The Basketball Girls and Jessie also participated in organized sports, a practice associated with boys, masculinity, and dominance (Adams and Bettis 2003; Edley and Wetherell 1997; Griffin 1995; Heywood and Dworkin 2003; Parker 1996; Shakib 2003; Theberge 2000). These girls were able to experience their bodies as agentic and powerful, much as boys might experience their bodies, because of their participation in sports. Their bodies weren't just objects to be ogled but active and powerful. Thus their sports participation, in large part, may have provided them with a different sense of their bodies than other teenage girls had.

The Basketball Girls', Jessie's, and the GSA Girls' different experiences of school status and different perceptions of the River High administration's homophobia lay in their collective levels of politicization (or lack thereof) about their sexuality and gender presentation as well as their ability to redefine themselves as actors in their social worlds. While none were strangers to the disciplinary system, they seemed to get in trouble for two very different reasons. The Basketball Girls got in trouble because they acted like boys. They were loud and disruptive and flouted basic school rules and teachers' authority. While they drew on hip-hop styles associated with African American males, they didn't embody this racialized or sexed status, so their "cool pose" was less of an actual threat.

The GSA Girls, in contrast, were punished for opposing the school in a more subtle and politicized way that revealed the embedded sexism and homophobia embodied in the school's day-to-day activities. Their distinctive ability to connect homophobia and sexism landed them in a different place in the school system than that occupied by Jessie and the Basketball Girls. At homecoming, the GSA Girls directly confronted the school's heterosexism during one of its most heterosexual rituals. The Basketball Girls and Jessie, on the other hand, participated wholeheartedly in various school rituals, and the Basketball Girls actively mocked

National Coming Out Day and used the word *gay* as a pejorative on a regular basis.

A close examination of the girls who challenged gender conventions in interaction and personal style demonstrates that theorists of masculinity need to take seriously the idea of female masculinity because it illustrates masculinity as practices enacted by both male and female bodies instead of as the domain of men. However, to look at girls who "act like boys" only as a challenge to a binary gender system is to miss the complex and contradictory ways gendered and sexualized power operates. A variety of masculinity practices enacted by these girls seemed to combat the equation of male bodies and masculinity on several fronts. The Basketball Girls and Jessie garnered students' respect, notice, and admiration for bucking gender expectations. However, their gender practices sometimes came at the cost of dignity for normatively gendered girls as they engaged in dominance practices of fighting and objectifying girls that sometimes looked like boys' masculinity practices. The GSA Girls provided a coherent and sustained critique of the relationship between gender oppression and homophobia through their activism and gendered practices. That said, they didn't have the social power of the Basketball Girls and Jessie to call attention to this political critique of gender and sexual norms at River High. So it seems that, taken as a whole, their varieties of gender maneuvering all called attention, in the world of River High, to the fact that masculinity cannot be easily equated solely with male bodies.

CHAPTER SIX

Conclusion

*Thinking about Schooling, Gender,
and Sexuality*

Walking through the bustling hallways at River High, watching letterman jacket–clad students rush past, and listening to the morning announcements, I often felt as if I had stepped into a filmic representation
of the archetypal American high school. Teachers, students, and administrators let me know I wasn't alone in this perception of River High, as
they spoke proudly of "tradition" and "Cougar Pride." They demonstrated this pride through their energetic investments in school rituals of
homecoming, Mr. Cougar, prom, sports games, and assemblies. This
sense of normality rendered River High a particularly helpful case with
which to think through contemporary constructions of masculinity, sexuality, and inequality.

Up until this point, I realize, the story of masculinity at River High
must seem quite grim. Many of the behaviors students recognized as
masculine were sexist and homophobic and at best generally involved insulting others. In this concluding chapter I recap central themes in my
analysis of masculinity at River High. I also return to the theories of gender and sexuality I set out at the beginning of the book, adding to and re-
working them to better account for the masculinity processes I observed.

I conclude by looking at activism around issues of sexuality and gender in high school and suggesting avenues for social change.

MASCULINITY AT RIVER HIGH
Repudiation Rituals

As psychoanalytic theorists of gender identity have pointed out, processes of repudiation are central to a masculine sense of self (Butler 1995; Chodorow 1978; Dinnerstein 1976). Through school ceremonies, engagement with pedagogy, and interactional rituals, boys at River continually repudiated femininity, weakness, and, most importantly, the specter of the "fag." Such repudiations were alternatively, and often simultaneously, funny, as in the Mr. Cougar skit when Brent and Greg finally shed their fire-engine-red miniskirts, and earnestly serious, as when Pablo called Mitch a fag for merely inquiring about male dancers. Fags, for all that boys defined them as powerless, weak, and unmanly, seemed to wield an immense amount of power. A fag is profoundly unmasculine, yet possesses the ability to penetrate and thus render any boy unmasculine. More than femininity, more than powerlessness, more than childhood, the abject nature of the specter of the fag required constant, vigilant, earnest repudiation. These repudiations constituted, in large part, boys' daily relationships and communication rituals. Their humor, in particular, depended on continual joking about fags, imitation of fags, and transformation of one another into fags. The aggressiveness of this sort of humor cemented publicly masculine identities as boys collectively battled a terrifying, destructive, and simultaneously powerless Other, while each boy was, at the same time, potentially vulnerable to being positioned as this Other.[1]

Boys' repudiatory interaction rituals didn't occur in a vacuum. School ceremonies and authorities encouraged, engaged in, and reproduced the centrality of repudiation processes to adolescent masculinity. Mocking the unmasculine was central to school rituals such as Mr. Cougar. Boys ripped off skirts, transforming themselves from nerds to real men, and mocked their weaker, feminized rivals in sporting competitions. The administration not only approved of but also awarded trophies to the winners of these skits, thus cementing these refutations as synonymous with popularity, dominance, and masculinity. Similar masculinity processes happened in the classroom; teachers engaged in or at least tacitly approved of these repudiations by ignoring students' comments, and sometimes, as with Mr. Kellogg or Mr. McNally, teachers engaged in these processes of repudiation themselves.

Confirmation Rituals

In addition to rituals of repudiation, masculinity processes at River High included interactional and institutional rituals of confirmation. Through engaging in rituals of sexualized dominance, boys invested in and reproduced meanings of masculinity as heterosexual and agentic. Like processes of repudiation, confirmation processes were embedded in school ceremonies. Mr. Cougar skits centered on the ability of boys to "get girls," linking male popularity with control of girls' bodies and desires. In classrooms teachers garnered the favor of male students by drawing upon relationships between masculinity, heterosexuality, and sexual activity. For instance, Mrs. Mac assumed that only boys and not girls would be interested in absconding with the condoms after the safer-sex presentation. Teachers ignored dangerous forms of these confirmation processes when boys' sex talk took the form of blatant sexual harassment. In fact, I never heard a faculty member reprimand a boy for the sometimes offensive (and often nonsensical) ways they spoke about girls' bodies. Indeed, this type of symbolic violence permeated boys' discussions about girls.

In public spaces (though not necessarily when alone with their girlfriends, or even in one-on-one interviews with me),[2] boys repeatedly engaged in heterosexual discourses not so much to express desire, longing, or pleasure as to indicate that they could control girls' bodies. They "got girls" in ways that ranged from the seemingly benign to the, quite frankly, violent and dangerous. Having a girlfriend seems like a normal and mostly harmless teenage rite of passage. But in the context of the public interaction between heterosexuality and masculinity, having girlfriends becomes, in part, a form of "getting girls" through discursive violence and physical force in which having a girlfriend confirms some sort of baseline heterosexuality.

Certainly this does not mean that boys don't have girlfriends for whom they care deeply. Even Chad, the exemplar of masculinity at River High, told me, at length, during our interview, about how much he loved his girlfriend. Possessing intense emotions for one's girlfriend doesn't negate the fact that this same girlfriend may also serve as a masculinity resource, bolstering a boy's claim on heterosexuality. In public contexts, which is where manifestations of compulsive heterosexuality occur, boys tended to close off, hide, or otherwise deny emotional attachments to girls. Instead, many boys physically and verbally harassed girls sexually. Under the guise of flirting they manipulated girls' bodies by throwing them around and engaging in games of "uncle" in which girls squealed submissively in order for the "game" to end. While their private interactions with girls or even with each other might involve tender discussions of desire and emotion, public sex talk didn't indicate desire; instead it highlighted boys' control over girls' bodies. These rituals of mythic storytelling included boys' stories about the crazy things they could make girls' bodies do—fart, poop, orgasm, or bleed. These stories were simultaneously information-sharing ventures and masculinity processes. In talking about and interacting with girls this way, boys invested in and reproduced meanings of masculinity characterized and constituted by eroticized male dominance and sexualized female submission.

Race

These processes of confirmation and repudiation were characterized by racialized meanings and, more importantly, are ways of reproducing a gendered racial inequality. The findings in this book echo other research on masculinity indicating that masculinity varies with race and is constituted by and constitutes racialized meanings (Almaguer 1991; Bucholtz 1999; Fine et al. 1997; Kelley 2004; Majors 2001; Mercer 1994; Riggs 1991; Ross 1998; Zinn 1998). Indeed, racial and gendered meanings often cannot be understood if they are decoupled (Combahee River Collective 1981; Collins 1990; V. Smith 1994; Zinn and Dill 1996). Like many Americans, students at River High understood race primarily in terms of whiteness and blackness.³ While several of the students I observed and interviewed listed a number of racial/ethnic backgrounds—German, Puerto Rican, Hispanic, Chinese, El Salvadorian, Filipino, Irish, and Mexican, for instance—most regularly identified themselves and others as either white or black.

Research indicates that schools treat African American boys differently from white boys (J. Davis 1999; Ferguson 2000; Majors 2001). I saw several instances at River High in which school officials punished African American boys for behaviors that were expected of white boys. In part, the economic positionings of many of the African American boys at River rendered them more vulnerable to school surveillance. As Darnell pointed out to me, many African American youth at River didn't have cars, so they couldn't leave campus with the ease of white students. Thus they were rarely outside the purview of school authorities. Since many of them used relatives' addresses to attend River rather than the nearby Chicago High School, they suffered worse consequences for punishments due to the threat of expulsion. As a result, when they were singled out by school authorities, the threat of "deportation" to the "bad" school frequently loomed.

While African American boys didn't engage nearly as often in the fag discourse as did white boys, they seemed to suffer more for it, as when Kevin was suspended for accusing the wrestling team of wearing "faggot outfits." Similarly African American boys' enactments of compulsive heterosexuality were watched more closely as school authorities regulated when and how they could touch girls during the dance show. Finally, sexualized insults such as *fag* took on different meanings among African American boys at River. It was not that these boys were more progressive, but, because of a different cultural history and reliance on symbolic power as a result of their lack of institutional power, they didn't call each other fags for engaging in several activities considered unmasculine by white boys, such as dancing, touching, or caring about clothing. African American boys' relationships with the fag discourse and compulsive heterosexuality reflected their positioning in American society as simultaneously hypersexual, dangerous men and utterly failed men (Ross 1998). They were regarded as sexually threatening to other girls and white boys at River; at the same time they were structurally less powerful and rendered vulnerable by their lack of institutional and economic resources.

Homophobia

Even though the fag discourse is and isn't about homophobia, River High as an institution was deeply homophobic. Homophobia took the form of blatant antigay practices and, more commonly, the staging of taken-for-granted heteronormative school ceremonies and traditions. Rallies, yearbook photos, graduation, and dances all celebrated heterosexual gender difference, encoding inequality in what Judith Butler (1993) calls the "heterosexual matrix." In this ferociously heteronormative context GSA members had to struggle to get their club approved and have it recognized in school announcements. Several gay pride events, such as the Day of Silence and the celebration of National Coming Out Day, were barred from the campus. The school authorities didn't protect the most vulnerable gay students, such as Ricky, who was teased, taunted, and eventually threatened out of the school. Indeed, I felt the homophobia so strongly that I took my gay pride sticker off my car while I researched at River High.

Girls' Gender Strategies

Girls at River High adopted a variety of "gender strategies"[4] (Hochschild 1989) to deal with the masculinity processes of repudiation (the fag discourse) and confirmation (compulsory heterosexuality) in which they were frequently used as masculinity resources—capitulation, subversion, and criticism. Girls' popularity, for the most part, depended on successfully navigating masculine approval mechanisms. They received admiration and popularity by confirming heterosexualized gender identities encouraged by school rituals and traditions. Through this sort of capitulation girls traded their own subjectivity for boys' point of view. They giggled and laughed as boys made seemingly offensive comments about their looks, their bodies, and their sexuality. Like other teenage girls, girls at River focused on boys' sexual desire and practices, not their own (Tolman 2005).

Some girls adopted a seemingly subversive approach by engaging in masculinity processes themselves. Rebeca and Jessie were able to escape, to a certain extent, the objectification and dehumanization to which many of the girls at River were subjected. They successfully embodied masculinity themselves by dominating others, dressing like boys, competing like boys, fighting like boys, and dating girls as heterosexual boys did. They were able to draw upon the "cool pose" (Majors 2001) frequently embodied by African American boys identified with hip-hop culture. This embodiment of masculinity, combined with their extroversion and good looks, seemed to have allowed them to avoid being used as resources in masculinity processes.

Other girls also developed a variety of systemic and spontaneous "gender strategies" that allowed them to contest boys' treatment of them and other girls. Most girls who did this deployed a sort of off-the-cuff feminism that labeled individual boys as jerks for their practices of compulsive heterosexuality. The GSA Girls adopted a more systemic approach, linking sexism to issues of homophobia. In their daily interactions with each other, with boys, and with the school administration, the GSA girls bravely confronted sexism by holding poster campaigns and days of activism, celebrating non-normative gender practices, and happily identifying as gay.

THEORETICAL IMPLICATIONS

As I wrote earlier, these findings look pretty bleak. I have detailed the ways boys tortured girls and each other through a barrage of sexualized insults and the ways the school structure itself undergirded such interactions. However, within the rampant harassment and teasing present at River High, I saw several points of entry for thinking about alternative interactions, rituals, and gendered ways of being—political action, parody, and play. I use the term *play* to indicate serious play, like Thorne's (1993) notion of "gender play" or Geertz's (1973) concept of "deep play." Play, in this sense, is not just about fun but is a way of constructing the social world. The theme of play has lurked throughout the book but up until now has remained relatively latent. I found especially illuminating three key instances of gender play and parody at River: Brent and Craig's "Revenge of the Nerds" Mr. Cougar skit, the play of the boys acting in *Carousel*, and the practices of the GSA Girls.

Brent and Craig opened this book with their award-winning Mr. Cougar skit, "Revenge of the Nerds." In this miniplay Brent and Greg transformed themselves, with the help of a female personal trainer, from effeminate nerds into muscular, virile men. Through this transformation, which encouraged students to laugh at their effeminate performances and cheer at their dominance over girls and poor men of color, Brent and Craig drew on and reinforced meanings of masculinity through sexualized dominance. While this skit (like the other Mr. Cougar skits) was an example of gender play and parody in which boys imitated masculinity and femininity, their imitations reinforced prevailing notions of gender identities. They parodied, not dominant gender identities, but the "abject," engaging the student audience in their ritualized repudiations. This sort of "deep play" and parody does not challenge dominant meanings of gender, race, and class but rather reflects and reinforces them.

The boys in *Carousel*, while commissioned to perform similarly masculine men, parodied dominant meanings of masculinity. Instead of insulting one another, putting down girls, or trying to establish some sort of masculine dominance, these boys moved between a hypermasculinity and an abjected identity, laughing, singing, and dancing. They danced, pirouetted, and squealed but at the same time got to act like tough, swaggering sailors. These masculine and feminine practices did not cohere in one gendered identity. Rather, the boys combined gender markers and practices to create fluid and playful selves. Their parody of sailors indicated that masculinity and unmasculinity could exist concurrently. The boys drew alternatively and simultaneously from both masculine and feminine iconography and bodily comportments. This sort of parody highlights the importance of institutional spaces for such gender play. It was precisely the institutional space of the drama performance, not the football field or the social science classroom, that allowed these boys to explore and play with alternative identities. Playing with gender through parody in this way can challenge the way gendered power inheres in masculine and feminine identities (Richardson 1996).

The GSA Girls, as I highlighted in the previous chapter, exhibited the most politically coherent and stable form of gender play, parody, and political activism through their serious critique of gender sexual norms. They continually mixed gendered symbols and bodily practices, backing up these performances with a sense of social justice through which they confronted both sexism and homophobia. They cleverly embodied masculine positionings by turning masculinized insults back upon boys. By mixing gendered symbols, bodily comportments, and discourses, these girls called into question the opposition and even the usefulness of the categories of masculinity and femininity. Their gender was, as Sedgwick (1995) puts it, "orthogonal." Their masculinity and femininity were not ends of the same axis but rather occupied different axes, so that they could mix all sorts of gendered imagery and practices.

As these examples indicate, playing with gender and performative gender transgression are not progressive acts in and of themselves (Jackson 1996). Boys who dress up as girls on Halloween (as many of them do) don't challenge the gender order. Rather, they highlight exactly how much they are *not* girls. Craig and Brent used repudiatory parody and play to highlight the extent to which they were *not* fags or unmasculine. The Basketball Girls' form of gender play both reworked notions of masculinity as inherent in male bodies and reinscribed notions of masculinity as dominance. Play and parody can be progressive when they open up opportunities for alternative gender expressions and gender fluidity. Brady and the rest of the boys in the drama performance moved in and out of typically masculine positions, mocking ideas of masculinity as dominant while also embodying it without repudiating the specter of the fag. They enacted seemingly contradictory gender positions simultaneously. It is important to note that Graham and Heath (who had celebrated getting a kiss from a girl during a ritual of "getting girls") were both involved in drama productions and when in those spaces did not engage in the fag discourse or compulsive heterosexuality in the same way. In this sense, looking at the same boys in a variety of public spaces is important to understanding masculinity processes. The GSA Girls simultaneously occupied multiple gender positions, mixing both masculine and feminine styles. These sorts of gender play and parody emphasize fluidity and change while highlighting gender and sexuality as vectors of power and inequality.

Contemporary queer theorists and poststructural theorists see the concept of play (Lugones 1990) as central to social change. Identifying places and practices in which youth can try on different identities, explore varieties of gender practices, and mix them up opens possibilities for social change through a proliferation of gender identities, instead of locking girls and boys into strict gender identity practices that match up with their presumed genitalia. Theater as a symbolic and metaphorical space is important in this sense. It is a place where it is okay and even required to try on different characters. Boys and girls can step into and out of identities at will and in a less threatening way because they are "just acting." In this sense, playing with gender is an answer. But it is not *the* answer because masculinity and femininity are not arbitrary categories; rather, they are identities required of individuals. As I've shown throughout this book, they are the very identities that reinforce inequality (Jeffreys 1998). Thus there are limits to parody, play, and doing gender differently, and, as a result, play, even serious play, is not enough. It needs to be accompanied and undergirded by institutional change.

Looking at gender as "deep play" builds on the argument I laid out at the beginning of the book that masculinity isn't so much about men as about processes and practices we associate with male bodies. I argued that many theorists of masculinity were so invested in the centrality of the male body to definitions of masculinity that they sometimes missed the ways masculinity was created through sexualized processes among both boys and girls. By listening to what the students at River actually called masculinity and by thinking about masculinity as a process, in addition to looking at masculinity as the property of those with male bodies, I have shown how, in the world of River High, masculinity was defined as sexualized and publicly enacted dominance. This is not to say that youth at River didn't define masculinity as a description of boys' attitudes, behaviors, and interactional styles. They did. But they also defined masculinity as a publicly enacted interactional style that demonstrated heterosexuality and dominance while at the same time repudiating and mocking weakness, usually represented by femininity or the fag.

By attending to students' multiple definitions of masculinity (both as what boys do and as a description of a specific public interactional style), this analysis builds upon the "multiple masculinities" model. Theorists of masculinity have been helpful in identifying how masculinity is multiple—how different men enact different configurations of masculinity. What the interactional rituals of youth at River High indicate is that these students saw a constellation of behaviors, whether the actor was a boy or a girl, as masculine. Thus it is important to attend to the manipulation, deployment, and enactment of varieties of masculinity, not just as what men do, but as how respondents recognize it. Looking at masculinity this way differentiates studies of masculinity from studies of men and brings these studies of masculinity in line with feminist studies of gender. As such, the analysis of masculinity is moved from an endless categorization of masculinity (which is really more about categories of men) into a study of the creation of gendered selves and resistance to normative gender identities. Looking at masculinity this way helps integrate the masculinity literature with feminist theory and its focus on inequality and social change.

PRACTICAL STEPS

It is hard to base policy recommendations on poststructuralist theory and analysis, which often seems far removed from the "nitty-gritty" of lived experience. In its emphasis on deconstructing categories, feminist theory has often outpaced the slower movement toward social justice, which relies on those very categories to illustrate inequality (Bordo 1994). I have detailed above a more theoretical approach to solving some of the problems I outlined in this book. Now I suggest some policy changes that may facilitate more equitable conditions for adolescents. I focus these policy suggestions mostly on schools because while schools, as shown throughout this text, can be places of intense homophobia and sexism, they can also be places for "anti-discriminatory responses to marginalization" (Pallotta-Chiarolli 1999, 183). Organizations, individuals, and professionals from a range of disciplines have been mobilizing around issues of harassment, bullying, sexism, and homophobia in schools over the last decade. I suggest here helpful organizations, curricular changes, resources for parents and educators, and films aimed at helping to facilitate gender and sexual equity in schools.

Legal protections need to be in place to shield gay, lesbian, bisexual, transgendered, and other non-normatively gendered students. Both Brady and Riley invoked California's AB 537, which prevents discrimination in schools based on sexual or gender identity, in order to gain equal treatment. Brady relied upon it, in part, to create the GSA, and Riley later used it to bolster her claim that she be able to wear a black graduation robe rather than a yellow one. The California legislature is not alone in having passed such a law. The District of Columbia, Maine, Minnesota, and New Jersey have all enacted laws that prohibit harassment and/or discrimination based on sexual orientation and gender identity in school. Several other states—Connecticut, Massachusetts, Vermont, Washington, Wisconsin—have passed laws that prohibit harassment and discrimination based on sexual orientation in school but fail to protect alternative gender expressions. As the experiences of many non-normatively gendered students at River High indicate, these laws need to include gender expression, as alternative gender practices trigger much of the homophobic or sexually based teasing in adolescence. As of the writing of this book, twenty states have no provisions protecting gay, lesbian, bisexual, transgendered, or other non-normatively gendered students in school.

Though California has one of the most progressive laws about gay, lesbian, bisexual, and transgendered (GLBT) youth in the nation, this law, it seems, did not protect Ricky. Ricky's experience indicates that these laws had little effect on his ability to learn free from harassment. Teachers and administrators actually need to know about and enforce this legislation once it is in place. Had teachers and administrators actually heeded the law (or even been informed of it) and protected Ricky from threats of violence, he might have completed his education instead of dropping out to work as a female impersonator.

Presumably students (male and female) have been protected from sexual harassment since the passage of Title IX in 1972 (Orenstein 2002). However, as with AB 537, the deployment of Title IX leaves something to be desired. Sexual harassment is rampant at River High School, as the boys in chapter 4 demonstrate. Boys' sex talk and predatory behavior has become so normalized that teachers don't even recognize it as harassment but rather consider it harmless flirting. To implement these laws teachers and administrators must look with a new eye at student interactions, noting how both homophobic epithets and so-called flirtatious behaviors shore up normative gender and sexual identities and perpetuate unequal gender arrangements. Films such as *Flirting or Hurting* can help both educators and students recognize more equitable interactions.[5] Additionally, students who harass other students need to be punished, but they also need to be educated. It's not enough to reprimand or discipline a boy for making sexist comments or calling someone a fag. To simply punish students who are harassing other students without explaining larger issues of power and inequality leaves those who are harassing confused and angry, and, more importantly, doesn't necessarily change how youth think about power and inequality (Orenstein 2002).

Educators can also take proactive steps to make schools more equitable places. They need to create learning and social environments that are more supportive of gay, lesbian, bisexual, transgendered, and other non-normatively gendered youth. Administrators can modify both the social organization of the school and the curriculum content so that they are less homophobic and gender normative. Including a range of sexual and gender identities in school rituals and curricula will indicate to both GLBT and non-normatively gendered students as well as straight and normatively gendered students that school authorities don't tolerate gender- and sexuality-based harassment or violence.

Schools can modify homophobic and sexist social environments in several ways—by placing affirming posters in their classrooms, providing support for GSAs, sponsoring assemblies and speakers, and reorganizing highly gendered school rituals. Allowing the formation of GSAs is an especially effective and simple way to support GLBT, gender-variant youth and their allies.[6] There has been a veritable explosion of GSAs across the country over the past ten years. Students are initiating, forming, and sustaining these clubs in progressive cities like San Francisco and in solidly "red states" like Utah. Since courts ruled that these clubs are protected by the Federal Equal Access Act (which requires that schools allow noncurricular student groups access to the school), students have been banding together in support of gay and lesbian youth. According to the Gay, Lesbian, and Straight Education Network, there are at least three thousand GSAs nationwide. GSAs from every state, with the exception of North Dakota, have registered with the network. As Ricky's, Genevieve's, and Lacy's stories indicate, having a GSA at River was crucial for them. It provided a space for them to feel safe, create social networks, hear special speakers, plan social events, and learn. The presence of and activism stemming from GSAs are central to combating homophobic and sexist teasing, bullying, and violence in schools (Blumenfeld 1995). Administrators might also want to consider providing counseling and support groups for GLBT and gender-variant teens. Several advocates for gay and lesbian and non-normatively gendered teens indicate that school-sponsored support groups and specially trained counselors may alleviate some of the suffering of gay and lesbian students (Reynolds and Koski 1995; Uribe 1995).

Schools can also send the message that homophobia and sexism are unacceptable through school-sponsored assemblies and speakers. Schools bring in a number of speakers and sponsor a variety of assemblies each year. River High's administration, for instance, brings in guest speakers and performers to celebrate Black History Month, sponsors an annual Multi-Cultural Assembly, and stages emotionally intense programs such as "Every 15 Minutes," which simulates student deaths due to drunk-driving accidents. These programs are organized to teach students lessons about history, respect for difference, antiracism, and alcohol abuse. In addition to these sorts of assemblies and educational programming, schools should bring in speakers from feminist and gay rights organizations to talk about gay history, equal rights, and teasing. Studies have shown that after youth have witnessed gay people talking about their experience as gay people in formal settings, such as these sorts of school assemblies, they are less likely to express homophobic attitudes (Nelson and Krieger 1997). Bringing in feminist, gay, and lesbian speakers might also change the public attitudes at River High. Since schools already bring in many special speakers and put on special programs to combat other social ills, recognizing Women's History Month or National Coming Out Day would send an unambiguous message to students that the school, as an institution, opposed sexism and homophobia. Additionally the school could support GSA members' efforts to stage their own social interventions such as the "Day of Silence."

Similarly, school administrators need to take a serious look at the role of rituals such as dances, proms, homecoming, and Mr. Cougar, in their socialization project.[7] To the extent that these rituals are hetero-sexist, homophobic, and sexist they need to be reworked. The messages conveyed to students through these rituals should not be that the school advocates and in fact demands heterosexualized gender differ-ence. Rather, the rituals should be organized to reflect the diversity of gender and sexual identities among students. Small changes can make a big difference in terms of school rituals. For example, River High, like many other high schools, distributes lists of the names of all sen-ior girls for homecoming queen and all senior boys for Mr. Cougar. If schools are wedded to these sorts of popularity rituals, they could con-sider listing all student names for each competition, instead of decid-ing in advance the gender of each student and thus the gender of the homecoming queen or Mr. Cougar. They might also want to allow a Ms. Cougar or a homecoming king or to develop alternative gender-neutral titles. Students should be able to take same-gender dates, whether romantically or just as friends, to school dances and as escorts to the more formal rituals. Technically River High had no rule against this practice, but certainly Jessie didn't initially feel comfortable taking a same-gender date to these rituals. Clothing expectations should be applied equally to boy and girl students. Girls should not be required to wear different-colored robes for graduation, nor should they be forced to wear revealing off-the-shoulder drapes for their senior pic-tures. Finally, schoolwide performances (such as the Mr. Cougar skits) should be vetted for homophobic, sexist, or heterosexist content. The fag discourse should not be allowed to form the story line of these sorts of rituals.

In addition to these modifications to the social world of the school, educators need to look seriously at the inclusion (or lack thereof) of GLBT and gender-variant people in the school curriculum. Arthur Lip-kin (1995) makes the case that gays and lesbians can be included in a variety of areas in the curriculum. Inclusion of nonheterosexual and non-normatively gendered people in the official learning of the school would make sexual minority and gender-variant students feel less alone. It would also combat damaging or scary images of gays and lesbians in the mainstream media (Lipkin 1995). Additionally, learning about GLBT or gender-variant people will send a message to straight students about the school's stance on homophobic and sexist teasing. If students are encouraged to be less prejudiced, they may indeed experience more leeway with their own sexual and gender identities (Lipkin 1995).

Whether or not they are teaching specifically about sexuality or gender, teachers need to be aware of how they contribute to the "hidden curriculum" (Campbell and Sanders 2002; Letts and Sears 1999; J. Martin 1976) of the classroom. Teachers shouldn't try to garner masculine favor by allowing sexism or homophobia to go unchecked. For example, the boys who formed the Man Party in response to Mrs. Mac's class assignment should have been questioned about their plan and motivations for the party. Their desire to deny women the right to vote and to make fun of girls by showing how little they knew about women's history could have been used as a moment to teach about sexism, citizenship, and voting rights.

Organizations such as the Safe Schools Coalition, the California Teachers Association, and GALE-BC provide resources, lesson plans, and teaching tools for teachers to create less homophobic and gender-normative classrooms.[8] The California Teachers Association and the National Education Association partnered to produce a teachers' handbook entitled *Gay, Lesbian, Bisexual and Transgender Youth: Breaking the Silence.* The goal of this handbook is to educate teachers and school employees to ensure that all students receive "equal educational opportunity," though it stops short of encouraging change in values or beliefs. This informative and creative booklet provides discussion guidelines, statistics about sexual identities, definitions, exercises for students, and a variety of ways to include gays and lesbians in the curriculum. It is a model of what might be given to teachers at the beginning of each school year.

Finally, in terms of the earlier discussion of parody and play, providing support and spaces for gendered and sexualized difference and fluidity is key to changing the seemingly entrenched homophobia and sexism central to adolescent masculinity. Spaces should be created and sustained in which youth can think about the possibilities of crafting and inhabiting a variety of gender identities. This is exactly what, with little adult guidance, the kids were doing in both the GSA and the drama performances. They were carving out playful, political, and meaningful ways of redefining, in part by deconstructing, the social categories of girl and boy, masculinity and femininity. In GSA meetings the youth (gay, straight, boy, and girl) challenged the concept of "normal" through their interactions and in their dress styles. They threw "normal" in the face of the administration and other kids in the school by participating in a Day of Silence, by putting up posters, and by having announcements of their meetings read aloud over the loudspeaker. They made their difference public and they did so in a group, which afforded them more protection, and possibly power, than doing it individually. The boys in drama tried on a variety of gender identities, often simultaneously. The spaces for this sort of gendered and sexualized creativity and playfulness are central to challenging gender and sexuality norms in adolescence and high school. Schools need to ensure that drama programs, which are constantly under funding threats, continue and that GSAs are allowed to meet, relatively free from peer harassment.

High school is hard. Negotiating gender identities is hard. Figuring out sexuality is hard. It is up to adults to configure spaces that support youths' variety of gender and sexual expressions. It is also up to adults to protect young people from the vicious teasing and harassment rampant in most modern high schools. We can't accept that boys and girls are defining a masculinity based on damaging notions of power and domination. We can't accept that youth craft masculine identities through physically and verbally harassing girls and some boys. Much as adults have taken a stand, for the most part, against racist epithets in school, we need to take institutional and individual stands against sexist and homo phobic epithets. At both institutional and individual levels, we need to support boys and girls who enact non-normative gender and sexual identities. "Making our schools safe for sissies" (Rofes 1995, 79) can make them safer places for all students: masculine girls, feminine boys, and all those in between.

WHAT IF A GUY HITS ON YOU?

*Intersections of Gender, Sexuality, and Age
in Fieldwork with Adolescents*

"Yeah, she's writing a book on River guys," said sixteen-year-old Ray as he introduced me to a few of his friends in River High School's bustling main hallway.
Don, a tall, lanky basketball player, leaned casually against the stone pillar next
to me. "Damn," he said, smiling down at me, "I was gonna hit on you." Six
months into my research I had grown more accustomed to, although certainly
not comfortable with, this sort of response from boys at River High School. During my time in the field I often heard similar comments from boys interested in
dating me, asking my advice about their sexual adventures, or inquiring about my
own personal life. In this chapter I discuss unique challenges encountered by female researchers when studying adolescent boys. I focus particularly on how the
boys infused our interactions with sexual content and how I managed these interactions to maintain rapport while simultaneously enforcing a professional distance (and maintaining my own dignity). I did this through the creation of what
I call, building on Mandell's (1988) notion of a "least-adult" identity, a "least-
gendered" identity.

    The role of sexuality is understudied in ethnographic research in general, and
thoughtful analysis of it in methodological discussions of ethnographic research
among youth is nearly absent. While teenagers are almost obsessively studied as
sexual actors, most research focuses on sex education, "at-risk" behaviors, or non-
normative sexual identities (Kulkin, Chauvin, and Percle 2000; Medrano 1994;
Strunin 1994; Waldner-Haugrud and Magruder 1996) rather than the ways sexuality constructs daily lives. In researching teenage boys I found that sexuality was

not just a set of behaviors studied by researchers but part of the research process itself in that it mediated, complicated, and illuminated researcher-respondent interactions. Masculinizing processes in adolescence take place not only between peers but also between a female researcher and male respondents (Arendell 1997). As a female researcher, I was drawn into a set of objectifying and sexualizing rituals through which boys constructed their identities and certain school spaces as masculine. In the end I wasn't just studying their gender identities; I became part of the very process through which they constructed these identities.

River High boys directed their masculinity rituals primarily at their female peers, but occasionally they would involve me. In response, I tried to manage this use of me as a masculinity resource by creating a "least-gendered identity," positioning myself as a woman who possessed masculine cultural capital. I carefully crafted my identity and interactional style to show that I was a woman who knew about "guy" topics and could engage in the verbal one-upmanship so common among boys at River High. That said, at times I accepted their use of me as a potential sexual partner or sexual object in order to maintain rapport, as I did when Don said he wanted to "hit on" me. At other times, I responded differently to the boys by establishing an insider/outsider position in terms of age, gender, and sexuality. This liminal stance, and specifically my attempts to create a least-gendered identity, allowed me to maintain a good relationship with the boys. This strategy yielded more information than I would have gathered had I reacted like an offended, judgmental adult or a giggly, smiling teenage girl. However, it stopped short of actually challenging the practices in which boys engaged as they crafted masculine identities.

GOING BACK TO SCHOOL: NEGOTIATING INTERSECTIONS OF AGE AND GENDER

The first methodological challenge I encountered when researching adolescents was not exactly what I had expected: going back to high school. I had assumed that since I had already researched adolescents, it would be simple to do the same for this project (Pascoe 2003). However, I hadn't anticipated the difference between interviewing and actually existing among teenagers in their social worlds. I realized that this project was going to be different the first day I walked onto the River campus to begin conducting research at 8:00 on a warm Monday morning. I walked out of the office in front of the school, having just signed in to the guest log and grabbed my visitor pass. The visitor pass, a blue and white rectangle sporting my name and VISITOR across the top, was supposed to be worn in a conspicuous location. Not wanting to highlight my temporary and outsider status, and possibly feeling some of that high school pressure to "fit in," I stuck it in my bag. Striding down the open-air hallway to my first classroom observation, I heard a deep voice booming out behind me, "Hey you! Hey! Hey you! You! Who are you!" Frozen, having sudden flashbacks to my own high school experience and remembering narrow escapes while ditching classes and evading threats of detention, I turned around. A fifty-something African American gentleman built like a linebacker loomed over me. Looking down through his glasses, he asked, "Who are you?" Recovering quickly and remembering that I was finishing up my twenties, not my teens, I looked up and smiled, in a way I hoped was charming, as I responded, "I'm C. J., a researcher here." I showed him my slip and he said, "Okay, as long as you have that with you." He explained to me that he was the school's security guard. His name was George Johnson, but I soon called him Mr. J. just like the rest of the kids at River. Later, as I became a more familiar sight at the school, Mr. J. engaged in many of the same sexualizing processes as the boys did, often saying flirtatious things to me like "Well, my day suddenly got much brighter since *you* got here!" followed with a wink.

That moment of misidentification was the first of many: teachers thought I was a student, and students thought I was a new student, a teacher, or worse, a parole officer. Early in my research, as I sat in the back row of the auto shop class, a tall, lanky blond boy with spiky hair and a relaxed demeanor turned to me as the rest of the boys in the class zinged from one side of the room to the other and asked, "You new here?" I laughed and said, "Sort of. How old do you think I am?" "Uh, seventeen?" he answered. I laughed, explaining, "No, I'm a researcher. I'm almost thirty. I'm writing a book on you guys." He told me he hoped it was a good book.

Soon after that tall, lanky blond thought I was a new student, I found myself standing at a table with the "High School Democrats" as they tried to recruit students to their club. I stood next to the vice-president, Trevor, as he summoned David, the president, to introduce me. David looked at me quizzically as he walked over, and I, responding to his questioning look, said, "Who do you think I am?" David paused, looked at Trevor and said, "His mom?" I burst out laughing, as did Trevor. Somehow I had gone from late teens to late thirties in a matter of hours! I told him no, I was a researcher from Berkeley and I was writing a book on boys in his school.

I found I was anxious not to let the students know my actual age, fearing that I would lose some of the cachet inherent in my role as a Berkeley researcher. My concern about age was reflected in my clothing choices as well. I didn't want to dress like the teachers because I didn't want to be seen as an authority figure. However, because I didn't wear the extremely low-slung pants that the girls tended to wear and possibly because I walked with more confidence than did most teenage girls, students often mistook me for a teacher. Even though I wore baggy pants and a black T-shirt, one day as I was walking down the hallway two boys who had been joking around and using swear words looked at one another as one said, "Shhhh! She's a teacher."

Like these two boys, other students were wary of me. I spent one afternoon early in my fieldwork hanging out at Bob's, a small yellow burger shack around the corner from school, where kids ordered their food from a window and congregated around the eight picnic tables separated from the sidewalk by a tall wrought-iron black fence. The "bad" kids hung out here. Most dressed in dark baggy clothing, and many smoked. Quite frankly, some of them, with their spiky hair and multiple piercings, intimidated me. I had never hung out with these sorts of "bad" kids when I was in high school and still felt as if I might be punished for associating with them. Thinking about this fear of punishment, I asked a large white boy in a red and plaid black shirt, earrings, a slight mustache, and baggy pants if kids ever got in trouble for smoking. He said, "No. Every once in a while the cops would come by and tell us to put it out, but not usually." I told him I was writing a book on River and he looked a little surprised. He took me over to another group of three boys, one of them clutching a skateboard who looked at me and asked, "Who are you?" At this point I was intrigued by their categories, so I responded with "Who do you think I am?" He said "P.O." and I immediately thought—participant observer—and laughed to myself. In explanation, he offered, "Parole officer." I laughed out loud at this point. "No, I would probably make more money being a parole officer. Do they really come around here?" "Yeah, all the time," he answered.

I finally settled on telling the students I was "almost thirty." I tried to make it seem as if I was an adult but not too much older than them, more of a mediator between the adult world and their world. I negotiated a "least-adult" (Mandell 1988) identity, in which I was simultaneously like and not like the teens I was researching. Barrie Thorne (1993), in her research on elementary school children, provides vivid examples of how to enact a least-adult identity across generational lines.

In establishing and maintaining a least-adult identity, I had to repeatedly promise the boys that they wouldn't get in trouble for the things they told me. J. W., for instance, walked out of the weight room to ask what I was writing down in my notebook. I said I took notes on everything they did. He asked if I had written about a fight that had occurred the day before. I said yes and asked him if he was worried that he was going to get in trouble. He nodded. I told him that everything I wrote down was confidential; I couldn't get him in trouble at all. He said he was worried that I was going to tell his teacher. I told him, "No, I don't tell teachers about stuff that I saw that could get kids in trouble." I continued by saying that maybe if "*I* were in the middle of a fight or got hurt then I might tell somebody." J. W. asked, "What if a guy hits on you?" I laughed and said that I didn't tell teachers about that either. J. W., in this early interaction, began to lay the groundwork for later comments he would make about my body and sexuality by ensuring that he wouldn't get in trouble for saying them.

Once the boys got used to the fact that I was going to be hanging around, they took pains to make sure I was writing down what they thought was important. It took them a while to realize that I wouldn't tattle on them. They tested me on this claim by breaking the rules in front of me and then looking at me to see if I disapproved. One day I proved my mettle by refusing to tattle on them as they monkeyed around on the cable machine in the weight room. Mike, J. W., and Josh set the pin to lift the heaviest weights on the cable machine. This meant that the cables were so heavy that none of them had the strength individually to pull the weights off the ground. As Billy and I watched, Mike, J. W., and Josh all tried to perform chest flies with this enormous amount of weight. They aided each other by holding the lifter's arms in place while another boy put the handle on the lifter's arm. As they tried out the cables they discovered, much to their delight, that the weight was so heavy that, if a boy kept hold of the cables, he would be lifted off the ground. When J. W. tried to perform a chest fly, he lost the battle with the weights, allowed the cables to pull him up, and executed a back flip as they did so. As he performed more flips, the boys in the class gathered in a half-circle around him, urging him on.

I asked Jeff what he thought this gymnastic/weight-lifting performance was all about. He told me, echoing my claims from earlier in the book about how boys become masculine in groups, "Proving masculinity. They're only doing it because they're guys and they're around other guys. They prove how strong they are, and then, when everyone sees how strong they are, they don't mess with them." As if realizing, that he, too, didn't want to be messed with, soon after he had made this pronouncement, Jeff walked over to join in. By this time the crowd was so large that they kept looking to make sure Coach Ramirez wasn't paying attention. A group of boys helped Jeff grab onto the cable handles, and he tried desperately to hold onto them. The weights yanked little Jeff quickly into the air as he easily performed a back flip. He kept trying to do a front flip, which no boy had yet performed, and when he was unable to complete it he let the weights fly down as he let go. They clanked down so hard that the pin snapped in half. The boys scattered, yelling, "He broke it! He broke it!" Josh, standing next to me, started laughing, "Write it down! Write about guys doing dumb stuff!" Instead of fearing that I would tattle on them to Coach Ramirez, they wanted me to document their misdeeds. Thankfully, teachers never put me in the position to report on student behavior either.

Many of the boys in auto shop and the weight room came to pride themselves on their status as research subjects. Brook took a look at my big pad of paper, which I happened to be carrying that day because I had filled up the small one I usually carried with me. He cried, "She came in with the big notebook today!" Darren chimed in, "She knows we do too much to put in the small one!" Arnie said, amazed, "I can't believe you filled up a whole notebook." I said, "Yeah, between you guys and weight lifting." Arnie replied, "Yeah, *they're* really bad." The boys frequently equated "badness" with masculinity. They knew I was there to study masculinity and as a result thought that what I wrote down was "bad" stuff. For instance, Ryan said to me, "Your book is a lot today." I said, "Yeah, lots of good stuff." To which he responded, "About Josh?" Josh was pegged as one of the most masculine boys because he was one of the "baddest"; thus Ryan assumed I wrote more on days he acted up.

This constant documentation helped define me as an outsider, albeit a privileged one, an expert, someone who knew more about the boys than they knew about themselves. The boys highlighted my outsider status in auto shop as a substitute was engaging in futile attempts to calm down the class. The substitute, Mr. Brown, stated, for the tenth time, "Okay, guys and girls. Settle down, guys and girls." Brook responded, "Uh, it's all guys." Jeff said, looking at me, "Except for her." Brook countered, "She's an outsider. She takes notes." Both looked at me and we laughed. Brook and Jeff highlighted my liminal status—I wasn't *really* a girl because I was an outsider. All these instances go to show that negotiating age and authority differences is important when studying adolescents. I had to leave my "adultness" behind and refrain from admonishing them for behaving like teens. Their impressions of me were a source of data themselves as boys projected on to me adultness, femaleness, and the ability to punish them.

CREATING A LEAST-GENDERED IDENTITY

While I did not lift weights with the boys or work on cars with them, I did engage in gender practices that marked me as less like the girls in their peer groups.

I was not easily categorized, creating what I thought of as a "least-gendered identity." Establishing a least-gendered identity required drawing upon masculine cultural capital such as bodily comportment, my inability to be offended, living in a tough area, athleticism, and a competitive joking interactional style.

I first attempted to create a least-gendered identity by dressing and carrying myself differently than teenaged girls. Most girls at River High wore tight, fitted pants baring their hips or belly buttons. I, on the other hand, routinely wore low-slung baggy jeans or cargo pants (characterized by multiple large pockets), black T-shirts or sweaters, and puffy vests or jackets favored by those who identified with hip-hop culture. Similarly, I "camped up" my sexuality. I performed what might be identified as a soft-butch lesbian demeanor. I walked with a swagger in my shoulders, rather than in my hips (Esterberg 1996). I stood strong legged instead of shifting my weight from one leg to another. I used little flourish in my hand motions, instead using my arms in a traditionally masculine way—hands wide with stiff wrists. I smiled less. I also sat with my legs wide apart and crossed ankle over knee rather than knee over knee. This appearance muted my difference and helped me gain access to boys' worlds and conversations—if not as an honorary guy, at least as some sort of neutered observer who wouldn't be offended.

My athletic ability and interests also contributed to my least-gendered status. Boys and I often spoke of mountain biking, and we would sometimes get into injury comparison contests, trying to one-up each other with the grossest and most outlandish sporting incident—me talking about my concussions and revealing my scars, boys showing their stitches and scabs. The weight room teacher, Coach Ramirez, inadvertently helped establish my sporting identity with his introduction to his weight-lifting class. We had spoken on the phone before I had come to visit his class, and during our discussion we had talked about lifting weights, something I did on a regular basis. This had helped me establish rapport with him, as he was passionate about weight lifting and strength training. When he introduced me to the class, he told the boys I was a "weight lifter from U.C. Berkeley who has some things she wants to talk to you about." He encouraged them to ask me questions about weight lifting and form. I think this gave them the impression that I was a weight lifter from Berkeley in some official capacity as opposed to a graduate student who went to the gym several times a week and lifted weights to stay fit. While boys didn't come running to me for advice, I did tease them about their form (which, more often than not, was horrible), and we were able to joke back and forth about it, thus establishing rapport. This sort of masculine cultural capital—both the teasing (a hallmark of masculinity) (Kehily and

Nayak 1997; Lyman 1998) and the knowledge—allowed me to attain something of an insider/outsider status.

Describing where I lived to the boys at River High also bolstered my least-gendered status. I lived off a main thoroughfare in Oakland, California, famous for drug deals, prostitution, and gang fights. Indeed, during the time of my research a man was gunned down on the street outside my apartment. This actually gave me an entrée with some groups of boys, especially African American boys, who were slightly less willing to talk with me, regarding me as just another white member of the administration who could discover their real addresses and send them back to the "bad" school in the nearby Chicago district. I was standing outside the weight room watching a bunch of boys with whom I hadn't yet spoken. J. W. turned to them to introduce me, saying, "She lives in East Oakland." A chorus of "ooohs," "aaaahs," and "no ways!" followed this announcement. One of the boys in that group, Mike, later introduced me to a group of his friends, all African American boys, by pointing at me and saying, "She live in East Oakland." One of the boys in the group said, looking over short, blonde, female me, "No she don't." Mike challenged him, "Ask her." So, Dax did, in disbelief: "You live in East Oakland?" I smiled and said, "Yeah, between East 18th and East 14th." Talking about a recent murder, Rakim said, "She lives two blocks from where that guy was killed." The boys still looked skeptical. I asked Dax, "Why don't you believe that I live in Oakland?" "'Cause it's ghetto," he replied. I agreed, "Yes, it is ghetto." They all laughed uproariously as I said the word *ghetto*. Then they clamored asking, where was I *really* from. I told them that I was born in Orange County, a famously white conservative area in Southern California. This seemed to make much more sense to them. It seemed that they were picking up on a raced and classed identity—a whiteness that was at odds with my residence in such a tough neighborhood. Much as the boys perceived badness as masculinity, my living and surviving in a "bad" area helped me to establish credibility with them. From this point on these African American boys were much more likely to let me into their circles. Again, this sort of knowledge allowed me to be an insider in multiple ways, in terms of street credibility, racial identity, and age.

As I established a "least-gendered" identity, I disrupted the common understanding of sex-gender correspondence. Like many women who gain access to all-male domains, I distanced myself from more conventional forms of femininity (Herbert 1998). I purposefully distinguished myself from the other women in these boys' lives: mothers, teachers, and, most importantly, other teenage girls. I didn't wear makeup or tight clothing and I didn't giggle. I also selectively shared information about myself, emphasizing attributes such as mountain biking, weight lifting, guitar playing, and bragging about injuries. I intentionally left out topics that would align me with femininity, such as my love of cooking, my feminism, and my excitement about my upcoming commitment ceremony. Like the boys, I distanced myself from femininity, but I did not, like the boys, actively disparage femininity. In this sense creating a "least-gendered identity" involved a deliberately gendered research strategy.

NEGOTIATING SEXUALITY

I was not consistently successful in maintaining this least-gendered identity. Some boys insisted on positioning me as a potential sexual partner by drawing me into the sexualizing and objectifying rituals central to maintaining a masculine identity at River High. Being used as an identity resource in this way left me feeling objectified, scared, angry, and unsettled. As a strong, assertive woman who socializes primarily with other feminists, I found it disconcerting to have boys leer at me and ask invasive questions about my personal life. Despite my efforts to create a least-gendered identity, some of them set up a heterosexual dynamic between us, trying to transform me into a girl their age (or older, which might have been in some way "better") who might or might not be a future sexual conquest. It was as if, by making me concretely feminine, they could assert their masculinity as a socially dominant identity.

The first time this happened I was startled, and, looking back at my field notes, I have a hard time describing why I knew I was being positioned as a sexual object. During my second day of research at River High, I had presented my project to the auto shop class, saying to a room full of boys, "Hey, you're probably all wondering what I'm doing here. I'm writing a book on teenage guys. And I'm researching the guys at your school. I'm gonna be a doctor in two years, that's what this book is for. I'm gonna be at your football games, dances, and lunch and school, et cetera . . . for the next year. And I'll probably want to interview some of you." When a bunch of boys in the back of the room yelled out, "Rodriguez will do it, Rodriguez will do it!" and Rodriguez said lasciviously, "Yeah, I *totally* will," I felt warned that these boys were in a process of building dominant identities and that I, as a woman, was central to this process. As a result, I knew, early in my research, that I would have to figure out ways to deal with this sort of treatment while maintaining my rapport with them.

On a few occasions I felt physically intimidated by the boys as they invaded my space with their sheer size and manipulated my body with their strength. At one point during the Junior Prom David ran up to me and started "freaking" me. Freaking is a popular dance move in which students grind their pelvises together in time to the music as if to simulate sex. David was probably six feet tall (as compared to my five feet and two inches) and the size of a grown man, not a wiry adolescent. I had never been grabbed by a man in such a way, and I responded with a bit of panic. I tried to step back from him, but he wrapped his arms around me so that I couldn't escape his frantic grinding. I put my arms on his shoulders and gently pushed back, laughing nervously, saying, "This might be a little inappropriate, David," and saying I hoped he had a good night. I was desperately hoping no administrators saw it because I didn't want to get in trouble for sexually accosting one of the students, even though he had approached me.

Researching teens required maintaining rapport with two groups who often had different interests: students and administrators. I needed administrators to see me as a responsible (and thus nonsexual) adult while simultaneously appearing accessible, but not too much so, to the teens on the dance floor. Similarly, at another dance, a boy I didn't even recognize ran up to me, tightly grabbed both of my wrists, and pulled me toward the dancing throng, saying, "C'mon! You want to dance!" as a statement, not as a question. Again, I tried to hide my fear and exit the situation by laughing, but I had to struggle to pull my wrists out of his grip.

Other boys were even more physically aggressive, especially in primarily male spaces. In auto shop Stan, Reggie, and J. W. kept grabbing each others' crotches and then hurriedly placing their hands in a protective cup over their own, while giggling. After watching them for a while, I finally asked J. W. what they were doing. He explained, "It's cup check. Wanna play?" I must have looked shocked as he extended his hand toward my own crotch. Trying to maintain my calm I said, "No thanks." Looking slyly at me he tried again: "Wanna play titties?" suddenly shoving his hands toward my chest and twisting them around. I shook my head, dumbfounded. He turned and walked away as Stan and Reggie defensively put their hands over their genitals. I felt especially violated because he didn't just ask, "Want to play cup check?" He followed this question with a specifically gendered proposal, reaching for my chest. To protect myself from their violating touches, while at the same time maintaining a relationship with them, I laughed to mitigate discomfort and quietly exited the situation. In these instances I found no way to maintain some sort of least-gendered identity but rather tried to escape their sexualizing and objectifying processes without looking offended or flattered.

Josh was one of the boys whose actions I found most troubling. He often stood too close to me, eyed me lasciviously, and constantly adjusted his crotch when he was around me. I was repelled by these gestures and his heavily pimpled face. He was constantly seeking masculine positioning by talking about women's bodies in problematic ways. I had forged a decent relationship with his off-again, on-again girlfriend, Jessica, a striking blonde. She came up to me one morning in drama class to tell me that she and Josh had been talking about me the previous night on the phone. I looked surprised as she continued, saying that he had told her how he liked older women and he would like to "bang" me. After hearing this I felt exceedingly awkward and, quite frankly, vulnerable. It hadn't occurred to me that conversations about me were going on in my absence. I also realized that I was in a vulnerable position, not just in terms of sexual advances, but in terms of any stories these boys might choose to tell about me. Throughout my research Josh continued to allude to me as his sexual partner. In auto shop one day, when I rose from my seat to use the restroom in the school office, Josh yelled out, "You leaving already?" I looked at him and said, "Bathroom." He pointed to the grimy bathroom/changing room the boys used and said, "There's one here." I replied, "I don't think so." As I walked away, Josh looked around, adjusted his crotch, and followed me out saying, "I'll be back, fellas," to suggest that he was going to follow me and something sexual was going to happen. He had adjusted his crotch with a greasy hand, so falling back, he said, "My nuts are greasy!" and he stopped following me. Using the strategy I had by that time perfected, I just ignored him.

In instances where I couldn't escape or ignore my involvement in these sexualizing processes, I sometimes tried to respond as neutrally as possible while encouraging boys to continue to talk about their feelings. One day in the weight room J. W. was looking pensive, sheepish, or moping, I couldn't tell which. He finally sidled up to me and asked, in a saccharine, bashful voice, "Can I ask you a personal question?" This question always gave me pause. I had been asking them all sorts of personal questions and following their every word and deed. As a result I felt that I should reciprocate, to a certain extent, with information about myself. So I concluded, "Sure," thinking I could talk my way out of inappropriate questions about whether I was married or dating, which were the types of questions I was usually asked. Instead, he surprised me with a question I didn't fully understand but knew was inappropriate: "Have you ever had your walls ripped?" Frantically, I thought that I had to stall for time as I figured out how to respond to what I knew must be a lewd question. I assumed, given the context of the boys' previous discussions about making girlfriends bleed by "ripping" their walls, that it had something to do with their penises being so large that they produced bloody tears in their girlfriends' vaginal walls. I tried to respond with a relatively neutral answer: "What do you mean, walls ripped?" J. W. stammered, trying to answer the question. He began to look around desperately for help, asking other guys to help him define it. Since it isn't really possible to rip a girls' walls as often and as harshly as they bragged, none of them really knew what it actually meant. The boys all looked at him as if to say, "You've gotten yourself into your own mess this time" and laughed at him as they shook their heads "no." Finally, unable to continue to embarrass him and feeling incredibly awkward myself, I said, "I know what it means. Why do you want to know?" He responded, "'Cause I like to know if girls are freaky or not. I like freaky girls." I felt awkward at this point because it seemed as if I was being categorized as a potential sexual conquest. Instead of following that line of talk I redirected the question and asked him, "Have you ever ripped a girl's walls?" J. W. responded proudly, "Hell yeah." So I asked him, "How does it make you feel?" He spread his legs and looked down between them, gesturing: "I feel hella bad because they are bleeding and crying. It hurts them." This strategy of redirecting the offensive statement back toward the boys had the effect of producing rich data. While trying not to reveal information about myself or appear offended, I furthered the discussion by trying to engage him to talk about his feelings, which he did, to the extent that he was able.

By the end of my research, I frequently copied some of the boys' masculinizing strategies in my interactions with them, specifically the ways boys established themselves as masculine through discursive battles for dominance in which they jokingly insulted one another (Kehily and Nayak 1997; Lyman 1998). I began to engage in a similar strategy when the boys would begin to make sexualized comments to me. While I didn't invoke the fag discourse, I tried to verbally spar with them in a way that was both humorous and slightly insulting. For example, in auto shop, Brook asked for some grease to lubricate an engine part. In response, Josh looked at me and commented lewdly, "I got white grease, baby." Fed up with Josh's incessant comments and no longer needing to establish rapport, I mimicked the boys' interactional style. I looked at him and said scathingly, "What does that mean, Josh?" The surrounding boys looked stunned and then burst out laughing. Brook looked down at me and said "I'm startin' to like you. You're okay!" Josh, angry, ran across the yard yelling, "Faggots! I'm not talking to any of you!" I had "won" this interchange and some of the boys' respect by interacting in their masculinized manner. Josh didn't stay angry at me, but he actually did tone down his comments during the remainder of my time at River.

As with Josh, I finally became so weary of J. W.'s continual propositions that

I responded to him with a similar verbal insult. In the weight room I tried to walk past J. W. to get to the back of the room. Looking at me, he put his leg up on a weight bench to prevent me from walking past. I said, without a smile, "Very funny, J. W.," and turned to walk around him. Quickly he put his other leg up. I was now trapped between his legs. He looked at me and smiled as if he expected me to smile back. I tried my usual strategy of invoking humor and challenged him, "But can you put both legs up like that at the same time?" He said, loudly for the entire class to hear, "You'd like that, wouldn't you?" Ticked off and embarrassed that my approach hadn't worked, I said, witheringly, "You know, I was a teenager once and I dated teenage boys then. They weren't impressive then and they aren't now." The other boys laughed loudly, jumping in with their own insults. J. W. hung his head in embarrassment. I felt good, as if I had linguistically wrested sexual and gendered control of the situation from his grasp.

With both of the boys I engaged in the sort of verbal one-upmanship boys engaged in with each other. While they tried to pull me into their objectifying rituals, I had to deny them that control without raising my voice, condemning the sex talk, or revealing too much about my own personal life. Instead, I had to either highlight the illogic of what they were saying, as I did with Josh, or make it clear that they were immature. I refused to engage in the feminizing verbal war of the fag discourse the boys used to define themselves and one another. As a result I had few other options with which to encourage their respect and avoid becoming another sort of victimized girl, appearing flattered by their obscene overtures, or looking like an authority figure by scolding them. Deploying this competitive joking strategy worked when my least-gendered identity failed and I was pulled into their objectifying rituals. To this end I was able to play, in a sense, the "age card," reminding boys that they were young and childlike.

JUST ONE OF THE (MASCULINE) GIRLS

Of course, the negotiations around masculinity and sexuality at River High didn't take place just between me and groups of boys but also between me and groups of girls, specifically the Basketball Girls and the GSA Girls. After a bit of getting to know me, both groups wanted me as a part of "their" group—seeing me as someone who echoed their non-normative gender practices. Indeed, I too felt a kinship with these girls in a way I didn't with the boys. I saw my own gender practices reflected in their public identities. I also respected them, seeing them as somewhat heroic for refusing the gender pressures of normative femininity that weigh so heavily on teenage girls. Though, in many ways I marked myself and was marked by them as one of them, I had to delicately patrol boundaries of and information about my own identity because of the rampant homophobia at River High, even though these girls, like many of the boys, were keenly interested in my personal life. While many girls at River talked to me and were interested in my presence, they didn't necessarily try to bring me into their social worlds as did many of the boys, the Basketball Girls, or the GSA Girls. Both groups of girls, eventually, actively claimed me as one of them.

The GSA Girls took me into their world soon after I began my tenure at River High. In large part this was probably due to my explicit interest in studying gender, which reflected much of their own political and social focus. I was quickly and easily invited into their social circle as they brought me over to the local burger joint that constituted their lunchtime hangout. Soon after I met Lacy, she introduced me to many of the members of the GSA. I was seen as so integrated into their group that it was as if they sometimes forgot I was not a student. During the club fair at lunch as they recruited for new GSA members they shouted at me to join GSA. I laughed and said that if I were in high school I would. I felt both honored by their inclusion of me in their political activism and slightly worried about explicitly revealing my own politics. For the most part I was happy that these girls were brave enough to form such a group and pleased that I could serve as an adult ally.

The Basketball Girls were a slightly more difficult group to penetrate. In fact, the first time I saw them, during the CAPA performance at which Ricky danced, I was intimidated. I watched as a group of five tall girls dressed in baggy clothes strutted up to a thin, lanky boy selling candy and surrounded him. He shrank as they laughingly grabbed candy out of his box and tossed it over his head at one another. He feebly tried to retrieve it, moving from one girl to another in their mocking game of "Keep Away," eventually giving up and slinking away in defeat as the girls strutted away smugly with their new candy. After this incident I frequently saw the Basketball Girls at lunch, but for a while I was too nervous to approach them, thinking I might sabotage my opportunity for rapport if I didn't appear tough enough.

Eventually, Sarah, the blonde perky cheerleader I discussed in chapter 5, was able to introduce me to the Basketball Girls. She took my business cards and passed them along to the Basketball Girls. A few days later at a football game, she took me by the hand and introduced me to the Basketball Girls as they roughhoused on the bleachers. Once I introduced myself, they, for the most part, seemed excited about being interviewed and, like the GSA Girls, slowly brought me into their group.

One of the ways the Basketball Girls made me part of their group was through inquiring about and expecting me to engage in non-normative gender practices. For example, a certain handshake was a powerful symbol of group membership for the Basketball Girls. Unlike other girls at River, they greeted each other not with hugs but with elaborate handshakes. One afternoon Michelle reached out to shake my hand as I walked up to their lunch table. Not having paid attention to the intricacies of the handshake, I made several wrong moves. Michelle patiently walked me through the ritual, showing me the choreography. In subsequent interactions she greeted me with the handshake, but I frequently forgot the final move—the concluding "snap." Michelle often reprimanded me for this. One afternoon, as I left the girls at basketball practice, I engaged in the handshake ritual. Michelle snapped in conclusion. Noticing I didn't snap, she yelled, "You didn't snap!" I turned to walk away, raised my hand up, and snapped defiantly. The Basketball Girls and Michelle cracked up. The day I finally remembered to snap in greeting, Michelle smiled and hollered, "You remembered to snap!" This sort of denotation of group membership was much more common among the Basketball Girls and the GSA Girls than it was among the boys. They positioned me not as a sexual object but as one of them, if only marginally.

The Basketball Girls were also interested in other ways I was "different." They were interested, for example, in my fighting abilities. During our interview, Michelle asked me, "Have you ever gotten into a fight?" Though I don't consider fighting a central part of who I am and have never actually punched someone in anger, I had recently recovered a stolen bike during a relatively physical interchange with a man much larger than me. Hoping that this would suffice in establishing my "tough" credentials, I shared the stolen bike story with Michelle. She then pressed me for more details about my fighting ability, asking me if I had ever been in a fight "with a girl." Given that I hadn't ever fought with a woman, I tried to change the subject by responding, "I'd never hit a girl." Michelle concurred, answering, "That's like me, I've never hit a girl." She continued to inquire: "Can you fight? But do you, like, fistfight, or do you wrestle, or do you catfight?" Not having any idea how I fight, but being pretty sure I could throw a punch if I needed to, I bluffed, "No, I don't catfight. You have to have nails to catfight." That, seemed to satisfy Michelle's need to know that I was indeed tough and therefore like her.

The Basketball Girls also drew on racialized gender identities to mark me as one of them. One afternoon Rebeca and Shawna (a tangential member of the Basketball Girls) both claimed me as their "nigga" (a primarily African American term, in this case as a term of endearment denoting friendship and camaraderie [Kennedy 1999/2000]). As I stood in the front quad of the school, watching the Bomb Squad practice for the next performance to loud booming music, Shawna ran up to me and threw her arms around me yelling, "She's my nigga!" Rebeca, hearing and seeing Shawna stake this claim, ran up from the other side yelling, "She's *my* nigga!" I laughed and hugged them both back, happy to be included in such an intimate way, indeed in a way that crossed racial lines. However, I found that because of my own racial and class status I couldn't reciprocate in kind, since for me using the word *nigga* would be laden with racist history. This was not the only time that gender-non-normative girls at River insisted I wasn't white. Valerie, a Latina member of the GSA who stylistically had more in common with the Basketball Girls, insisted, "But you're not really white. You're not all conceited and preppy, you know." So the girls didn't rely just on our likeness in the gendered presentation of self but also on our likeness in terms of a racialized gender identity.

Both the Basketball Girls and the GSA Girls were intensely interested in my sexuality, but unlike the boys they were looking for similarity, not difference. They frequently asked probing questions to see if I was straight or gay. During my first conversation with Rebeca's girlfriend, Annie, we chatted about her current argument with Rebeca. I laughed and commented, "It's always more drama with women!" Alicia looked at me and asked if I dated women too. Though I did "date women too," I had decided, early in my research, not to discuss this part of my personal life with students or administrators at River High. In my response, I stuck with the line I had decided to use, explaining that I couldn't talk about some parts of my personal life until my research was over.

The GSA Girls put me in similar positions, expecting me to participate with them in discussions about other women. One afternoon at Bob's they engaged in a heated and playful debate over who was "hotter," Pink, Eve, or Angelina Jolie. Unable to come to a consensus, they turn to me to ask who I thought was the "hottest." Figuring it wouldn't be the same as outing myself and wanting to establish rapport, I said Pink and then revised my answer to jokingly include Britney Spears. They laughed at me for my clearly uncool preference.

Several times I had to evade answers about my sexual life. Shawna followed me out of the cafeteria after lunch, saying, "I have to ask you my question but I'm not sure how." I teased her asking, "Do you want to know how much I weigh?" Shawna responded, "No," and the other Basketball Girls laughed. Being silly, and concerned about what she wanted to know, I threw out a few more joking questions: "How old I am? What my favorite color is? How many kids I have?" As Shawna and I continued to walk, the other girls fell away and she asked me, "So are you into girls?" I said back, "What makes you ask that?" She murmured, "I dunno," as she shuffled uncomfortably. "'Cause you wear that big jacket and 'cause the way you like move and talk and stuff and 'cause you used to have your hair all short." I nodded to indicate that I understood why she was asking that question and responded by saying that I could answer her when I was done with my research in December. Much as with the boys, I found it difficult to avoid some questions about my personal life. However, my feminist challenge in this sense was not to avoid condemning their sexist behavior. Rather, I found myself wanting to be "out" to these girls as a role model and an ally because there were no other out gay adults at River High.

The GSA Girls had similar questions, though it seems that they had a more secure sense that I was gay. For instance, one day I was complaining about my cats, who had made a mess of my apartment the night before. Lacy asked, "Why don't you just get rid of them?" Thinking about my partner's dedication to our pets, I quickly answered, "There are multiple reason for that." Lacy smiled slyly and said, "Significant other?" I smiled in response and changed the subject. Additionally, they frequently teased me about my "roommate" with knowing winks. At Winter Ball both Lacy and Genevieve asked me, laughing, what my "roommate" was doing that night.

As I concluded my research I did let each of the GSA Girls know that I was gay and had a partner. Of course, it seemed they already knew that, and I was just formalizing it. That said, it was challenging for me as I conducted my research to know how "out" to be, especially when I would grow outraged at the school's treatment of the GSA Girls. It was hard to let the GSA Girls know that my allegiance lay with them, yet not risk the antagonism of the school authorities.

A FEMINIST CHALLENGE
IN ADOLESCENT RESEARCH

Crafting a researcher identity when studying teens is difficult because adolescence is such a chaotic life period. When conducting research with adults, a researcher most likely has a general sense of the ways he or she is defined. Interacting with adults, even in social worlds very different from one's own, usually involves age-defined shared categorizations, ways of interacting, and manners. Though in any setting doing fieldwork across lines of difference can lead to misunderstandings and unintended interactions, age differences bring up a unique set of issues (Baker 1983; Weber, Miracle, and Skehan 1994).

In adulthood the self is relatively settled. It is not so in adolescence. The self is so in flux during the teenage years that the psychologist Erik Erikson (1959/1980) called adolescence a time of "normative crisis." An adolescent's task, according to developmental theorists like Erikson, is "identity consolidation." This task requires that teens figure out "who they are." As teens categorize themselves, they categorize others as well. The researcher, in this setting, becomes part of their meaning-making systems and identity work. As a researcher I was not necessarily perceived by them according to the way I tried to present myself, which is generally the way I am perceived by adults. Rather, I became one of the resources they mobilized to create identity and make meaning.

When I simply conducted interviews, as opposed to gathering data through observations, less identity negotiation was required of me. My identity was more or less firm. I was a researcher, tied to a prestigious university. However, as I spent much of the boys' daily lives with them, they challenged my own assumptions about my identity, and I had to meet those challenges with my own identity strategies. During my time with them my ascribed identity was ever-shifting and I had to adapt. Sometimes these identities suited my purpose, but other times I was stuck in a role I didn't want. I was alternatively a teacher, a mother, a girl, an outsider, a note taker, an author, a student, a potential sexual partner, or a confidant.

Being mobilized as an identity resource was quite jarring. When boys positioned me as a potential sexual partner, none of them seemed concerned about my thoughts or desires about my own sexual availability. In trying to create a "least-gendered identity" or responding by copying their joking strategy, I was able to maintain rapport with them, maintain my own self-respect, and earn some of theirs. I distanced myself in terms of both gender and age from being a "girl" or a "boy" by refraining from girlish squealing or joining in boys' objectification of girls, a strategy that would probably not have worked for me. I also distanced myself from recognizably adult behaviors by refraining from expressing disapproval of dirty talk, expressing offense, or attempting to enforce discipline. Instead, I struck a balance, not joining in with this sort of talk and not reporting it to school faculty. By occupying a less gendered and less age-defined position, I was able to maintain rapport with the boys, while also helping to preserve some of the more troubling aspects of gender inequalities in this school.

Using the masculine capital I had at my deployment often meant that I didn't challenge sexist and homophobic behavior among the teenage boys. This is a challenge for feminist researchers studying adolescent masculinity—maintaining rapport with boys while not validating their belief systems and gender prejudices.

I walked a tightrope in managing my allegiance to other teenage girls and my need to gather data from the boys who mocked them. When I could, I used masculine joking strategies to best other boys without simultaneously invoking feminizing or homophobic insults. I also had to maintain a balance between distancing myself from femininity and not disparaging it. While I may have challenged gender stereotypes by decoupling sex and gender in utilizing masculine interactional strategies and cultural capital, this research approach failed to challenge the sexist underpinnings of masculine identities at River High.

The other feminist challenge I encountered was around my personal and political concerns in terms of the non-normatively gendered girls at River High. These girls were carving out new ways of being teenage girls in which they played with, maneuvered around, and challenged conventional gender and sexual norms. I saw them both as the products of years of feminist activism and as reflections of myself in high school. When I couldn't be as honest about my own life or as active around my political beliefs as I wanted to, I felt frustrated, drained and, quite frankly, as if I were betraying them.

Researchers' own subjectivities are central to ethnographic research, as feminist methodologists have long demonstrated (Arendell 1997; Boreland 1991; Harding 1987). Paying attention to my own feelings and desires as the boys drew me into their masculinizing rituals helped me to recognize processes of masculinity I otherwise might have missed. In this way my own feelings and experiences were central to the data I gathered. My own horror at being involved in these processes led to a gendered identity strategy that both elicited more information from the boys and frequently stopped short of challenging their sexism.

NOTES

CHAPTER 1

1. This is not to say that women don't possess this sort of subjectivity, but these qualities are what students at River High associate with masculinity.

2. While trying to retain the insight that there are multiple masculinities that vary by time and place, I self-consciously use the singular *masculinity* in this text because students at River talk about masculinity as a singular identity that involves practices and discourses of sexualized power and mastery.

3. I make this claim on the basis of the administrators' opinions and my respondents' descriptions of their parents' jobs.

CHAPTER 2

1. That said, gender identities and sexual norms are not simply unidirectional socialization processes. Youth also contribute to and reconfigure "official" teachings about gender and sexuality. They contribute their own knowledge and contest official school norms and teachings (Trudell 1993). I address these challenges to authority and received wisdom in later chapters.

2. Other authors call this the "hidden curriculum" (Campbell and Sanders 2002; Letts and Sears 1999; J. Martin 1976). I choose to use Trudell's term because I think what is going on in high school is less about uncovering the hidden than it is about the informal way teachers and students structure sexuality by drawing on popular and shared definitions.

3. While I never initiated conversations about "sexual identity development" in my interviews, students talked about sex all the time in both formal and informal settings. So much of this book is composed of these discussions.

4. There always seemed to be tension over the dress code. It was continually experienced by students as an infringement on their right to free expression.

5. River High was not unique in establishing policies that encouraged a gender-differentiated heterosexuality; indeed, social policy frequently constitutes heterosexuality as both normal and natural (Carabine 1998).

6. They called it the "Wrestling World" after a real event that happened each spring at River High. The sports director was a former pro wrestler. He invited his current pro-wrestler colleagues to come to River to put on a show for the community, an immensely popular event that sold out quickly.

7. Ricky was one of the few "out" gay boys at the school. Ironically, he played a hyperheterosexualized role in this dance routine. This may have something to do with why the administrators allowed him to dance so sensually. However, a white boy and girl danced together in one other routine that included extensive cross-gender touching.

8. While none of the students I asked could tell me *why* they were frustrated about being called the Pep Squad, my guess is the connotations of the name were problematic. *Pep squad* invokes a bunch of smiling *white* girls with blond ponytails performing for the student body. This group of black students adopted a name that deployed the hip-hop vernacular of "da bomb," meaning something really great, to connote a tougher, more streetwise, more legitimate club name.

9. The term *sexual and gender regimes* in the title of this section is a modification of R. W. Connell's (1996) idea of "gender regimes," which he uses to refer to the sum of gender relations in a given school.

CHAPTER 3

1. In fact, two of my colleagues, both psychotherapists, suggested that the boys exhibited what we could think of as a sort of "Fag Tourette's Syndrome."

2. Though River was not a particularly violent school, it may have seemed like that to Ricky because sexuality-based harassment increases with grade level as gender differentiation becomes more intense. As youth move from childhood into adolescence there is less flexibility in terms of gender identity and self-presentation (Shakib 2003).

3. There were two other gay boys at the school. One, Corey, I learned about

after a year of fieldwork. While he wasn't "closeted," he was not well known at the school and kept a low profile. The other out gay boy at the school was Brady. While he didn't engage in the masculinity rituals of the other boys at River High, he didn't cross-dress or engage in feminine-coded activities as did Ricky. As such, when boys talked about fags, they referenced Ricky, not Brady or Corey.

CHAPTER 4

1. This is not to say that similar enactments of dominance and control don't occur among gay men. But such behavior is out of the scope of this study, since there were not enough self-identified gay boys at this school from which to draw conclusions about the way sexual discussions and practices interacted with masculinity for gay boys.

2. I am also indebted to Michael Kimmel's (1987) argument that masculinity itself must be compulsively expressed and constantly proven, something he calls "compulsive masculinity."

3. Chris Rock is a popular comedian. This routine is a fictionalized account in which he both plays himself and imitates Michael Jackson. The "Neverland" Chris Rock refers to is Michael Jackson's whimsical ranch in California.

4. Heath's behavior is a good illustration of how a boy's engagement with the "fag discourse" might vary by context. While in drama performances neither he nor Graham engaged in the fag discourse, outside that context both of them did.

5. That said, if anyone called this sort of behavior sexual harassment, it would more likely be girls than boys, since women are more likely than men to label so-called flirtatious behaviors as harassment (Quinn 2002)

6. *Whore*, however, is equivalent to *fag* only in that both boys and girls agree it is the worst insult one can direct toward a girl, much as *fag* is for a boy. That said, girls do not frantically lob the insult *whore* at one another in order to shore up a feminine identity the way boys do with *fag* regarding a masculine identity. Both *fag* and *whore*, however, do invoke someone who has been penetrated, which is a powerless position.

7. Muscles, in many boys' interviews, were central to understandings of oneself and others as masculine. Later in the chapter we see that boys are obsessed with size; in just about every realm, bigger is better.

8. Transitional periods are the time when students are most at risk for harassment and bullying (N. Stein 2002).

9. Jack Daniels, a relatively inexpensive whiskey.

10. The research on smiling and giggling as practices of submission is mixed. Most of the research indicates that the meanings invoked by a smile depend on the context in which it is given, by whom and to whom (LaFrance 2002; Mast and Hall 2004).

CHAPTER 5

1. Though after my research ended, toward the end of her senior year, Riley started to identify as transgendered.

2. While they recognized themselves as distinct groups, they did not have a label for themselves, nor did others. The majority of youth at River High did not use group labels, with the exception of the term *jocks*, to describe others in their school. For a more thorough discussion of the importance of the category of "jock" in high school, see Pascoe (2003).

3. See Best (2000, 2004), Gordon, Holland, and Lahelma (2000), Bettie (2003), Kehily (2000), and K. Martin (1996) for discussions of adolescent female femininity.

4. Several girls followed this same routine at each formal dance I attended. They would wear formal dress for the pictures and quickly change into jeans and/or more comfortable shoes.

5. While these terms were originated by Joseph Howell (1973), I take this description from Julie Bettie's (2003) discussion of teenage girls at Waretown High.

CHAPTER 6

1. Janet Halley (1993) examines how those who are thrown out of the discursive and legal category of "heterosexual" lose definitional power over their own identity. Much as the threat of the "fag" disciplines boys into certain behavioral practices, the threat of being excluded from the category "heterosexual" functions as a bribe to keep people silent and thus reinforces the false unity of the category itself.

2. Indeed, part of what students recognize as masculinity is its very public nature. That is, masculinity, according to the youth at River High, is what happens when boys (and some girls) are in groups, not necessarily what happens when they are in private.

3. Youth at River did identify a third racial/ethnic group—youth from Mexico who didn't speak English. They were a small group who primarily kept to

themselves. Unfortunately, I didn't speak any Spanish, so I was unable to include them in this study.

4. Hochschild (1989) uses the phrase *gender strategies* to refer to the ways that men and women develop a plan of action with which to solve a problem given current gender norms. Though she uses it to describe the way men and women negotiate work and housework, it is equally apt in this instance. Drawing upon definitions of femininity and masculinity, girls deploy a variety of gender strategies to deal with often-damaging masculinity practices.

5. Another helpful resource for educational films is Women's Educational Media (www.womedia.org). They distribute a film entitled *It's Elementary: Talking about Gay Issues in School* as part of their "Respect for All" project.

6. Several organizations provide resources for forming Gay/Straight Alliances and for supporting gender-variant youth: the Gay, Lesbian, and Straight Education Network (www.glsen.org), The Gay Straight Alliance Network (www.gsanetwork.org), and GenderPAC (www.gpac.org).

7. The institute for Gay and Lesbian Strategic Studies makes suggestions for school reform in their publication "Going beyond Gay Straight Alliances to Make Schools Safe for Lesbian, Gay, Bisexual and Transgender Students," accessible at www.iglss.org/pubs/highlights/highlights.html.

8. These sorts of curricular resources are produced by the Safe Schools Coalition (www.safeschoolscoalition.org), Gay and Lesbian Educators of British Columbia (www.galebc.org), and Southern Poverty Law Center (www.tolerance .org/teach).

REFERENCES

Adams, Natalie Guice, and Pamela J. Bettis. 2003. *Cheerleader! An American Icon.* New York: Palgrave Macmillan.

Adler, Patricia A., Steven J. Kless, and Peter Adler. 1992. "Socialization to Gender Roles: Popularity among Elementary School Boys and Girls." *Sociology of Education* 65, no. 3:169–87.

Almaguer, Tomas. 1991. "Chicano Men: A Cartography of Homosexual Identity and Behavior." *Differences* 3, no. 2:75–100.

American Association of University Women. 2001. *Beyond the "Gender Wars": A Conversation about Girls, Boys, and Education.* Washington, DC. American Association of University Women Educational Foundation.

Arendell, Terry. 1997. "Reflections on the Researcher-Researched Relationships: A Woman Interviewing Men." *Qualitative Sociology* 20, no. 3:341–68.

Baker, Carolyn. 1983. "A 'Second Look' at Interviews with Adolescents." *Journal of Youth and Adolescence* 12, no. 6:501–19.

Baker, Janet G., and Harold D. Fishbein. 1998. "The Development of Prejudice towards Gays and Lesbians by Adolescents." *Journal of Homosexuality* 36, no. 1:89–100.

Bederman, Gail. 1995. *Manliness and Civilization: A Cultural History of Gender and Race in the United States, 1880-1917.* Chicago: University of Chicago Press.

Ben-Amos, Ilana Krausman. 1995. "Adolescence as a Cultural Invention: Philippe Ariès and the Sociology of Youth." *History of the Human Sciences* 8, no. 2:66–89.

Bersani, Leo. 1987. "Is the Rectum a Grave?" *AIDS: Cultural Analysis/Cultural Activism*, no. 43:197–222.

Best, Amy. 2000. *Prom Night: Youth, Schools, and Popular Culture*. New York: Routledge.

———. 2004. "Girls, Schooling, and the Discourse of Self-Change: Negotiating Meanings of the High School Prom." In *All about the Girl: Power, Culture, and Identity*, edited by Anita Harris, 195–204. New York: Routledge.

Bettie, Julie. 2003. *Women without Class: Girls, Race, and Identity*. Berkeley: University of California Press.

Blumenfeld, Warren J. 1995. " 'Gay/Straight' Alliances." In *The Gay Teen: Educational Practice and Theory for Lesbian, Gay, and Bisexual Adolescents*, edited by Gerald Unks, 211–24. New York: Routledge.

Bordo, Susan. 1994. *Unbearable Weight: Feminism, Western Culture, and the Body*. Berkeley: University of California Press.

Boreland, Katherine. 1991. " 'That's Not What I Said': Interpretive Conflict in Oral Narrative Research." In *Women's Words: The Feminist Practice of Oral History*, edited by Sherna Berger Gluck and Daphne Patai, 63–76. New York: Routledge.

Briggs, Jean L. 1998. *Inuit Morality Play: The Emotional Education of a Three-Year-Old*. New Haven: Yale University Press.

Brogan, Jim. 1995. "Gay Teens in Literature." In *The Gay Teen: Educational Practice and Theory for Lesbian, Gay and Bisexual Adolescents*, edited by Gerald Unks, 67–78. New York: Routledge.

Brown, Lyn Mikel. 1998. "Voice and Ventriloquation in Girls' Development." In *Standpoints and Differences: Essays in the Practice of Feminist Psychology*, edited by Karen Henwood, Christine Griffin, and Ann Phoenix, 91–114. Thousand Oaks, CA: Sage Publications.

———. 2003. *Girlfighting: Betrayal and Rejection among Girls*. New York: New York University Press.

Bucholtz, Mary. 1999. "You Da Man: Narrarating the Racial Other in the Production of White Masculinity." *Journal of Sociolinguistics* 3, no. 4:443–60.

Burn, Shawn Meghan. 2000. "Heterosexuals' Use of 'Fag' and 'Queer' to Deride One Another: A Contributor to Heterosexism and Stigma." *Journal of Homosexuality* 40, no. 2:1–11.

Butler, Judith. 1993. *Bodies That Matter: On the Discursive Limits of "Sex."* New York: Routledge.

———. 1995. "Melancholy Gender/Refused Identification." In *Constructing Masculinity*, edited by Maurice Berger, Brian Wallis, and Simon Watson, 21–36. New York: Routledge.

———. 1999. *Gender Trouble: Feminism and the Subversion of Identity*. New York: Routledge.

Califia, Pat. 1994. "Butch Desire." In *Dagger: On Butch Women*, edited by L. Burana and L. Roxie Due, 220–24. San Francisco: Cleis Press.

California Teachers Association. 2002. *Gay, Lesbian, Bisexual, and Transgender Youth: Breaking the Silence.* Teachers' Handbook. Component of the California Teachers Association High Risk Program. Burlingame: California Teachers Association.

Campbell, Patricia B., and Jo Sanders. 2002. "Challenging the System: Assumptions and Data behind the Push for Single-Sex Schooling." In *Gender in Policy and Practice*, edited by Amanda Datnow and Lea Hubbard, 31–46. New York: Routledge.

Carabine, Jean. 1998. Heterosexuality and Social Policy. In *Theorising Heterosexuality*, edited by D. Richardson, 55–74. Buckingham: Open University Press.

Carrigan, T., B. Connell, and J. Lee. 1987. "Towards a New Sociology of Masculinity." In *The Making of Masculinities: The New Men's Studies*, edited by H. Brod, 63–102. Boston: Allen and Unwin.

Chodorow, Nancy. 1978. *The Reproduction of Mothering: Psychoanalysis and the Sociology of Gender.* Berkeley: University of California Press.

———. 1995. "Gender as a Personal and Cultural Construction." *Signs* 20, no. 3:516–44.

———. 2000. "Individuals in History and History through Individuals." In *Born into a World at War*, edited by Nancy Blackmun and Maria Tymoczko, 127–51. Manchester: St. Jerome.

Collins, Patricia Hill. 1990. *Black Feminist Thought: Knowledge, Consciousness, and the Politics of Empowerment.* New York: Routledge.

Coltrane, Scott. 2001. "Selling the Indispensable Father." Paper presented at the conference "Pushing the Boundaries: New Conceptualizations of Childhood and Motherhood," Temple University, Philadelphia.

Combahee River Collective. 1982. "A Black Feminist Statement." In *But Some of Us Are Brave*, edited by G. T. Hull, P. B. Scott, and B. Smith, 13–22. Old Westbury, NY: Feminist Press.

Connell, R. W. 1995. *Masculinities.* Berkeley: University of California Press.

———. 1996. "Teaching the Boys: New Research on Masculinity and Gender Strategies for Schools." *Teachers College Record* 98, no. 2:206–35.

———. 1998. "Masculinities and Globalization." *Men and Masculinities* 1, no. 1:3–23.

Cooper, Marianne. 2000. "Being the 'Go-to Guy': Fatherhood, Masculinity and the Organization of Work in Silicon Valley." *Qualitative Sociology* 23, no. 4:379–405.

Corbett, Ken. 2001. "Faggot = Loser." *Studies in Gender and Sexuality* 2, no. 1:3–28.

Craig, Steve. 1992. *Men, Masculinity, and the Media.* Research on Men and Masculinities Series 1. Newbury Park, CA: Sage Publications.

Curry, Timothy Jon. 2004. "Fraternal Bonding in the Locker Room: A Profeminist Analysis of Talk about Competition and Women." In *Men's Lives*, edited by Michael Messner and Michael Kimmel, 204–17. Boston: Pearson.

Davies, Jude. 1995. " 'I'm the Bad Guy?' *Falling Down* and White Masculinity in Hollywood." *Journal of Gender Studies* 4, no. 2:145–52.

Davis, Angela. 1981. *Women, Race and Class.* New York: Vintage Books, 1981.

Davis, James Earl. 1999. "Forbidden Fruit: Black Males' Constructions of Transgressive Sexualities in Middle School." In *Queering Elementary Education: Advancing the Dialogue about Sexualities and Schooling*, edited by William J. Letts IV and James T. Sears, 49–59. Lanham, MD: Rowan and Littlefield.

Dinnerstein, Dorothy. 1976. *The Mermaid and the Minotaur: Sexual Arrangements and Human Malaise.* New York: Harper Perennial.

Donaldson, Mike. 1993. "What Is Hegemonic Masculinity?" *Theory and Society* 22, no. 5:643–57.

Durkheim, Emile. 1995. *The Elementary Forms of Religious Life.* New York: Free Press.

Eckert, Penelope. 1989. *Jocks and Burnouts: Social Categories and Identity in the High School.* New York: Teachers College Press.

Eder, Donna, Catherine Colleen Evans, and Stephen Parker. 1995. *School Talk: Gender and Adolescent Culture.* New Brunswick: Rutgers University Press.

Edley, Nigel, and Margaret Wetherell. 1997. "Jockeying for Position: The Construction of Masculine Identities." *Discourse and Society* 8, no. 2:203–17.

Emerson, Rana A. 2002. " 'Where My Girls At?' Negotiating Black Womanhood in Music Videos." *Gender and Society* 16, no. 1:115–35.

Epstein, Debbie. 1997. "Boyz' Own Stories: Masculinities and Sexualities in Schools." *Gender and Education* 9, no. 1:105–15.

Epstein, Steven. 1994. "A Queer Encounter." *Sociological Theory* 12:188–202.

Erikson, Erik. 1959/1980. *Identity and the Life Cycle.* New York: W. W. Norton.

Esterberg, Kristin G. 1996. " 'A Certain Swagger When I Walk': Performing Lesbian Identity." In *Queer Theory/Sociology*, edited by Steven Seidman, 259–79. Cambridge: Blackwell.

Faderman, Lillian. 1991. *Odd Girls and Twilight Lovers: A History of Lesbian Life in Twentieth-Century America.* New York: Columbia University Press.

Fausto-Sterling, Ann. 1995. "How to Build a Man." In *Constructing Masculinity*, edited by Maurice Berger, Brian Wallis, and Simon Watson, 127–34. New York: Routledge.

Ferguson, Ann. 2000. *Bad Boys: Public Schools in the Making of Black Masculinity.* Ann Arbor: University of Michigan Press.

Fine, Gary Alan. 1989. "The Dirty Play of Little Boys." In *Men's Lives*, edited by Michael Kimmel and Michael Messner, 171–79. New York: Macmillan.

Fine, Michelle, Lois Weis, Judi Addelston, and Julia Marusza. 1997. "(In)Secure Times: Constructing White Working-Class Masculinities in the Late 20th Century." *Gender and Society* 11, no. 1:52–68.

Foley, Douglas. 1990. "The Great American Football Ritual: Reproducing Race, Class and Gender." *Sociology of Sport Journal* 7:111–35.

Foucault, Michel. 1990. *The History of Sexuality.* Vol. 1. Translated by Robert Hurley. New York: Vintage Books.

Francis, Becky, and Christine Skelton. 2001. "Men Teachers and the Construction of Heterosexual Masculinity in the Classroom." *Sex Education* 1, no. 1:9–21.

Freud, Sigmund. 1905. *The Basic Writings of Sigmund Freud.* Translated by A. A. Brill. New York: Modern Library.

Gagne, Patricia, and Richard Tewksbury. 1998. "Conformity Pressures and Gender Resistance among Transgendered Individuals." *Social Problems* 45, no. 1:81–101.

Gamson, Joshua, and Dawne Moon. 2004. "The Sociology of Sexualities: Queer and Beyond." *Annual Review of Sociology* 30:47–64.

Gardiner, Judith Kegan. 2003. "Gender and Masculinity Texts: Consensus and Concerns for Feminist Classrooms." *NWSA Journal* 15, no. 1:147–57.

Geertz, Clifford. 1973. *The Interpretation of Cultures.* New York: Basic Books.

Gilbert, Rob. 1998. *Masculinity Goes to School.* New York: Routledge.

Gordon, Tuula, Janet Holland, and Elina Lahelma. 2000. "Friends or Foes? Interpreting Relations between Girls in School." In *Genders and Sexualities in Education*, edited by G. Walford and C. Hudson, 7–25. Amsterdam: JAI.

Griffin, Pat. 1995. "Homophobia in Sport." In *The Gay Teen: Educational Practice and Theory for Lesbian, Gay, and Bisexual Adolescents*, edited by Gerald Unks, 53–65. New York: Routledge.

Griswold, Wendy. 1994. *Cultures and Societies in a Changing World.* Sociology for a New Century. Thousand Oaks, CA: Pine Forge Press.

Halberstam, Judith. 1998. *Female Masculinity.* Durham: Duke University Press.

Halley, Janet E. 1993. "The Construction of Heterosexuality." In *Fear of a Queer Planet: Queer Politics and Social Theory*, edited by Michael Warner, 82–102. Minneapolis: University of Minnesota Press.

Hallinan, Maureen T., and Richard A. Williams. 1990. "Students' Characteristics and the Peer-Influence Process." *Sociology of Education* 63 (April): 122–32.

Hand, Jeanne Z., and Laura Sanchez. 2000. "Badgering or Bantering? Gender Differences in Experience of, and Reactions to, Sexual Harassment among U.S. High School Students." *Gender and Society* 14, no. 6:718–46.

Harding, Sandra G. 1987. *Feminism and Methodology: Social Science Issues.* Bloomington: Indiana University Press.

Hartmann, Heidi. 1976. "Capitalism, Patriarchy and Job Segregation by Sex." *Signs* 1:137–70.

Henley, Nancy. 1977. *Body Politics: Power, Sex, and Nonverbal Communication.* Englewood Cliffs, NJ: Prentice-Hall.

Herbert, Melissa S. 1998. *Camouflage Isn't Only for Combat: Gender, Sexuality and Women in the Military.* New York: New York University Press.

Heward, Christine. 1990. "Like Father, Like Son: Parental Models and Influences in the Making of Masculinity at an English Public School, 1929–1950." *Women's Studies International Forum* 13, no. 1/2:139–49.

Heywood, Leslie, and Shari L. Dworkin. 2003. *Built to Win: The Female Athlete as Cultural Icon.* Sport and Culture Series. Minneapolis: University of Minnesota Press.

Hird, Myra J., and Sue Jackson. 2001. "Where 'Angels' and 'Wusses' Fear to Tread: Sexual Coercion in Adolescent Dating Relationships." *Journal of Sociology* 37, no. 1:27–43.

Hochschild, Arlie Russell. 1989. *The Second Shift.* New York: Avon.

Howell, Joseph. 1973. *Hard Living on Clay Street: Portraits of Blue-Collar Families.* Garden City, NY: Anchor.

Ingraham, Chrys. 1999. *White Weddings: Romancing Heterosexuality in Popular Culture.* New York: Routledge.

Jackson, Stevi. 1996. "Heterosexuality and Feminist Theory." In *Theorising Heterosexuality*, edited by Diane Richardson, 21–38. Buckingham: Open University Press.

Jaggar, Alison. 1983. *Feminist Politics and Human Nature.* Totowa, NJ: Rowman and Allanheld.

Jeffreys, Sheila. 1996. "Heterosexuality and the Desire for Gender." In *Theorising Heterosexuality*, edited by Diane Richardson, 75–90. Buckingham: Open University Press.

Jenefsky, Cindy, and Diane Helene Miller. 1998. "Phallic Intrusion: Girl-Girl Sex in Penthouse." *Women's Studies International Forum* 21, no. 4:375–85.

Julien, Isaac, and Kobena Mercer. 1991. "True Confessions: A Discourse on Images of Black Male Sexuality." In *Brother to Brother: New Writings by Black Gay Men*, edited by Essex Hemphill, 167–73. Boston: Alyson Publications.

Kandiyoti, Denise. 1988. "Bargaining with Patriarchy." *Gender and Society* 2, no. 3:274–90.

Kehily, Mary Jane. 2000. "Understanding Heterosexualities: Masculinities, Embodiment and Schooling." In *Genders and Sexualities in Educational Ethnography*, edited by Geoffrey Walford and Caroline Hudson, 27–40. Amsterdam: JAI.

Kehily, Mary Jane, and Anoop Nayak. 1997. " 'Lads and Laughter': Humour and the Production of Heterosexual Masculinities." *Gender and Education* 9, no. 1:69–87.

Kelley, Robin D. G. 2004. "Confessions of a Nice Negro, or Why I Shaved My Head." In *Men's Lives*, edited by Michael Kimmel and Michael Messner, 335–41. Boston: Allyn and Bacon.

Kennedy, Randall L. 1999/2000. "Who Can Say 'Nigger'? . . . And Other Considerations." *Journal of Blacks in Higher Education* 26 (Winter): 86–96.

Kimmel, Michael S. 1987. "The Cult of Masculinity: American Social Character and the Legacy of the Cowboy." In *Beyond Patriarchy: Essays by Men on Pleasure, Power, and Change*, edited by Michael Kaufman, 235–49. New York: Oxford University Press.

———. 1996. *Manhood in America: A Cultural History*. New York: Free Press.

———. 1999. " 'What about the Boys?' What the Current Debates Tell Us—and Don't Tell Us—about Boys in School." *Michigan Feminist Studies* 14:1–28.

———. 2001. "Masculinity as Homophobia: Fear, Shame, and Silence in the Construction of Gender Identity." In *The Masculinities Reader*, edited by Stephen Whitehead and Frank Barrett, 266–87. Cambridge: Polity Press.

———. 2003. "Adolescent Masculinity, Homophobia, and Violence: Random School Shootings, 1982–2001." *American Behavioral Scientist* 46, no. 10:1439–58.

Kindlon, Dan, and Michael Thompson. 1999. *Raising Cain: Protecting the Emotional Life of Boys*. New York: Ballantine.

King, J. L. 2004. *On the Down Low: A Journey into the Lives of Straight Black Men Who Sleep with Men*. New York: Broadway Books.

Kinney, David A. 1993. "From Nerds to Normals: The Recovery of Identity among Adolescents from Middle School to High School." *Sociology of Education* 66, no. 1:21–40.

Kulkin, Heidi S., Elizabeth A. Chauvin, and Gretchen A. Percle. 2000. "Suicide among Gay and Lesbian Adolescents and Young Adults: A Review of the Literature." *Journal of Homosexuality* 40, no. 1:1–29.

LaFrance, Marianne. 2002. "Smile Boycotts and Other Body Politics." *Feminism and Psychology* 12, no. 3:319–23.

Lehne, Gregory. 1998. "Homophobia among Men: Supporting and Defining the Male Role." In *Men's Lives*, edited by Michael Kimmel and Michael Messner, 237–49. Boston: Allyn and Bacon.

Lemert, Charles. 1996. "Series Editor's Preface." In *Queer Theory/Sociology*, edited by Steven Seidman, vii–xi. Cambridge: Blackwell.

Letts, William J., IV, and James T. Sears, eds. 1999. *Queering Elementary Education: Advancing the Dialogue about Sexualities and Schooling*. Lanham, MD: Rowan and Littlefield.

Light, Richard. 2000. "From the Profane to the Sacred: Pre-game Ritual in Japanese High School Rugby." *International Review for the Sociology of Sport* 35, no. 4:451–63.

Lipkin, Arthur. 1995. "The Case for a Gay and Lesbian Curriculum." In *The Gay Teen: Educational Practice and Theory for Lesbian, Gay and Bisexual Adolescents*, edited by Gerald Unks, 31–52. New York: Routledge.

Lugones, Maria. 1990. "Playfulness, 'World'-Traveling, and Loving Perception." In *Making Face, Making Soul = Haciendo Caras: Creative and Critical Perspectives by Feminists of Color*, edited by Gloria Anzaldua, 390–402. San Francisco: Aunt Lute Books.

Lyman, Peter. 1998. "The Fraternal Bond as a Joking Relationship: A Case Study of the Role of Sexist Jokes in Male Group Bonding." In *Men's Lives*, edited by Michael Kimmel and Michael Messner, 171–93. Boston: Allyn and Bacon.

Mac an Ghaill, Martain. 1996. "What about the Boys—Schooling, Class and Crisis Masculinity." *Sociological Review* 44, no. 3:381–97.

Mackinnon, Catherine A. 1982. "Feminism, Marxism, Method and the State: An Agenda for Theory." *Signs* 7, no. 2:515–44.

Mahay, Jenna, Edward O. Laumann, and Stuart Michaels. 2005. "Race, Gender and Class in Sexual Scripts." In *Speaking of Sexuality: Interdisciplinary Readings*, edited by J. Kenneth Davidson Sr. and Nelwyn B. Moore, 144–58. Los Angeles: Roxbury.

Majors, Richard. 2001. "Cool Pose: Black Masculinity and Sports." In *The Masculinities Reader*, edited by Stephen Whitehead and Frank Barrett, 208–17. Cambridge: Polity Press.

Mandell, Nancy. 1988. "The Least Adult Role in Studying Children." *Journal of Contemporary Ethnography* 16, no. 4:433–67.

Martin, Emily. 1997. "The Egg and the Sperm." In *Situated Lives: Gender and*

Culture in Everyday Life, edited by Louise Lamphere, Helena Ragone, and Patricia Zavella, 85–98. New York: Routledge.

Martin, Jane. 1976. "What Should We Do with a Hidden Curriculum When We
Find One?" *Curriculum Inquiry* 6, no. 2:135–51.

Martin, Karin. 1996. *Puberty, Sexuality and the Self: Girls and Boys at Adolescence.*
New York: Routledge.

Martino, Wayne. 1999. " 'Cool Boys,' 'Party Animals,' 'Squids' and 'Poofters':
Interrogating the Dynamics and Politics of Adolescent Masculinities in
School." *British Journal of Sociology of Education* 20, no. 2:239–63.

Mast, Marianne Schmid, and Judith A. Hall. 2004. "When Is Dominance Related
to Smiling? Assigned Dominance, Dominance Preference, Trait Dominance,
and Gender as Moderators." *Sex Roles* 50, no. 5/6:387–400.

Medrano, Luisa. 1994. "AIDS and Latino Adolescents." In *Sexual Cultures and the
Construction of Adolescent Identities*, edited by Janice M. Irvine, 100–114.
Philadelphia: Temple University Press.

Mercer, Kobena. 1994. *Welcome to the Jungle: New Positions in Black Cultural Studies.* New York: Routledge.

Messner, Michael. 1993. " 'Changing Men' and Feminist Politics in the United
States." *Theory and Society* 22, no. 5:723–27.

———. 2002. *Taking the Field: Women, Men and Sports.* Minneapolis: University
of Minnesota Press.

———. 2004a. "Barbie Girls versus Sea Monsters: Children Constructing Gender." In *Men's Lives*, edited by Michael A. Messner and Michael S. Kimmel,
87–102. Boston: Pearson.

———. 2004b. "On Patriarchs and Losers: Rethinking Men's Interests." Paper
presented at the Berkeley Journal of Sociology Conference: Rethinking Gender, University of California, Berkeley, March.

———. 2005. "Becoming 100% Straight." In *Gender through the Prism of Difference*, edited by Maxine Baca Zinn, Pierrette Hondagneu-Sotelo, and Michael
Messner, 227–32. New York: Oxford University Press.

Modell, John. 1989. *Into One's Own: From Youth to Adulthood in the United States,
1920–1975.* Berkeley: University of California Press.

Moran, Jefferey. 2000. *Teaching Sex: The Shaping of Adolescence in the 20th Century.*
Cambridge, MA: Harvard University Press.

Morgan, David. 1992. *Discovering Men.* New York: Routledge.

Neilsen, Joyce McCarl, Glenda Walden, and Charlotte A. Kunkel. 2000. "Gendered Heteronormativity: Empirical Illustrations in Everyday Life." *Sociological Quarterly* 41, no. 2:283–96.

Nelson, Eileen S., and Shirley L. Krieger. 1997. "Changes in Attitudes toward Homosexuality in College Students: Implementation of a Gay Men and Lesbian Peer Panel." *Journal of Homosexuality* 33, no. 2:63–81.

Orenstein, Peggy. 2002. "Striking Back: Sexual Harassment at Weston." In *The Jossey-Bass Reader on Gender in Education,* edited by Susan M. Bailey, 459–75. San Francisco: Jossey-Bass.

Owens, Laurence, Rosalyn Shute, and Philip Slee. 2005. " 'In the Eye of the Beholder . . . ': Girls', Boys' and Teachers' Perceptions of Boys' Aggression to Girls." *International Education Journal* 5, no. 5:142–51.

Paechter, Carrie. 2006. "Masculine Femininities/Feminine Masculinities: Power, Identities and Gender." *Gender and Education* 18, no. 3:253–63.

Pallotta-Chiarolli, Maria. 1999. "Diary Entries from the 'Teachers' Professional Development Playground': Multiculturalism Meets Multisexualities in Australian Education." *Journal of Homosexuality* 36, no. 3/4:183–205.

Parker, Andrew. 1996. "The Construction of Masculinity within Boys' Physical Education." *Gender and Education* 8, no. 2:141–57.

Parsons, Talcott. 1954. *Essays in Sociological Theory.* New York: Free Press.

Pascoe, C. J. 2003. "Multiple Masculinities? Teenage Boys Talk about Jocks and Gender." *American Behavioral Scientist* 46, no. 10:1423–38.

Peirce, Jennifer. 1995. *Gender Trials: Emotional Lives in Contemporary Law Firms.* Berkeley: University of California Press.

Perry, Pamela. 2002. *Shades of White: White Kids and Racial Identities in High School.* Durham: Duke University Press.

Pleck, Joseph H. 1987. "The Theory of Male Sex-Role Identity: Its Rise and Fall, 1936 to the Present." In *The Making of Masculinities: The New Men's Studies,* edited by Harry Brod, 21–38. Boston: Allen and Unwin.

Plummer, David C. 2001. "The Quest for Modern Manhood: Masculine Stereotypes, Peer Culture and the Social Significance of Homophobia." *Journal of Adolescence* 24, no. 1:15–23.

Pollack, William S. 1998. *Real Boys: Rescuing Our Sons from the Myths of Boyhood.* New York: Random House.

Price, Jeremy. 1999. "Schooling and Racialized Masculinities: The Diploma, Teachers and Peers in the Lives of Young, African American Men." *Youth and Society* 31, no. 2:224–63.

Quantz, Richard A. 1999. "School Ritual as Performance: A Reconstruction of Durkheim's and Turner's Uses of Ritual." *Educational Theory* 49, no. 4:493–513.

Quinn, Beth A. 2002. "Sexual Harassment and Masculinity: The Power and Meaning of 'Girl Watching.' " *Gender and Society* 16, no. 3:386–402.

Renold, Emma. 2000. " 'Coming Out': Gender, (Hetero)Sexuality and the Primary School." *Gender and Education* 12, no. 3:309–26.

———. 2004. " 'Other' Boys: Negotiating Non-hegemonic Masculinities in the Primary School." *Gender and Education* 16, no. 2:247–66.

Reynolds, Amy L., and Michael J. Koski. 1995. "Lesbian, Gay, and Bisexual Teens and the School Counselor: Building Alliances." In *The Gay Teen: Educational Practice and Theory for Lesbian, Gay and Bisexual Adolescents*, edited by Gerald Unks, 85–94. New York: Routledge.

Rich, Adrienne. 1986. "Compulsory Heterosexuality and Lesbian Existence." In *Blood, Bread and Poetry*, 23–74. New York: W. W. Norton.

Richardson, Diane. 1996. "Heterosexuality and Social Theory." In *Theorising Heterosexuality*, edited by Diane Richardson, 1–20. Buckingham: Open University Press.

Riggs, Marlon. 1991. "Black Macho Revisited: Reflections of a Snap! Queen." In *Brother to Brother: New Writings by Black Gay Men*, edited by Essex Hemphill, 253–60. Boston: Alyson Publications.

Risman, Barbara, and Kristen Myers. 1997. "As the Twig Is Bent: Children Reared in Feminist Households." *Qualitative Sociology* 20, no. 2:229–52.

Robinson, Kerry. 2005. " 'Queering' Gender: Heteronormativity in Early Childhood Education." *Australian Journal of Early Childhood* 30, no. 2:19–28.

Robinson, Victoria. 1996. "Heterosexuality and Masculinity." In *Theorising Heterosexuality*, edited by Diane Richardson, 109–24. Buckingham: Open University Press.

Rofes, Eric. 1995. "Making Our Schools Safe for Sissies." In *The Gay Teen: Educational Practice and Theory for Lesbian, Gay and Bisexual Adolescents*, edited by Gerald Unks, 79–84. New York: Routledge.

Rosaldo, Michelle, and Louise Lamphere. 1974. "Introduction." In *Woman, Culture and Society*, edited by Michelle Rosaldo and Louise Lamphere. Stanford: Stanford University Press.

Ross, Marlon B. 1998. "In Search of Black Men's Masculinities." *Feminist Studies* 24, no. 3:599–626.

Rubin, Gayle. 1984. "Thinking Sex: Notes for a Radical Theory of the Politics of Sexuality." In *Pleasure and Danger: Exploring Female Sexuality*, edited by Carol Vance, 267–319. London: Pandora.

Schalet, Amy. 2000. "Raging Hormones, Regulated Love: Adolescent Sexuality and the Constitution of the Modern Individual in the United States and the Netherlands." *Body and Society* 6, no. 1:75–105.

Schippers, Mimi. 2002. *Rockin' out of the Box*. New Brunswick: Rutgers University Press.

Scott, Joan Wallach. 1999. *Gender and the Politics of History*. New York: Columbia University Press.

Sedgwick, Eve Kosofsky. 1995. " 'Gosh, Boy George, You Must Be Awfully Secure in Your Masculinity!' " In *Constructing Masculinity*, edited by Maurice Berger, Brian Wallis, and Simon Watson, 11–20. New York: Routledge.

Seidman, Steven. 1996. "Introduction." In *Queer Theory/Sociology*, edited by Steven Seidman, 1–29. Oxford: Blackwell.

Shakib, Sohaila. 2003. "Female Basketball Participation: Negotiating the Conflation of Peer Status and Gender Status from Childhood through Puberty." *American Behavioral Scientist* 46, no. 4:1405–22.

Skelton, Christine. 1996. "Learning to Be 'Tough': The Fostering of Maleness in One Primary School." *Gender and Education* 8, no. 2:185–97.

Smith, George W. 1998. "The Ideology of 'Fag': The School Experience of Gay Students." *Sociological Quarterly* 39, no. 2:309–35.

Smith, Valerie. 1994. "Split Affinities: The Case of Interracial Rape." In *Theorizing Feminism*, edited by Anne Herrmann and Abigail Stewart, 155–70. Boulder, CO: Westview Press.

Sommers, Christina. 2000. *The War against Boys: How Misguided Feminism Is Harming Our Young Men*. New York: Simon and Schuster.

Spade, Joan Z. 2001. "Gender and Education in the United States." In *Gender Mosaics: Social Perspectives*, edited by Dana Vannoy, 85–93. Los Angeles: Roxbury.

Stein, Arlene. 1997. *Sex and Sensibility: Stories of a Lesbian Generation*. Berkeley: University of California Press.

Stein, Arlene, and Ken Plummer. 1994. " 'I Can't Even Think Straight': Theory and the Missing Sexual Revolution in Sociology." *Sociological Theory* 12, no. 2:178–87.

Stein, Nan. 2002. "Bullying as Sexual Harassment." In *The Jossey-Bass Reader on Gender in Education*, edited by S. M. Bailey, 409–28. San Francisco: Jossey-Bass.

———. 2005. "No Laughing Matter: Sexual Harassment in K-12 Schools." In *Transforming a Rape Culture*, edited by Emilie Buchwald, Pamela R. Fletcher, and Martha Roth, 311–33. Minneapolis: Milkweed Editions.

Strunin, Lee. 1994. "Culture, Context, and HIV Infection: Research on Risk

Taking among Adolescents." In *Sexual Cultures and the Construction of Adolescent Identities*, edited by Janice M. Irvine, 71–87. Philadelphia: Temple University Press.

Suransky, Valerie Polakow. 1982. *The Erosion of Childhood*. Chicago: University of Chicago Press.

Tait, Gordon. 2000. *Youth, Sex and Government*. New York: Peter Lang.

Tanenbaum, Leora. 1999. *Slut! Growing Up Female with a Bad Reputation*. New York: Seven Stories Press.

Theberge, Nancy. 2000. *Higher Goals: Women's Ice Hockey and the Politics of Gender*. Albany: State University of New York Press.

Thorne, Barrie. 1993. *Gender Play: Boys and Girls in School*. New Brunswick: Rutgers University Press.

———. 2002. "Gender and Interaction: Widening the Conceptual Scope." In *Gender in Interaction: Perspectives on Femininity and Masculinity in Ethnography and Discourse*, edited by Bettina Baron and Helga Kotthoff, 3–18. Philadelphia: John Benjamins.

Tolman, Deborah L. 2005. "Found(ing) Discourses of Desire: Unfettering Female Adolescent Sexuality." *Feminism and Psychology* 15, no. 1: 5–9.

Trudell, Bonnie Nelson. 1993. *Doing Sex Education: Gender Politics and Schooling*. New York: Routledge.

Turner, Victor. 1966. *The Ritual Process: Structure and Anti-Structure*. Ithaca: Cornell University Press.

Tyack, David, and Elisabeth Hansot. 1990. *Learning Together: A History of Coeducation in American Public Schools*. New Haven: Yale University Press.

Uribe, Virginia. 1995. "Project 10: A School-Based Outreach to Gay and Lesbian Youth." In *The Gay Teen: Educational Practice and Theory for Lesbian, Gay and Bisexual Adolescents*, edited by Gerald Unks, 203–10. New York: Routledge.

U.S. Bureau of the Census. 2000. "Census 2000 Demographic Profile Highlights." American Fact Finder. http://factfinder.census.gov/ (accessed September 8, 2006).

Waldner-Haugrud, Lisa K., and Brian Magruder. 1996. "Homosexual Identity Expression among Lesbian and Gay Adolescents: An Analysis of Perceived Structural Associations." *Youth and Society* 27, no. 3:313–33.

Walford, Geoffrey. 2000. "Introduction." In *Genders and Sexualities in Educational Ethnography*, edited by Geoffrey Walford and Caroline Hudson, 1–6. Amsterdam: JAI.

Walters, Andrew S., and David M. Hayes. 1998. "Homophobia within Schools:

Challenging the Culturally Sanctioned Dismissal of Gay Students and Colleagues." *Journal of Homosexuality* 35, no. 2:1–23.

Warner, Michael. 1993. "Introduction." In *Fear of a Queer Planet: Queer Politics and Social Theory*, edited by Michael Warner, vii–xxxi. Minneapolis: University of Minnesota Press.

Weber, Linda, Andrew Miracle, and Tom Skehan. 1994. "Interviewing Early Adolescents: Some Methodological Considerations." *Human Organization* 53, no. 1:42–47.

Weeks, Jeffrey. 1996. "The Construction of Homosexuality." In *Queer Theory/Sociology*, edited by Steven Seidman, 41–63. Cambridge: Blackwell.

West, Candace, and Don Zimmerman. 1991. "Doing Gender." In *The Social Construction of Gender*, edited by Judith Lorber, 102–21. Newbury Park, CA: Sage Publications.

Whitehead, Stephen, and Frank Barrett. 2001. "The Sociology of Masculinity." In *The Masculinities Reader*, edited by Stephen Whitehead and Frank Barrett, 1–26. Malden, MA: Blackwell.

Wilchins, Riki. 2003. "Do You Believe in Fairies?" *Advocate*, February 4, 72.

Willis, Paul. 1981. *Learning to Labor: How Working Class Kids Get Working Class Jobs*. New York: Columbia University Press.

Wood, Julian. 1984. "Groping Towards Sexism: Boy's Sex Talk." In *Gender and Generation*, edited by Angela McRobbie and Mica Nava, 54–84. London: Macmillan.

Woody, Elisabeth L. 2002. "Constructions of Masculinity in California's Single-Gender Academies." In *Gender in Policy and Practice*, edited by Amanda Datnow and Lea Hubbard, 280–303. New York: Routledge.

Zinn, Maxine Baca. 1998. "Chicano Men and Masculinity." In *Men's Lives*, edited by Michael Messner and Michael Kimmel, 25–34. New York: Macmillan.

Zinn, Maxine Baca, and Bonnie Thornton Dill. 1996. "Theorizing Difference from Multiracial Feminism." *Feminist Studies* 22, no. 2:321–31.

INDEX

AB 537 (California assembly bill), 141, 167–68

abject identity, 14–15, 81, 104, 114, 163–64

abortion, 50

abstinence, sexual, 30–31

abstinence-only programs, 29

Adam, 103

administration: and compulsive heterosexuality, 97–98, and fag identity, 65, 71; and female researchers, 184, and formal gender/sexuality curriculum, 28–31; and gender/sexuality regimes, 50 51; and GSA Girls, 143, 147, 173; and informal gender/sexuality curriculum, 34–35, 39; and legal protections, 141, 167–68; and masculine girls, 131–32, 141–42; and policing of gender/sexuality, 46–49; and ritualized interactions, 42–43, 46, 48–49, 196n7

adolescence as social category, 15–16

African American boys, 18, 20; and compulsory heterosexuality, 84, 95–96; and fag identity, 54–55, 58, 60–61, 69, 71–77; and female researchers, 182; and school as institution, 5, 46–49, 160–62

African American girls, 18, 20, 46, 48–49, 96, 118

age/gender, intersections of, 176–80, 182, 187

AIDS, 33

Alan, 34

alcohol, 88, 102, 197n9

Allen, 118

"All for You" skit, 148–49

Ally, 142, 146

alternative ethos, 140

American Pie, 85

Ana, 125, 127–28

Angela, 31–32, 56, 88

Angelica, 148–49

Annie, 122, 125–26, 147, 190

antihomophobic attitudes, 24, 147

army fatigues, 140

Arnie, 56–57, 180

Arturo, 33–34

Asian Club, 21

Asians, 19–21, 48, 116, 133–40, 160

assemblies, 30, 39, 41, 48, 65, 74, 92, 170. *See also names of assemblies*

astronaut skirt, 106

athleticism, 46, 120, 140, 154, 181

"at-risk" behaviors, 28–29, 175

Text:	10/15 Janson
Display:	Janson
Compositor:	Binghamton Valley Composition
Indexer:	Sharon Sweeney
Printer and binder:	Maple-Vail Manufacturing Group